Early praise for *Text Processing with Ruby*

It is rare that a programming language can be unequivocally stated to be the right tool for a job. But when it comes to scanning, extracting, and transforming text, Ruby is that tool, and Rob Miller is the right guide to instruct you in the most effective and efficient application of it.

➤ **Avdi Grimm**
Author, *Confident Ruby*; Head Chef, RubyTapas.com

This is a fun, readable, and very useful book. I'd recommend it to anyone who needs to deal with text—which is probably everyone.

➤ **Paul Battley**
Developer, maintainer of text gem

While Ruby has become established as a Web development language, thanks to Rails, it's an excellent language for working with text as well. *Text Processing with Ruby* covers the nuts and bolts of what I believe is a natural domain for Ruby, all the way from bringing text into the environment via files, the Web, and other means through to parsing what it says and sending it back out again.

➤ **Peter Cooper**
Editor of *Ruby Weekly*, Cooper Press

I'd recommend this book to anyone who wants to get started with text processing. Ruby has powerful tools and libraries for the whole ETL workflow, and this book describes everything you need to get started and succeed in learning.

➤ **Hajba Gábor László**
Developer

A lot of people get into Ruby via Rails. This book is really well suited to anyone who knows Rails, but wants to know more *Ruby*.

➤ **Drew Neil**
Director, Studio Nelstrom, and author of *Practical Vim*

Text Processing with Ruby

Extract Value from the Data That Surrounds You

Rob Miller

The Pragmatic Bookshelf

Dallas, Texas • Raleigh, North Carolina

Pragmatic Bookshelf

Our Pragmatic courses, workshops, and other products can help you and your team create better software and have more fun. For more information, as well as the latest Pragmatic titles, please visit us at *https://pragprog.com*.

The team that produced this book includes:

Jacquelyn Carter (editor)
Potomac Indexing, LLC (index)
Cathleen Small; Liz Welch (copyedit)
Dave Thomas (layout)
Janet Furlow (producer)
Ellie Callahan (support)

For international rights, please contact *rights@pragprog.com*.

Printed in the United States of America.
ISBN-13: 978-1-68050-070-7
Printed on acid-free paper.
Book version: P1.0—September 2015

Contents

Acknowledgments ix
Introduction xi

Part I — Extract: Acquiring Text

1. Reading from Files 3
   Opening a File 3
   Reading from a File 4
   Treating Files as Streams 7
   Reading Fixed-Width Files 12
   Wrapping Up 18

2. Processing Standard Input 19
   Redirecting Input from Other Processes 19
   Example: Extracting URLs 22
   Concurrency and Buffering 25
   Wrapping Up 27

3. Shell One-Liners 29
   Arguments to the Ruby Interpreter 30
   Prepending and Appending Code 35
   Example: Parsing Log Files 37
   Wrapping Up 39

4. Flexible Filters with ARGF 41
   Reading from ARGF as a Stream 42
   Modifying Files 45
   Manipulating ARGV 47
   Wrapping Up 49

5. **Delimited Data** 51
Parsing a TSV 52
Delimited Data and the Command Line 56
The CSV Format 58
Wrapping Up 62

6. **Scraping HTML** 63
The Right Tool for the Job: Nokogiri 63
Searching the Document 64
Working with Elements 72
Exploring a Page 77
Example: Reading a League Table 80
Wrapping Up 88

7. **Encodings** 89
A Brief Introduction to Character Encodings 90
Ruby's Support for Character Encodings 92
Detecting Encodings 98
Wrapping Up 99

Part II — Transform: Modifying and Manipulating Text

8. **Regular Expressions Basics** 103
A Gentle Introduction 104
Pattern Syntax 105
Regular Expressions in Ruby 108
Wrapping Up 114

9. **Extraction and Substitution with Regular Expressions** . . 115
Matching Against Patterns 115
Global Match Variables 117
Extracting Multiple Matches 119
Transforming Text 122
Wrapping Up 126

10. **Writing Parsers** 127
Simple Parsers with StringScanner 128
Example: Parsing a Config File 132
Rule-Based Parsers 135

Example: Parsing RTF Files 143
Wrapping Up 153

11. **Natural Language Processing** **155**
What Is Natural Language Processing? 155
Example: Extracting Keywords from Articles 156
Example: Fuzzy Searching 161
Wrapping Up 169

Part III — Load: Writing Text

12. **Standard Output and Standard Error** **173**
Simple Output 173
Formatting Output with printf 178
Redirecting Standard Output 182
Wrapping Up 187

13. **Writing to Other Processes and to Files** **189**
Writing to Other Processes 189
Writing to Files 193
Temporary Files 195
Wrapping Up 198

14. **Serialization and Structure: JSON, XML, CSV** **199**
JSON 200
XML 205
CSV 207
Wrapping Up 211

15. **Templating Output with ERB** **213**
Writing Templates 214
Example: Generating a Purchase Ledger 217
Evaluating Templates 218
Passing Data to Templates 221
Controlling Presentation with Decorators 224
Wrapping Up 226

Part IV — Appendices

A1. **A Shell Primer** 229
Running Commands 229
Controlling Output 230
Exit Statuses and Flow Control 232

A2. **Useful Shell Commands** 235
Index 245

Acknowledgments

Thanks to my long-suffering partner, Gillian, for enduring a year of lost weekends, late nights, and generally having a sullen and distracted boyfriend who woke up in the middle of the night in a cold sweat, having had another nightmare about character encodings. Who knew writing a book could be so stressful?

Many thanks to Alessandro Bahgat, Paul Battley, Jacob Chae, Peter Cooper, Iris Faraway, Kevin Gisi, Derek Graham, James Edward Gray II, Avdi Grimm, Hajba Gábor László, Jeremy Hinegardner, Kerri Miller, and Drew Neil for their helpful technical review comments, questions, and suggestions—all of which shaped this book for the better.

Thanks to Rob Griffiths, Mark Rogerson, Samuel Ryzycki, David Webb, Lewis Wilkinson, Alex Windett, and Mike Wright for ensuring there was no chance I got too big for my football boots.

Finally, the amazing folks at Pragmatic. Thanks to Susannah Davidson Pfalzer for taking a chance on me and my daft idea. Thanks to Jackie Carter for her incredible patience in guiding a first-time author through the editing process, and for contributing much to the structure and readability of the book. And thanks to Andy and Dave for creating a truly brilliant publisher that I'm proud to be even a tiny a part of.

Introduction

Text is everywhere. Newspaper articles, database dumps, spreadsheets, the output of shell commands, keyboard input; it's all text, and it can all be processed in the same fundamental way. Text has been called "the universal interface," and since the early days of Unix in the 1960s this universal interface has survived and flourished—and with good reason.

Unlike binary formats, text has the pleasing quality of being readable by humans as well as computers, making it easy to debug and requiring no distinction between output that's for human consumption and output that's to be used as the input for another step in a process.

Processing text, then, is a valuable skill for any programmer today—just as it was fifty years ago, and just as it's likely to be fifty years hence. In this book I hope to provide a practical guide to all the major aspects of working with text, viewed through the lens of the Ruby programming language—a language that I think is ideally suited to this task.

About This Book

Processing text is generally concerned with three things. The first concern is acquiring the text to be processed and getting it into your program. This is the subject of Part I of this book, which deals with reading from plain text files, standard input, delimited files, and binary files such as PDFs and Word documents.

This first part is fundamentally an exploration of Ruby's core and standard library, and what's possible with `IO` and its derived classes like `File`. Ruby's history and design, and the high-level nature of these tasks, mean that we don't need to dip into third-party libraries much, but we'll use one in particular—Nokogiri—when looking at scraping data from web pages.

The second concern is with actually processing the text once we've got it into the program. This usually means either extracting data from within the text, parsing it into a Ruby data structure, or transforming it into another format.

The most important subject in this second stage is, without a doubt, regular expressions. We'll look at regular expression syntax, how Ruby uses regular expressions in particular, and, importantly, when *not* to use them and instead reach for solutions such as parsers.

We'll also look at the subject of natural language processing in this part of the book, and how we can use tools from computational linguistics to make our programs smarter and to process data that we otherwise couldn't.

The final step is outputting the transformed text or the extracted data somewhere—to a file, to a network service, or just to the screen. Part of this process is concerned with the actual writing process, and part of it is concerned with the form of the written data. We'll look at both of these aspects in the third part of the book.

Together, these three steps are often described as "extract, transform, and load" (ETL). It's a term especially popular with the "big data" folks. Many text processing tasks, even ones that seem on the surface to be very different from one another, fall into this pattern of three steps, so I've tried to mirror that structure in the book.

In general, we're going to explore why Ruby is an excellent tool to reach for when working with text. I also hope to persuade you that you might reach for Ruby sooner than you think—not necessarily just for more complex tasks, but also for quick one-liners.

Most of all, I hope this book offers you some useful techniques that help you in your day-to-day programming tasks. Where possible, I've erred toward the practical rather than the theoretical: if it does anything, I'd like this book to point you in the direction of practical solutions to real-world problems. If your day job is anything like mine, you probably find yourself trawling through text files, CSVs, and command-line output more often than you might like. Helping to make that process quick and—dare I say it?—fun would be fantastic.

Who This Book Is For

Throughout the book, I try not to assume an advanced understanding of Ruby. If you're familiar with Ruby's syntax—perhaps after having dabbled with Rails a little—then that should be enough to get by. Likewise, if Ruby is your first programming language and you're looking to learn about data processing, you should be able to pick things up as you go along—though naturally this book is about teaching text processing more than it is about teaching Ruby.

While the book starts with material likely to be familiar to anyone who's written a command-line application in Ruby, there's still something here for the more advanced user. Even people who've worked with Ruby a lot aren't necessarily aware of the material covered in Chapter 3, *Shell One-Liners*, on page 29, for example, and I see far too many developers reaching for regular expressions to parse HTML rather than using the techniques outlined in Chapter 6, *Scraping HTML*, on page 63.

Even experienced developers might not have written parsers before (covered in Chapter 10, *Writing Parsers*, on page 127), or dabbled in natural language processing (as we do in Chapter 11, *Natural Language Processing*, on page 155)—so hopefully those subjects will be interesting regardless of your level of experience.

How to Read This Book

Although the book follows a structure of extractions first, transformations second, and loading third, the chapters are relatively self-contained and can be read in any order you wish—so feel free to dive into a later chapter if you're particularly interested in the material it covers.

I've tried to include in each of the chapters material of interest even to more advanced Rubyists, so there aren't any chapters that are obvious candidates to skip if you're at that end of the skill spectrum.

If you're not familiar with how to use the command line, there's a beginner's tutorial in Appendix 1, *A Shell Primer*, on page 229, and a guide to various commands in Appendix 2, *Useful Shell Commands*, on page 235. These appendixes will give you more than enough command-line knowledge to follow all of the examples in the book.

About the Code

All of the code samples in the book can be downloaded from the book's website.[1] They've been tested in Ruby 2.2 running on OS X, Linux, and Cygwin on Microsoft Windows, but they should run just fine on any version of Ruby after 2.0 (released in February 2013).

The book assumes that you're running in a Unix-like environment. Users of Mac OS X, Linux, and BSD will be right at home. Microsoft Windows users, though, will only be able to get the most out of some sections of the book by

1. https://pragprog.com/book/rmtpruby/text-processing-with-ruby

installing Cygwin.[2] Cygwin provides a Unix-like environment on Windows, including a full command-line environment and Unix shell. This gives Windows users access to the core text processing utilities referenced in this book. This is particularly true of the chapters on shell one-liners, writing flexible filters with ARGF, and writing to other processes.

Online Resources

The page for this book on the Pragmatic Bookshelf website[3] contains a discussion forum, where you can post any comments or questions you might have about the book and make suggestions for any changes or expansions you'd like to see in future editions. If you discover any errors in the book, you can submit them there, too.

Rob Miller
August 2015

2. https://www.cygwin.com/
3. https://pragprog.com/book/rmtpruby/text-processing-with-ruby

Part I

Extract: Acquiring Text

The first part of our text processing journey is concerned with getting text into our program. This text might reside in files, might be entered by the user, or might come from other processes; wherever it comes from, we'll learn how to read it.

We'll also look at taking structure from the text that we read, learning how to parse CSV files and even scrape information from web pages.

CHAPTER 1

Reading from Files

Our first concern when processing text is to get the text into our program, and perhaps the most common place to source text is from the humble file. Whether it's log files from a server, exports from database, or text you've written yourself, there's lots of information that lives on the filesystem. Learning to read from files effectively opens up a world of text to process.

Throughout the course of this chapter, we'll look at how we can use Ruby to reach text that resides in files. We'll look at the basics you might expect, with some methods to straightforwardly read files in one go. We'll then look at a technique that will allow us to read even the biggest files in a memory-efficient way, by treating files as streams, and look at how this can give us random access into even the largest files. Let's take a look.

Opening a File

Before we can do something with a file, we need to *open* it. This signals our intent to read from or write to the file, allowing Ruby to do the low-level that make that intention actually happen on the filesystem. Once it's done those things, Ruby gives us a File object that we can use to manipulate the file.

Once we have this File object, we can do all sorts of things with it: read from the file, write to it, inspect its permissions, find out its path on the filesystem, check when it was last modified, and much more.

To open a file in Ruby, we use the open method of the File class, telling it the path to the file we'd like to open. We pass a block to the open method, in which we can do whatever we like with the file. Here's an example:

```
File.open("file.txt") do |file|
  # ...
end
```

Because we passed a block to open, Ruby will automatically close the file for us after the block finishes, freeing us from doing that cleanup work ourselves. The argument that open passes to our block, which in this example I've called file, is a File object that points to the file we've requested access to (in this case, file.txt). Unless we tell Ruby otherwise, it will open files in *read-only mode*, so we can't write to them accidentally—a safe default.

Kernel#open

In the real world, it's common to see people using the global open method rather than explicitly using File.open:

```
open("file.txt") do |file|
  # ...
end
```

As well as being shorter, which is always nice, this convenient method is actually a wrapper for a number of different types of IO objects, not just files. You can use it to open URLs, other processes, and more. We'll cover some more uses of open later; for now, use either File.open or regular open as you prefer.

There's nothing in our block yet, so this code isn't very useful; it doesn't actually do anything with the file once it's opened. Let's take a look at how we can read content from the file.

Reading from a File

Once we've opened a file, the next step is to read its contents. We'll start with the simplest way to do this—reading the whole file into a string, allowing us to perform many kinds of processing with the text contained in the file. We'll then look at how we can break the file's content up into lines and loop through them, a task that's frequently necessary when processing log files, when processing text written by people, and in many other situations.

Reading a Whole File at Once

The easiest way to access the contents of a file in Ruby is to read the entire file in one go. It's not always the right solution, especially when working with bigger files, but it makes sense in many cases.

We can achieve this by using the read method on our File object:

```
File.open("file.txt") do |file|
  contents = file.read
end
```

The read method returns for us a string containing the file's contents, no matter how large they might be.

Alternatively, if all we're doing is reading the file and we have no further use for the File object once we've done so, Ruby offers us a shortcut. There's a read method on the File class itself, and if we pass it the name of a file, then it will open the file, read it, and close it for us, returning the contents:

```
contents = File.read("file.txt")
```

Whichever method we use, the result is that we have the entire contents of the file stored in a string. This is useful if we want to blindly pass those contents over to something else for processing—to a Markdown parser, for example, or to insert it into a database, or to parse it as JSON. These are all very common things to want to do, so read is a widely used method.

For example, if our file contained some JSON data, we could parse it using Ruby's built-in JSON library:

```
require "json"

json = File.read("file.json")
data = JSON.parse(json)
```

Often, though, we want to do something with the contents ourselves. The most common task we're likely to face is to split the file into lines and do something with each line. Let's look at a simple way to achieve this.

Line-by-line Processing

Lots of plain-text formats—log files, for instance—use the lines of a file as a way of structuring the content within them. In files like this, each line represents a distinct item or *record*. It's about the simplest way to separate data, but this kind of structure is more than enough for many use cases, so it's something you'll run into frequently when processing text.

One example of this sort of log file that you might have encountered before is from the popular web server Apache. For each request made to it, Apache will log some information: things like the IP address the request came from, the date and time that the request was made, the URL that was requested, and so on. The end result looks like this:

```
127.0.0.1 - [10/Oct/2014:13:55:36] "GET / HTTP/1.1" 200 561
127.0.0.1 - [10/Oct/2014:13:55:36] "GET /images/logo.png HTTP/1.1" 200 23260
192.168.0.42 - [10/Oct/2014:14:10:21] "GET / HTTP/1.1" 200 561
192.168.0.91 - [10/Oct/2014:14:20:51] "GET /person.jpg HTTP/1.1" 200 46780
192.168.0.42 - [10/Oct/2014:14:20:54] "GET /about.html HTTP/1.1" 200 483
```

Let's imagine we wanted to process this log file so that we could see all the requests made by a certain IP address. Because each line in the file represents one request, we need some way to loop over the lines in the file and check whether each one matches our conditions—that is, whether the IP address at the start of the line is the one we're interested in.

One way to do this would be to use the readlines method on our File object. This method reads the file in its entirety, breaking the content up into individual lines and returning an array:

```
File.open("access_log") do |log_file|
  requests = log_file.readlines
end
```

At this point, we've got an array—requests—that contains every line in the file. The next step is to loop over those lines and only output the ones that match our conditions:

```
File.open("access_log") do |log_file|
  requests = log_file.readlines

  requests.each do |request|
    if request.start_with?("127.0.0.1 ")
      puts request
    end
  end
end
```

Using each, we loop over each request. We then ask the request if it starts with 127.0.0.1, and if the response is true, we output it. Lines that don't start with 127.0.0.1 will simply be ignored.

While this solution works, it has a problem. Because it reads the whole file at once, it consumes an amount of memory at least equal to the size of the file. This will hold up okay for small files, but as our log file grows, so will the memory consumed by our script.

If you think about it, though, we don't actually need to have the whole file in memory to solve our problem. We're only ever dealing with one line of the file at any given moment, so we only really need to have that particular line in memory. For some problems it's necessary to read the whole file at once, but this isn't one of them. Let's look at how can we rework this example so that we only read one line at a time.

Treating Files as Streams

We've seen that reading the entire contents of a file isn't always the best solution. For a start, it forces us to keep the entire contents of the file in memory. This might merely be wasteful with smaller files, but it can turn out to be plain impossible with much larger ones. Imagine wanting to process a 50GB file on a computer that has only 4GB of memory; it would be impossible for us to read the entire file at once.

The solution is to treat the file as a stream. Instead of reading from the beginning of the file to the end in one go, and keeping all of that information in memory, we read only a small amount at a time. We might read the first line, for example, then discard it and move onto the second, then discard that and move onto the third, and so on until we reach the end of the file. Or we might instead read it character by character, or word by word. The important thing is that at no point do we have the full file in memory: we only ever store the little bit that we're processing.

This enables us to work with enormous files—gigabytes in size, if necessary—without consuming anywhere near that much memory. By varying exactly what that "bit by bit" is, we can also step through the file in a way that reflects its structure. If we know that the file has many lines, each of which represents a record, then we can read one line at a time. If we know that the file is one enormous line, but that fields are separated by commas, we can read up to the next comma each time, processing the text one field at a time.

Streaming Files Line by Line

Let's revisit our web server log example, where we outputted only those requests that came from a certain IP address, and see how we can adapt it to use streaming. Luckily, the solution is straightforward—in fact, it's actually easier than the method that reads the whole file into memory.

The `File` object yielded to our block has a method called `each_line`. This method accepts a block and will step through the file one line at a time, executing that block once for each line.

```
File.open("access_log") do |log_file|
  log_file.each_line do |request|
    if request.start_with?("127.0.0.1 ")
      puts request
    end
  end
end
```

That's it. The each_line method allows us to step through each line in the file without ever having more than one line of the file in memory at a time. This method will consume the same amount of memory no matter how large the file is, unlike our first solution.

Just like with File.read, Ruby offers us a shortcut that doesn't require us to open the file ourselves: File.foreach. Using it trims the previous example down a little:

```
File.foreach("access_log") do |request|
  if request.start_with?("127.0.0.1 ")
    puts request
  end
end
```

On my machine, working on a 5,000,000-line, 315MB file, the stream method uses 18MB of memory, while the non-streaming version uses 706MB—an increase of almost forty times. As the size of the file you're dealing with increases, the streaming method won't use any more memory, whereas the readlines method will. So if you're dealing with files that are more than a few kilobytes in size, and if the processing that you're doing doesn't require you to have the whole file in memory at once, each_line will result in a noticeably more efficient solution.

Enumerable Streams

The each_line method of the File class is aliased to each. This might not seem particularly remarkable, but it's actually tremendously useful. This is because Ruby has a module called Enumerable that defines methods like map, find_all, count, reduce, and many more. The purpose of Enumerable is to make it easy to search within, add to, delete from, iterate over, and otherwise manipulate collections. (You've probably used methods like these when working with arrays, for example.)

Well, a file is a collection too. By default, Ruby considers the elements of that collection to be the lines within the file, so because File includes the Enumerable module, we can use all of its methods on those lines. This can make many processing operations simple and expressive, and because many of Enumerable's methods don't require us to consume the whole file—they're *lazy*, in other words—we often retain the performance benefits of streaming, too.

To explore what this means, we can revisit our log example. Let's imagine you wanted to group all of the requests made by each IP address, and within that group them by the URL requested. In other words, you want to end up with a data structure that looks something like this:

```
{
  "127.0.0.1" => [
    "/",
    "/images/logo.png"
  ],
  "192.168.0.42" => [
    "/",
    "/about.html"
  ],
  "192.168.0.91" => [
    "/person.jpg"
  ]
}
```

Here's a script that uses the methods offered by Enumerable to achieve this:

requests-by-ip.rb

```
requests =
  File.open("data/access_log") do |file|
    file
      .map { |line| { ip: line.split[0], url: line.split[5] } }
      .group_by { |request| request[:ip] }
      .each { |ip, requests| requests.map! { |r| r[:url] } }
  end
```

We open the file just like we did previously. But instead of using each_line to iterate over the lines of the file, we use map. This loops over the lines of the file, building up an array as it does so by taking the return value of the block we pass to it. Here our block is using split to separate the lines on whitespace. The first of these whitespace-separated fields contains the IP, and the sixth contains the URL that was requested, so the block returns a hash. The result of our map operation is therefore an array of hashes that contain only the information about the request that we're interested in—the IP address and the URL.

Next, we use the group_by method. This transforms our array of hashes into a single hash. It does so by checking the return value of the block that we pass to it; all the elements of the array that return the same value will be grouped together. In this case, our block returns the IP part of the request, which means that all of the requests made by the same IP address will be grouped together.

The data structure after the group_by operation looks something like this:

```
{
  "127.0.0.1" => [
    {:ip=>"127.0.0.1", :url=>"/"},
    {:ip=>"127.0.0.1", :url=>"/images/logo.png"}
  ],
```

```
  "192.168.0.42" => [
    {:ip=>"192.168.0.42", :url=>"/"},
    {:ip=>"192.168.0.42", :url=>"/about.html"}
  ],
  "192.168.0.91" => [
    {:ip=>"192.168.0.91", :url=>"/person.jpg"}
  ]
}
```

This is almost what we were after. The problem is that we have both the IP address and the URL of the request, rather than just the URL. So the next step in our chain uses each to loop over these IP address and request combinations. It then uses map! to replace the array of hashes with just the URL portion, leaving us with an array of strings.

The final result is exactly what we wanted:

```
{
  "127.0.0.1" => [
    "/",
    "/images/logo.png"
  ],
  "192.168.0.42" => [
    "/",
    "/about.html"
  ],
  "192.168.0.91" => [
    "/person.jpg"
  ]
}
```

This transformation is relatively complex, but it was easily achieved with Ruby's enumerable methods. Each step in the chain of methods performs one particular transformation on the data, getting us closer and closer to the final structure that we're after. If you can break your problem down into small steps like these, then you'll find that you can get Ruby to do much of the work for you. When processing text, you'll find yourself writing *collection pipelines* like this fairly frequently, so it's definitely worth getting acquainted with Enumerable and the functionality that it offers you.

Other Streaming Methods

Although it's most common to want to stream files line by line, it's not your only option. As well as each_line, Ruby also offers a general streaming method in the form of each.

By default, each behaves exactly like each_line, looping over the lines in the file. But it also accepts an argument allowing you to change the character on which it will split, from a newline to anything else you might like.

Let's imagine we had a file with only a single line in it, but that contained many different records separated by commas:

```
this is field one,this is field two,this is field three
```

To process this file as a stream, we could pass a comma character to each, thereby telling it to give us a new record each time it encountered a comma:

```
File.open("commas.txt") do |file|
  file.each(",") do |record|
    puts record
    # >> "this is field one,"
    #    "this is field two,"
    #    "this is field three"
  end
end
```

Instead of giving us a new record whenever it encountered a new line, as each_line did and as is the default behavior of each, we now get a new record each time Ruby sees a comma. This allows us to process this type of file with all the benefits of streaming.

Another commonly used streaming method is each_char, which will yield to us each character in the file. So if we wanted to see how many b characters were in a file, we could use each_char:

```
n = 0
File.open("file.txt") do |file|
  file.each_char do |char|
    n += 1 if char == "b"
  end
end

puts "#{n} b characters in file.txt"
```

Again, this method has all of the benefits of other streaming examples; we only ever have a single character in memory at one time, so we can process even the largest of files.

Like many enumerating methods in Ruby, if we don't pass a block to methods like each_char and each, they'll return for us an Enumerator. That means we can also use these other streaming methods with all of the collection-related methods Enumerable offers us simply by calling them on the Enumerator that's returned for us.

For example, we could rewrite the previous example, where we quite verbosely initialized our n variable and incremented it manually, by using Enumerable's count method:

character-count.rb
```
n =
  File.open("file.txt") do |file|
    file.each_char.count { |char| char == "b" }
  end

puts "#{n} b characters in file.txt"
```

The count method accepts a block and will return the number of values for which the block returned true. This is exactly what our previous code was doing, but this way is a little shorter and a little neater, and reveals our intentions more clearly.

IO: Ruby's Input/Output Class

All of the methods we've seen so far—read, each_line, each_char, and so on—aren't actually defined by the File class itself. They're defined by the class that File inherits from: IO.

This might seem like an academic distinction, but it has an important benefit: it means that other types of IO in Ruby have those same methods, too. Files, streams, sockets, Unix pipelines—all of these things are fundamentally similar, and it's in IO that these similarities are gathered into one abstraction. In the words of Ruby's own documentation, IO is "the basis for all input and output in Ruby." By learning to read from files, then, you'll learn both principles and concrete methods that will translate to all the other places from which you might want to acquire text.

If you know how to write output to the screen, then—using puts—you already know how to write to a file: by calling puts on the file object. Our screen and a file are both IO objects—of two different kinds—so the way we interact with them is the same. This similarity will be very useful throughout our text processing journey.

Reading Fixed-Width Files

Another way of processing files without consuming them whole is to consume a fixed number of bytes. It's much like the streaming examples that we've seen, where we read from the file until we encountered a newline or until we encountered a comma. But instead of reading until we hit a particular character, we read, say, ten bytes from the current position, receiving a string containing those ten bytes.

This might seem an inflexible and impractical way of doing things. After all, how can we know at how many bytes from the start of the file we'll find the information we want? But this sort of processing has several real-world applications and has an important performance characteristic that gives it many of the benefits of a "proper" database system, so it's worth exploring. Let's see how we can use it.

The Data File

In this section, we'll be playing with some scientific data. The National Oceanic and Atmospheric Administration (NOAA) releases data on the surface temperature of four regions in the Pacific Ocean, as measured every week since 1990, offering for download a text file that looks like this:[1]

```
03JAN1990     23.4-0.4     25.1-0.3     26.6 0.0     28.6 0.3
10JAN1990     23.4-0.8     25.2-0.3     26.6 0.1     28.6 0.3
17JAN1990     24.2-0.3     25.3-0.3     26.5-0.1     28.6 0.3
```

...and so on for many hundreds more rows.

Let's imagine we wanted to dig into this data. We might want to find out what the warmest week was, or plot the results on a graph, or just show what the temperature of a particular region was last week. To do any of these things, we need to parse the data and get it into our script.

First, a quick explanation of the data. The first column contains the date of the week in which the measurements were taken. The other four columns represent different regions of the ocean. For each of them we have two numbers: the first representing the recorded temperature, and the second representing the departure from the expected temperature that this recording represents (the "sea surface temperature anomaly"). In the first row, then, the first region recorded a temperature in the week of 3 January 1990 of 23.4 degrees, which is an anomaly of -0.4 degrees.

The pleasing visual quality that this data has—the fact that all the columns in the table line up neatly—will help us in this task. If we were to count the characters across each line, we'd see that each field started at exactly the same place in each row. The first column, containing the date of the week in question, is always twelve characters long. The next number is nine characters long, always, and the following number is always four characters, regardless of whether it has a negative sign. This nine/four pattern repeats three more times for the other three regions.

In trying to get this data into our script, let's look at how to read the first row of data.

1. The data is available on the NOAA website: http://www.cpc.ncep.noaa.gov/data/indices/wksst8110.for.

Reading a Fixed Number of Bytes

We know that in the file we're looking at, each column is a fixed size. That means to read each one, we just need to read a different number of bytes, and to do this we need to revisit a method that we've already looked at: read.

Previously, we used read in its basic form, without any arguments, which read the entire file into memory. But if we pass an integer as the first argument, read will read only that many bytes forward from the current position in the file.

So, from the start of the file, we could read in each field in the first row as follows:

noaa-first-row-simple.rb

```
File.open("data/wksst8110.for") do |file|
  puts file.read(10)
  4.times do
    puts file.read(9)
    puts file.read(4)
  end
end
# >>  03JAN1990
# >>      23.4
# >> -0.4
# >>      25.1
# >> -0.3
# >>      26.6
# >>  0.0
# >>      28.6
# >>  0.3
```

We first read ten bytes, to get the name of the week. Then we read nine bytes followed by four bytes to extract the numbers, doing this four times so that we extract all four regions.

From here, it's not much work to have our script continue through the rest of the file, slurping up all of the data within and converting it into a Ruby data structure—in this case, a hash:

noaa-all-rows.rb

```
File.open("data/wksst8110.for") do |file|
  weeks = []

  until file.eof?
    week = {
      date:  file.read(10).strip,
      temps: {}
    }
```

```
    [:nino12, :nino3, :nino34, :nino4].each do |region|
      week[:temps][region] = {
        temp: file.read(9).to_f,
        change: file.read(4).to_f
      }
    end

    file.read(1)

    weeks << week
  end

  weeks
  # => [{:date=>"03JAN1990",
  #      :temps=>
  #       {:nino12=>{:temp=>23.4, :change=>-0.4},
  #        :nino3=>{:temp=>25.1, :change=>-0.3},
  #        :nino34=>{:temp=>26.6, :change=>0.0},
  #        :nino4=>{:temp=>28.6, :change=>0.3}}},
  #     {:date=>"10JAN1990",
  #      :temps=>
  #       {:nino12=>{:temp=>23.4, :change=>-0.8},
  #        :nino3=>{:temp=>25.2, :change=>-0.3},
  #        :nino34=>{:temp=>26.6, :change=>0.1},
  #        :nino4=>{:temp=>28.6, :change=>0.3}}},
  #     {:date=>"17JAN1990",
  #      :temps=>
  #       {:nino12=>{:temp=>24.2, :change=>-0.3},
  #        :nino3=>{:temp=>25.3, :change=>-0.3},
  #        :nino34=>{:temp=>26.5, :change=>-0.1},
  #        :nino4=>{:temp=>28.6, :change=>0.3}}},
  # ...snip...
end
```

The logic is fundamentally the same as when reading the first row. To loop over all the rows in the file, there are two main changes: first, we loop `until` we hit the end of the file by checking `file.eof?`; it will return true when the end of the file is reached and therefore end our loop. The other addition is the call to `file.read(1)` at the end of the row; this will consume the newline character at the end of each line. We're also using `strip` to strip the whitespace from the week name, and `to_f` to convert the temperature numbers to floats.

This method works and is fast. But by only using `read` to consume a fixed numbers of bytes, we haven't seen the most important advantage of treating the file in this way: the fact that it offers us random access to the records within the file.

Seeking Through the File

Until now we've looked at advancing through the file as a stream, starting at the beginning and moving through the whole file. But just as we can use read to advance through and *consume* a portion of the file, we can also move to a specific location without consuming anything. This is a fast way to skip data that we're not interested in.

To continue with our temperature data, let's imagine we wanted to be able to access a particular week. Not necessarily the first one and not all of them at once, but instead just a single row from within the records.

Well, because each of the columns within the data has a fixed width, that means that all of the rows do, too. Adding up the columns, including the newline at the end, gives us 10 + 4 * (9 + 4) + 1 = 63 characters, so we know that each of our records is 63 bytes long.

If we used seek to skip 63 bytes into the file, then our first call to read would begin reading from the second record:

noaa-skip-first-row.rb

```
File.open("data/wksst8110.for") do |file|
  file.seek(63)
  file.read(10)
  # => " 10JAN1990"
end
```

As we can see, our first call to read returns for us the date of the second week in the file, not the first. Using this method, we can now skip to arbitrary records—the first, the tenth, the thousandth, whatever we like—and read their data.

The most important part of this is that seeking happens in *constant time*. That means that it takes the same amount of time no matter how large the file is and no matter how far into the file we want to seek. We've finally uncovered the amazing benefit to fixed-width files like this—that we gain the ability to access records within them at random, so it's no slower to find the 303rd record than it is to find the third—or even the 300,003rd.

In the final version of our script, then, we can write a get_week method that will retrieve a record for us given an index for that record (1 for the first, 2 for the second, and so on):

noaa-seek.rb

```
def get_week(file, week)
  file.seek((week - 1) * 63)

  week = {
    date:  file.read(10).strip,
    temps: {}
  }

  [:nino12, :nino3, :nino34, :nino4].each do |region|
    week[:temps][region] = {
      temp: file.read(9).to_f,
      change: file.read(4).to_f
    }
  end

  week
end

File.open("data/wksst8110.for") do |file|
  get_week(file, 3)
  # => {:date=>"17JAN1990",
  #     :temps=>
  #      {:nino12=>{:temp=>24.2, :change=>-0.3},
  #       :nino3=>{:temp=>25.3, :change=>-0.3},
  #       :nino34=>{:temp=>26.5, :change=>-0.1},
  #       :nino4=>{:temp=>28.6, :change=>0.3}}}
  get_week(file, 303)
  # => {:date=>"18OCT1995",
  #     :temps=>
  #      {:nino12=>{:temp=>20.0, :change=>-0.8},
  #       :nino3=>{:temp=>24.1, :change=>-0.9},
  #       :nino34=>{:temp=>25.8, :change=>-0.9},
  #       :nino4=>{:temp=>28.2, :change=>-0.5}}}
  get_week(file, 1303)
  # => {:date=>"17DEC2014",
  #     :temps=>
  #      {:nino12=>{:temp=>22.9, :change=>0.1},
  #       :nino3=>{:temp=>26.0, :change=>0.8},
  #       :nino34=>{:temp=>27.4, :change=>0.8},
  #       :nino4=>{:temp=>29.4, :change=>1.0}}}
end
```

Here we use the get_week method to fetch the third, 303rd, and 1,303rd records. With this method we can treat the data within the file almost as though it was a data structure within our script—like an array—even though we haven't had to read any of it in. This allows us to randomly access data within even the largest of files in a very fast and efficient way.

One important caveat is that read and seek operate at the level of bytes, not characters. You'll learn more about the difference between the two in Chapter 7, *Encodings*, on page 89, but it's worth noting that if you're using a multibyte character encoding, like UTF-8, then using seek carelessly might leave you in the middle of a multibyte character and might mean that you get some gibberish when you try to read data.

You should therefore use these methods only when you know that you're dealing solely with single-byte characters or when you know that the location you're seeking to will never be in the middle of a character—as in our temperature data example, where we're seeking to the boundaries between records.

Despite this limitation of seek, hopefully you can see the benefit of using a fixed-width file like this. We can retrieve any value, no matter how big the file is, without reading any unnecessary data; we have what's called *random access* to the data within. To retrieve the tenth record, we just need to seek 567 bytes from the start of the file; to retrieve the 703rd, we just need to seek 44,226 bytes from the start; and so on. The wonderful thing is that no matter how large our file gets, this operation will always take the exact same amount of time—even if we've got hundreds of megabytes of data. That's why it's sometimes worth putting up with the limitations of such a format: it's both very simple and very fast.

Wrapping Up

That's about it for reading files. We looked at how to open a file and what we can do with the resulting File object. We covered reading files in one go and processing them like streams, and why you'd prefer one or the other. We explored how we can use the methods offered by Enumerable to transform and manipulate the content of files. We looked at line-by-line processing and reading arbitrary numbers of bytes, and how we can seek to arbitrary locations in the file to replicate some of the functionality of a database.

With these techniques, we've gained an impressive arsenal for reading text from files large and small. Next, we'll take our newfound knowledge of streams and apply it to another source of text: standard input.

CHAPTER 2

Processing Standard Input

We've looked at how we can use Ruby to read data that exists on the filesystem. Another common source of information, though, is direct input to a script. This might be text that users input using their keyboard, or it might be text that's redirected to your script from another process. From the perspective of Ruby, these two different types of input are actually the same thing, processed in the same way.

This source of input is called *standard input*, and it's one of the foundations of text processing. Along with its output equivalents *standard output* and *standard error*, it enables different programs to communicate with one another in a way that doesn't rely on complex protocols or unintelligible binary data, but instead on straightforward, human-readable text.

Learning how to process standard input will allow you to write flexible and powerful utilities for processing text, primarily by enabling you to write programs that form part of *text processing pipelines*. These chains of programs, linked together so that each one's output flows into the input of the next, are incredibly powerful. Mastering them will allow you to make the most both of your own utilities and of those that already exist, giving you the most text processing ability for the least amount of typing possible.

Let's take a look at how we can write scripts that process text from standard input, slotting into pipeline chains and giving us flexibility, reusability, and power.

Redirecting Input from Other Processes

Standard input can be used to read text from the keyboard. You might have used it that way when learning Ruby, prompting users for input and storing the text they typed:

```
print "What's your name? "
name = $stdin.gets.chomp
puts "Hi, #{name}!"
```

Here we ask standard input—$stdin—for a line of input using the gets method, using chomp to remove the trailing newline. This gives us a string, which we store in name.

This simplistic use of standard input isn't particularly useful, let's face it. But it's actually only half of the story. Standard input isn't just used to read from the keyboard interactively; it can also read from input that's been redirected—or *piped*—to your script from another process.

The ultimate goal here is to be able to use your scripts in *pipeline chains*. These are chains of programs strung together so that the output from the first is fed into the input of the second, the output of the second becomes the input of the third, and so on. Here's an example:

```
$ ps ax | grep ruby | cut -d' ' -f1
```

Here we use three separate commands, each of which performs a different individual task, and combine them to perform quite a complex operation. In this case, that operation is to fetch all of the processes running on the system, search for ones that contain ruby in their name, and then display the first whitespace-separated column of the output (which contains the process ID). That's actually quite a feat, and it was achieved without writing a script; we can do all of that processing just by typing a command into our shell.

That example used preexisting commands to do its work. But we can write our own programs that slot into such workflows. Imagine that we frequently wanted to convert sections of text to uppercase. We know how to convert text to uppercase in Ruby, so we could write a script that works like this:

```
$ echo "hello world" | ruby to-uppercase.rb
HELLO WORLD
```

...and that also works like this:

```
$ hostname | ruby to-uppercase.rb
ROB.LOCAL
```

In other words, we could write a program that converts any text it receives on standard input to uppercase, then outputs that converted text. It won't know where the text is coming from (for example, the echo command we saw previously versus the hostname command)—it accepts anything you pass to it. This gives you great flexibility in how you use the script, opening up ways of using it that you might not have foreseen when writing it.

This flexibility is what makes such scripts useful. Your goal, or at least a pleasant side effect of processing text in this way, is to build up a library of such scripts so that, if you encounter the same problem again, you can just slot the script you wrote last time into the new pipeline chain and be on your way. The to-uppercase.rb script is a good example of this: you might need to write it from scratch the first time you encounter the problem of converting input to uppercase, but after that it can be used again and again in completely different situations.

Actually writing our to-uppercase.rb script is pretty straightforward. In fact, we don't need to know anything more than we learned when prompting users for their name. That's because Ruby doesn't distinguish between standard input that comes from the keyboard and standard input that's redirected; you can just read blindly from standard input. Likewise, you don't have to care whether your output is being written to the screen or being piped to another process; you can just write blindly to standard output. The shell will take care of redirections for you.

To write our to-uppercase.rb example, we need to read from standard input, convert that text to uppercase, and then output it to standard output. In Ruby, that's one line:

```
puts $stdin.read.upcase
```

Saving this script as to-uppercase.rb, we've got everything we need. We can run it like this:

```
$ echo "hello world" | ruby to-uppercase.rb
HELLO WORLD
$ hostname | ruby to-uppercase.rb
ROB.LOCAL
$ whoami | ruby to-uppercase.rb
ROB
```

We now have a script that reads from standard input, modifies what it receives, and outputs it to standard output. It's general purpose. It doesn't know or care where its input comes from, but it processes the input happily regardless.

Countless examples of this type of tool already exist, distributed with Unix-like operating systems: grep, for example, which outputs only lines that match a given pattern, or sort, which outputs an alphabetically sorted version of its input. The scripts you write yourself will be right at home with these standard Unix utilities as part of your text processing pipelines.

Example: Extracting URLs

In the previous example, we used read to read all the standard input in one go. But as we saw with files, reading everything into memory in one gulp often isn't the best idea, especially when our input begins to grow in size.

It was also annoying in the previous example that we had to type ruby to-uppercase.rb. Other commands are short and snappy—cut, grep—but we had to type what feels like a lot of superfluous information.

For our next example, we're going to write a script that extracts URLs from the input passed to it, outputting any that it finds and ignoring the rest of the input. So, if we passed it the following text:

```
Alice's website is at http://www.example.com
While Jane's website is at https://example.net and contains a useful blog.
```

we'd expect to have these URLs extracted from it:

```
http://www.example.com
https://example.net
```

This script will be called urls, and once we've written it we'll be able to use it in any pipeline we like. Because it will treat its input as a stream, we'll be able to use it on whatever input we like, no matter how large it is. So we'll be able to extract the URLs from a text file:

```
$ cat file.txt | urls
```

Or extract the URLs from within a web page:

```
$ curl http://example.com | urls
```

Let's take a look at what we need to do to write the urls script.

The Shebang

Up until now we've only run our Ruby scripts by telling the Ruby interpreter the name of the file to execute. But when we're using ordinary Unix commands, such as grep or uniq, we just specify them as commands in their own right. Ideally, we want to be able to do the same with our URL extractor. It would be annoying if we had to type ruby urls.rb or something similar each time we wanted to use it, especially if we're going to be using it a lot.

But if we just called our script urls, how would our shell know that it was a Ruby script and know to pass its contents to Ruby to execute? The answer is, because we tell it to, and we tell it using a special line at the top of our script called the shebang. In this case, we'd use:

```
#!/usr/bin/env ruby
```

The special part is the #!—it's this that gives the line its name ("hash" + "bang"). Since the Ruby interpreter might be in different places on different people's computers, we use a command called env to tell the shell to use ruby, wherever ruby might be.

The presence of this shebang allows us to save our script as a file called urls and run it directly, rather than as ruby urls. The final step in this process is to allow the file to be executed. We can do this with the chmod command:

```
$ chmod +x urls
```

That's it. We can now call ./urls from within the directory our urls file resides in, and it will execute our script as Ruby code.

If we wanted to be able to call our version from anywhere, not just from the directory in which it's saved, we could put it into a directory that's within our PATH—/usr/local/bin, for example. Many people create a directory under their home directory—typically called bin—and put that into their path, so that they have a place to keep all of their own scripts without losing them among the ones that came with their system or that they've installed from elsewhere.

Putting the script in a directory that's in your PATH will make it feel just like any other text processing command and make it really easy to use wherever you are. If you think you'll use a particular script regularly, then don't hesitate to put it there. The only thing you need to do is to make sure the name of the script doesn't clash with an existing command that you still want to be able to use—otherwise, you'll run your script when you type the command, rather than whatever command originally had that name. So don't call it ls or mv!

Looping Over Lines

When writing scripts like these, we'll often want to loop over the input we're passed one line at a time. That way, we don't need to read the whole input into memory at once, which would be less scaleable and would also slow down the other parts of our pipeline chain.

Just like the File objects we saw in the previous chapter, $stdin has an each_line method that allows us to iterate over the lines in our input:

```
$stdin.each_line do |line|
  # ...
end
```

Wherever possible, we should try to treat standard input as a stream. If our script is used to process a large amount of data, this stream processing will mean that we can pass our output along to the next stage in the process as and when we process it. If our script is the last stage in the pipeline, that means the user sees output more quickly; and if we're earlier in the pipeline, then it means the next part of the pipeline can be doing its processing while we're working on our next chunk.

The Logic

Unlike our to-uppercase.rb example, we're not actually interested in printing the line of output, even in a modified form. Instead we want to extract any URLs we find in it and then output those. To do that, we'll use a regular expression. We'll be covering these in depth in Chapter 8, *Regular Expressions Basics*, on page 103, so don't worry too much about them now:

urls
```
#!/usr/bin/env ruby

$stdin.each_line do |line|
  urls = line.scan(%r{https?://\S+})
  urls.each do |url|
    puts url
  end
end
```

Here we use String's scan method to extract everything that looks like a URL. Then, we loop over them—after all, there might be multiple URLs in a single line—and output each one of them.

Running the Script

If we invoke our script as follows, assuming that we've put it in our PATH, we'll see the output we're expecting:

```
$ printf "hello\nworld http://www.example.com/\nhttps://example.net/" | urls
http://www.example.com/
https://example.net/
```

We now have the general-purpose URL-matcher that we were after, and it took only a few lines of Ruby code! That's great. We can now find all the URLs in a file:

```
$ cat some-file.txt | urls
http://www.example.org.uk
https://example.co.uk
«snip»
```

Or all the URLs in a log file from our web server:

```
$ cat /var/log/webserver/access | urls
https://example.com/about-us
http://www.example.com/contact
https://example.com/about-us
«snip»
```

Of course, we're not limited to having our script be the final stage in the pipeline. We could use it as an intermediary step—for example, to fetch a web page, extract the URLs from it, and then download each of those URLs:

```
$ curl http://example.com | urls | xargs wget
```

Hopefully you can imagine many scenarios where having such a script and other tools like it would come in handy. Before long, if you're anything like me, you'll have built up quite the collection of them, each in true Unix fashion built to do one thing—but to do it well.

Concurrency and Buffering

When thinking about pipeline chains, you could be forgiven for thinking that they're executed in sequence; that is, that the first command generates all of its output, then the second command takes that input and outputs whatever it needs to, and then after that the third process does its bit, and so on.

In reality, though, that's not the case. All of the programs in the pipeline chain run simultaneously, and data flows between them bit by bit—just like water through a real pipe. While the second process is working with the first chunk of information, the first process is generating another chunk; by the time the first chunk is through to the third or fourth process in the pipeline, the first process may be onto the third, tenth, or hundredth chunk.

The amazing thing about this concurrency is that the processes themselves need know nothing about it. It's all taken care of by the operating system and the shell, leaving the individual process to worry only about fetching input and producing output.

We can prove this concurrency by typing the following into our command line:

```
$ sleep 5 | echo "hello, world"
hello, world
```

If the tasks were executed in series, we'd see nothing for five seconds, and only then would `hello, world` appear on our screen. But instead, because the `echo` command starts at the same time as `sleep`, we see the output immediately.

When we request more data from standard input—when calling `$stdin.gets`, for example—Ruby will do one of two things. If it has input available in its buffer, it will pass it on immediately. If it doesn't, though, it will block, waiting until the process before it in the pipeline has generated enough output.

What constitutes "enough output" is up to the operating system, but the upshot is that input will be passed to your script in chunks; on a Linux system, for example, those chunks will be 65,536 bytes in size. If the process before you generates 65,535 bytes and then waits ten seconds before generating some more output, then your process will wait ten seconds before receiving any input at all.

This can be frustrating when the input you're receiving is in many small chunks, especially if those small chunks are slow to generate. One example is the `find` command, which searches the filesystem for files matching given conditions. It might generate hundreds of filenames per second, or it might generate one per minute, depending on how many files you're searching through and how many of them match your conditions.

If we pipe the result of a `find` into this script, it will be a long time before the script actually receives any input, and because this buffering happens at the output stage, not the input stage, there's nothing we can do about it. Our supposedly concurrent pipeline sometimes doesn't behave concurrently at all.

While we have no control over the behavior of other programs, if we're writing programs ourselves that generate slow output like `find` does, then we can remove this buffering by telling our standard output stream to behave synchronously. To illustrate the change, here's a script that uses the default behavior and therefore has its output buffered:

stdout-async.rb

```
100.times do
  "hello world".each_char do |c|
    print c
    sleep 0.1
  end
  print "\n"
end
```

If we run this script and pipe the output into `cat`:

```
$ ruby stdout-async.rb | cat
```

then we'll see the problem: nothing happens for a very, very long time. Because we're outputting a character only every 0.1 seconds, it would take us 410 seconds to fill up a 4,096-byte buffer and a staggering two hours to fill up a 65,536-byte buffer, so we see nothing until the program ends.

The synchronous version of the script avoids this problem:

stdout-sync.rb
```
$stdout.sync = true

100.times do
  "hello world".each_char do |c|
    print c
    sleep 0.1
  end
  print "\n"
end
```

Here we set `$stdout.sync` to `true`, telling our standard output stream not to buffer but instead to flush constantly. If we pipe the input from this script into `cat`, we'll see a character appear every 0.1 second. Although the script will take the same amount of time in total to execute, the next program in the pipeline will have the chance to work with the output immediately, potentially speeding up the overall time the pipeline takes.

Wrapping Up

We looked now at how to use standard input to obtain input from users' keyboards, how to redirect the output of other programs into our own, and how powerful text processing pipelines can be. We saw the value of small tools that perform a single task and how they can be composed together in different ways to perform complex text processing tasks. We learned how to write scripts that can be directly executed and that can process standard input as a stream and so can work with large quantities of input.

We used standard input so far from the perspective of scripts—simple ones, at times, but scripts nevertheless. Sometimes, though, we don't want to have to go to the trouble of writing a full-fledged script to process some data. Wouldn't it be nice to have the flexibility of Ruby in throwaway one-liners that we write in our shell? The next chapter looks at how we can do just that.

CHAPTER 3

Shell One-Liners

We've looked at processing text in Ruby scripts, but there exists a stage of text processing in which writing full-blown scripts isn't the correct approach. It might be because the problem you're trying to solve is temporary, where you don't want the solution hanging around. It might be that the problem is particularly lightweight or simple, unworthy of being committed to a file. Or it might be that you're in the early stages of formulating a solution and are just trying to explore things for now.

In such cases, it would be advantageous to be able to process text from the command line, without having to go to the trouble of committing your thoughts to a file. This would allow you to quickly throw together text processing pipelines and scratch whatever particular itch that you have—either solving the problem directly or forming the foundation of a future, more solid solution.

Such processing pipelines will inevitably make use of standard Unix utilities, such as `cat`, `grep`, `cut`, and so on. In fact, those utilities might actually be sufficient—tasks like these are, after all, what they're designed for. But it's common to encounter problems that get just a little too complex for them, or that for some reason aren't well suited to the way they work. At times like these, it would nice if we could introduce Ruby into this workflow, allowing us to perform the more complex parts of the processing in a language that's familiar to us.

It turns out that Ruby comes with a whole host of features that make it a cinch to integrate it into such workflows. First, we need to discover how we can use it to execute code from the command line. Then we can explore different ways to process input within pipelines and some tricks for avoiding lengthy boilerplate—something that's very important when we're writing scripts as many times as we run them!

Arguments to the Ruby Interpreter

You probably learned on your first day of programming Ruby that you can invoke Ruby from the command line by passing it the filename of a script to run:

```
$ ruby foo.rb
```

This will execute the code found in foo.rb, but otherwise it won't do anything too special. If you've ever written Ruby on the command line, you'll definitely have started Ruby in this way.

What you might not know is that by passing options to the ruby command, you can alter the behavior of the interpreter. There are three key options that will make life much easier when writing one-liners in the shell. The first is essential, freeing you from having to store code in files; the second and third allow you to skip a lot of boilerplate code when working with input. Let's take a look at each them in turn.

Passing Code with the -e Switch

By default, the Ruby interpreter assumes that you'll pass it a file that contains code. This file can contain references to other files (require and load statements, for example), but Ruby expects us to pass it a single file in which execution will begin.

When it comes to using Ruby in the shell, this is hugely limiting. We don't want to have to store code in files; we want to be able to compose it on the command line as we go.

By using the -e flag when invoking Ruby, we can execute code that we pass in directly on the command line—removing the need to commit our script to a file on disk. (It might be helpful to remember -e as standing for *evaluate*, because Ruby is evaluating the code we pass contained within this option.) The universal "hello world" example, then, would be as follows:

```
$ ruby -e 'puts "Hello world"'
Hello world
```

Any code that we could write in a script file can be passed on the command line in this way. We could, though it wouldn't be much fun, define classes and methods, require libraries, and generally write a full-blown script, but in all likelihood we'll limit our code to relatively short snippets that just do a couple of things. Indeed, this desire to keep things short will lead to making choices that favor terseness over even readability, which isn't usually the choice we make when writing scripts.

This is the first step toward being able to use Ruby in an ad hoc pipeline: it frees us from having to write our scripts to the filesystem. The second step is to be able to read from input. After all, if we want our script to be able to behave as part of a pipeline, as we saw in the previous chapter, then it needs to be able to read from standard input.

The obvious solution might be to read from `STDIN` in the code that we pass in to Ruby, looping over it line by line as we did in the previous chapter:

```
$ printf "foo\nbar\n" | ruby -e 'STDIN.each { |line| puts line.upcase }'
FOO
BAR
```

But this is a bit clunky. Considering how often we'll want to process input line by line, it would be much nicer if we didn't have to write this tedious boilerplate every time. Luckily, we don't. Ruby offers a shortcut for just this use case.

Streaming Lines with the -n Switch

If we pass Ruby the `-n` switch as well as `-e`, Ruby will act as though the code we pass to it was wrapped in the following:

```
while gets
  # execute code passed in -e here
end
```

This means that the code we pass in the `-e` argument is executed once for each line in our input. The content of the line is stored in the `$_` variable. This is one of Ruby's many global variables, sometimes referred to as *cryptic globals*, and it always points to the last line that was read by `gets`.

So instead of writing the clunky looping example that we saw earlier:

```
$ printf "foo\nbar\n" | ruby -e 'STDIN.each { |line| puts line.upcase }'
FOO
BAR
```

we can simply write:

```
$ printf "foo\nbar\n" | ruby -ne 'puts $_.upcase'
FOO
BAR
</code>
<p> There's more to <inlinecode>$_</inlinecode> than this, though.
  Ruby also defines some global methods that either act on
```

```
  <inlinecode>$_</inlinecode> or have it as a default argument.
  <ic>print</ic> is one of them: if you call it with no arguments,
  it will output the value of <inlinecode>$_</inlinecode>. So we
  can output the input that we receive with this short script:
</p>
[code language="session"]
$ printf "foo\nbar\n" | ruby -ne 'print'
foo
bar
```

This implicit behavior is particularly useful for filtering down the input to only those lines that match a certain condition—only those that start with f, for example:

```
$ printf "foo\nbar\n" | ruby -ne 'print if $_.start_with? "f"'
foo
```

This kind of conditional output can be made even more terse with another shortcut. As well as print, regular expressions also operate implicitly on $_. We'll be covering regular expressions in depth in Chapter 8, *Regular Expressions Basics*, on page 103, but if in the previous example we changed our start_with? call to use a regular expression instead, it would read:

```
$ printf "foo\nbar\n" | ruby -ne 'print if /^f/'
```

This one-liner is brief almost to the point of being magical; the subject of both the print statement and the if are both completely implicit. But one-liners like this are optimized more for typing speed than for clarity, and so tricks like this—which have a subtlety that might be frowned upon in more permanent scripts—are a boon.

There are also shortcut methods for manipulating input. If we invoke Ruby with either the -n or -p flag, Ruby creates two global methods for us: sub and gsub. These act just like their ordinary string counterparts, but they operate on $_ implicitly.

This means we can perform search and replace operations on our lines of input in a really simple way. For example, to replace all instances of COBOL with Ruby:

```
$ echo 'COBOL is the best!' | ruby -ne 'print gsub("COBOL", "Ruby")'
Ruby is the best!
```

We didn't need to call $_.gsub, as you might expect, since the gsub method operates on $_ automatically. This is a really handy shortcut.

Handy shortcuts are nice to have, but these techniques are fundamentally useful, too. This line-by-line looping that we achieve with -n enables many types of processing. We've seen *conditional output*, where we output only those lines that match certain criteria, and we've seen *filtering*, where we output a modified form of our input. Many scripts involve both of these steps, sometimes even multiple times.

In a full-blown script, we might not consider these to be distinct steps in a process, worthy of considering separately. We certainly wouldn't write multiple scripts, one to handle each one of them. But it can often help when writing a one-liner to frame things in this way. For example, let's take the following text file, which contains the names of students and their scores on a test:

```
Bob 40
Alice 98
Gillian 100
Fred 67
```

Let's imagine we want to output the name of any student who scored more than 50 on the test (sorry, Bob). There are two steps here: conditional output, to select only those students who scored more than 50; and filtering, to show only the name, rather than the name and score together. With a one-liner, it makes sense to treat those two things separately.

The first step is typically to output the contents of the file. This is an important psychological step, if nothing else, because it validates that the data is there and is in the format we're expecting:

```
$ cat scores.txt
Bob 40
Alice 98
Gillian 100
Fred 67
```

Next, we need to perform our filtering step. In this case, we need to take the second word of the line, convert it to a number, and check whether it's greater than 50:

```
$ cat scores.txt | \
  ruby -ne 'print if $_.split[1].to_i > 50'
Alice 98
Gillian 100
Fred 67
```

(The \ characters at the end of the line escape the line break, meaning that when you press Enter a newline is inserted rather than the shell executing the command you've typed. They're included here just to keep lines shorter on the page; although you can type them into your shell, in practice you wouldn't.)

Finally we perform our filter step, to output only the names:

```
$ cat scores.txt | \
  ruby -ne 'print if $_.split[1].to_i > 50' | \
  ruby -ne 'puts $_.split.first'
Alice
Gillian
Fred
```

Although we could potentially have performed these two steps together, breaking up the problem in this way has two important advantages. The first is performance: the two steps will run in parallel, so on greater input we might see a speedup. The second, though, is that we might discover that a particular step can be performed with an existing tool—in which case there's no need write any code of our own. That's the case here, in fact. We could have used cut for the second step:

```
$ cat scores.txt | \
  ruby -ne 'print if $_.split[1].to_i > 50' | \
  cut -d' ' -f1
Alice
Gillian
Fred
```

Here we tell cut that we want to delimit text by the space character, and to take the first field. If we keep our commands small and have them do just one job, then they're easier to compose together—either with more scripts of our own or with commands that already exist. That means solving problems more quickly and with less typing, which is always one of our goals when programming.

The -n switch is very useful, but Ruby has more one-liner gifts. There's another useful option that makes it even easier to write filter scripts.

Printing Lines with the -p Switch

We've seen that, when writing scripts to perform filter operations on input, we're very often taking a line of input, making a modification to it, and then outputting it. This pattern is common enough that Ruby offers us another switch to help: -p.

Used instead of -n, the -p switch acts similarly in that it loops over each of the lines in the input. However, it goes a bit further: after our code has finished, it always prints the value of $_. So, we can imagine it as:

```
while gets
  # execute code passed in -e here
  puts $_
```

```
end
```

Generally, it's useful when the code we pass using -e does something that modifies the current line, but where that output isn't conditional—in other words, where we're expecting to modify and output every line of the input.

So, returning to our find-and-replace example, we could use gsub! to modify the contents of $_:

```
$ echo 'COBOL is the best!' | ruby -pe '$_.gsub!("COBOL", "Ruby")'
Ruby is the best!
```

However, we can go shorter still. This operation is so common that Ruby provides a shortcut for it:

```
$ echo 'COBOL is the best!' | ruby -pe 'gsub("COBOL", "Ruby")'
Ruby is the best!
```

We know that the global gsub method operates on $_, but it also modifies it. In that sense, it operates like $_.gsub!. So after our call to gsub, $_ has been modified, and the implicit puts outputs our transformed text.

Prepending and Appending Code

When we use switches like -n and -p, the code that we pass runs in a loop. This avoids the need to write looping code ourselves, but it also presents a problem: all the code we pass will be executed repeatedly, once for each line in the input. Sometimes that's fine, but if we want to do something only once—for example, some initial setup code or something right at the end to summarize what we've worked on—then we're out of luck. Variables we initialize will be initialized (and so reset) on every line. Anything we output will be output for every line, not just once at the start or end.

We can sidestep this issue using two language constructs Ruby provides for us generally, not just for use with one-liners: BEGIN and END blocks.

Using BEGIN Blocks

If we want to execute some code once and once only, at the beginning of our script, we can use BEGIN blocks. They're an idiom borrowed from Awk, via Perl, and allow us—regardless of where we define them—to execute the associated code at the start of the script. In the case of our one-liners, even though the BEGIN block is technically being defined every time the loop runs, the code within the block will be executed only once. Ruby is clever enough to know that they're the same each time.

There are many uses for this. Perhaps the most common is to initialize variables. For example, if we wanted to output a number before each line, starting from 1 and proceeding upward, we could initialize a variable in a BEGIN block:

```
$ printf "foo\nbar\nbaz\n" | \
  ruby -ne 'BEGIN { i = 1 }; puts "#{i} #{$_}"; i += 1'
```

Here, we initialize i to 1 at the start of the script. The BEGIN block executes only once, so it is ignored on subsequent loops. We can then increment i, producing the following output:

```
1 foo
2 bar
3 baz
```

We can achieve the same effect, if we're only initializing variables, by using the conditional assignment operator:

```
$ printf "foo\nbar\nbaz\n" | \
  ruby -ne 'i ||= 1; puts "#{i} #{$_}"; i += 1'
```

In this case i will be assigned to 1 only if it doesn't already have a value. That means our assignment will take place on the first line of input, but then never again; we won't continually reset the value back to 1.

Ordinarily BEGIN blocks can be confusing to read, since they might potentially be defined in a totally different place from the point that they're executed. But in one-liners, where readability plays second fiddle to writability and terseness, and where the quantity of code is small, they're a valuable tool and worth using.

Using END Blocks

The opposite of wanting to execute something at the beginning of a script is, of course, executing something at the end. For this, we have the predictably named END block. Perhaps less used than the BEGIN blocks in one-liners, END blocks can be useful to make a final transformation before finishing our script. For example, if we wanted to write a script that treated its input as a list of numbers and provided a total of all of them, we could combine a BEGIN and an END block:

```
$ printf "12\n76\n42" | \
  ruby -ne 'BEGIN { n = 0 }; n += $_.to_i; END { puts n }'
130
```

This way we perform the addition on every line in the input, but only output the total after we've finished processing the final line.

Another example might be to output the longest line in our input. We don't know until we've reached the end of our input which line is the longest. (After all, the next line could always be longer than the previous longest.) So we need to keep track of which the longest line is and then output it at the end:

```
$ printf "a\nbb" | \
  ruby -ne 'l ||= $_; l=$_ if $_.length > l.length; END { puts l }'
```

That is: set a variable l to the contents of the first line of input. Then, on subsequent lines, update the value of l to the contents of the current line if its length is greater than that of the previous longest line. Finally, in an END block, output the value of l; by the end of the script, it will contain the longest line in the input.

With BEGIN and END blocks, and with our newfound knowledge of Ruby's command-line switches, we have everything we need to write powerful one-liners that use Ruby to process text. It's time to look at something a little more practical, so we can see how this translates to real life.

Example: Parsing Log Files

Generally the one-liners that you might find yourself writing fall into two categories: problems that are too simple or too temporary to ever commit to a file, or problems that are exploratory in nature, where you might eventually write a script but aren't ready to do so just yet.

Let's look at an example of the latter, a case of exploring a file to gather information about its contents. The file we'll be looking at is a log file for the popular web server software Apache. Its error logs look something like this:

```
[Tue Dec 30 15:25:20 2014] [error] Directory index forbidden
[Tue Dec 30 15:26:11 2014] [notice] caught SIGTERM, shutting down
[Tue Dec 30 15:26:14 2014] [notice] Digest: generating secret ...
[Tue Dec 30 15:26:14 2014] [notice] Digest: done
[Tue Dec 30 15:26:14 2014] [notice] Apache (Unix) -- resuming normal operations
```

Imagine we're looking at the error log and want to see the most common errors in it. We don't care about notices (things like the server restarting); we just want to look at errors and to know which ones are happening most often. But we don't want to have to write complicated logic for counting the number of occurrences of each error message ourselves. Such problems have already been solved, and the logic would take us far too long to write. Let's take a look at how we can write a one-liner in our shell that uses Ruby, in combination with other Unix utilities, to solve our problem.

First, let's extract just the error messages. This definitely seems like a job for Ruby. Some time spent with a regular expression, and we'll soon cut it down to size:

```
$ cat error_log | ruby -ne '$_ =~ /^\[.+\] \[error\] (.*)$/ and puts $1'
```

Here we ignore the date and time, make sure that the line refers to an error (rather than a notice), and then capture the error message. We then print the contents of that capture, but only if there actually was a match. (Don't worry if the regular expression syntax isn't clear; we'll look at regular expressions in more detail in Chapter 8, *Regular Expressions Basics*, on page 103.)

This combines conditional output with filtering, giving us an output of all the error messages and only the error messages—no extraneous output. We've fulfilled the first part of our task, extracting the error messages. We now need to count how many times each one of them appears in the log. We could continue to use Ruby for this, but it's not the best tool for the job; standard Unix utilities already exist for counting lines in output, so we should use those.

Those utilities are sort and uniq:

```
$ cat error_log \
  | ruby -ne '$_ =~ /^\[.+\] \[error\] (.*)$/ and puts $1' \
  | sort | uniq -c
```

Sorting our log entries ensures that the same entries appear next to one another, allowing uniq to exclude all of the duplicates. The -c argument to uniq then tells it to output how many times each duplicate line occurred.

The output of our one-liner at this point will look something like this:

```
1653 Directory index forbidden
 560 File does not exist bar.jpg
 579 File does not exist baz.png
 564 File does not exist foo.txt
1674 caught SIGTERM, shutting down
```

We're almost there. This output shows us all the errors that occur in the log and the number of times they occur. But the output is unsorted; there may be many different errors, many of which might occur only once, and the errors that occur the most might get lost among all the other output. We need to sort the lines so that the errors with the most occurrences appear at the top of the list.

For this, we can turn again to sort. Instead of sorting the lines as straightforward strings, though, we need to treat them as numbers:

```
$ cat error_log \
  | ruby -ne '$_ =~ /^\[.+\] \[error\] (.*)$/ and puts $1' \
  | sort | uniq -c | sort -rn
```

The -rn arguments tell sort to sort in descending order and to sort "naturally" (that is, to treat 10 as greater than 2, even though an ordinary string sort wouldn't agree).

Our iterative process has gotten us closer and closer to solving our problem. In fact, we're there. A final nicety might be to show only the top ten errors, rather than the complete list, and for this we can use head:

```
$ cat error_log \
  | ruby -ne '$_ =~ /^\[.+\] \[error\] (.*)$/ and puts $1' \
  | sort | uniq -c | sort -rn | head -n 10
```

head outputs lines from the start of its input. In this case we pass -n 10 to it to instruct it to output the first ten lines of input it receives.

We now see the desired output, with the most common errors listed first:

```
1674 caught SIGTERM, shutting down
1653 Directory index forbidden
 579 File does not exist baz.png
 564 File does not exist foo.txt
 560 File does not exist bar.jpg
```

This is a great example of how, by combining a Ruby one-liner with some preexisting utilities, we were able to do a fairly complex bit of processing while only needing to write code for the part of the problem that was novel. We used Ruby to do the heavy lifting of extracting the information, then transformed it using common Unix utilities. The script took a matter of minutes to write, and we only had to write the minimum part of it—we didn't need to write code to handle the sorting or counting, for example. Because we didn't have to bother committing it to disk anywhere, we could just use it to do some ad hoc exploration of the data, modifying the code as we went.

Wrapping Up

We've now further developed our text processing toolkit. No longer are we restricted to writing Ruby code to be executed in the form of scripts. By harnessing the power of Ruby's interpreter and its -e flag, we can pass code to Ruby directly from the command line.

But Ruby goes even further than that to help us. We can use the -n and -p flags to loop automatically over the lines in standard input, and in the latter case automatically output it. These flags allow us to very straightforwardly write snippets of Ruby code that filter standard input, slotting neatly into text processing pipelines.

This allows us to write quick and straightforward snippets that solve both simple problems and exploratory ones. This way of processing standard input is a useful one. Next, we'll look at another useful idiom—writing utilities that work with both standard input and files, the ultimate flexibility.

CHAPTER 4

Flexible Filters with ARGF

In text processing utilities that act as filters and are designed to be run from the command line, it's common—standard, even—to accept input both from standard input and from files. Take perhaps the simplest of all such tools: cat. If you pass it standard input, it outputs standard input:

```
$ echo "hello from standard input" | cat
hello from standard input
```

If, on the other hand, you pass it filenames as arguments, it will output the contents of those files:

```
$ echo "hello from file one" > one.txt
$ echo "hello from file two" > two.txt
$ cat one.txt two.txt
hello from file one
hello from file two
```

This behavior is a great courtesy to the end users of the tool: it gives it an enormous flexibility and allows it to be used in as many situations as possible. Virtually every Unix text filter utility works in this way, from cat and grep to sed and awk.

Thankfully, Ruby makes it easy to write tools that behave in the same courteous and flexible way: ARGF. Related, as its name might suggest, to ARGV—the array of arguments passed on the command line—ARGF allows you not to care where your input is coming from. Ruby will take care of figuring out whether to read from files passed on the command line or from standard input.

Thanks to ARGF, then, writing utilities that can handle input both from standard input and from files turns out to be no more difficult than writing ones that can handle just one of them. But that's not all. With ARGF, several other behaviors become easier, such as directly modifying the files you're processing or straightforwardly working with both a constant set of files and the variable ones passed on the command line. Let's dive in and see what ARGF can do.

Reading from ARGF as a Stream

The simplest way to use ARGF is by treating it as a single stream of text and looping over each line in that stream.

Like other streams in Ruby, ARGF responds to each_line. We've seen this before, both when working with standard input and when working with files. In the former case, we called each_line on $stdin, and in the latter, we called each_line on a file object. In this case, we call ARGF.each_line, and just like in those other examples the block that we pass to ARGF.each will be invoked once per line in the stream.

With ARGF, the contents of that stream either are the same as $stdin or are a continuous reading of all the files passed on the command line.

Here's an example, then, of the simplest possible use of ARGF:

```
# argf.rb
ARGF.each_line do |line|
  puts line
end
```

If we run the previous script with arguments, like so:

```
$ ruby argf.rb foo.txt bar.txt baz.txt
```

then Ruby will assume that each of the arguments is a file, and ARGF will read from each of the files in turn, from left to right. That means that our script is equivalent to:

```
ARGV.each do |file|
  File.open(file).each_line do |line|
    puts line
  end
end
```

If one of the files doesn't exist, Ruby will throw its standard ENOENT error, like so:

```
$ ruby argf.rb nonexistent.txt
argf.rb:1:in `each': No such file or directory - nonexistent.txt (Errno::ENOENT)
  from argf.rb:1:in `<main>'
```

Where ARGF becomes more useful, however, is in what it does when no arguments are specified. In this case, Ruby will read from standard input instead. That means that our example script is *also* equivalent to:

```
$stdin.each_line do |line|
  puts line
end
```

This enables us to pipe input into our script:

```
$ printf "foo\nbar" | ruby argf.rb
foo
bar
```

More usefully, this means that we could pipe the input from another process into our script and do something interesting with it. We've allowed for the same text processing pipelines that we achieved when processing just standard input, but also added the ability to read from files.

You may have noticed that this "simplest possible" script is functionally equivalent to `cat`. It will output sequentially the contents of all files passed to it, or it will echo back standard input passed to it.

Two Behaviors

Although `ARGF` has two possible behaviors—two sources of input—it might be surprising to learn that it won't behave in both ways at the same time. For example, if we call our argf.rb script as follows:

```
$ echo "hello from a file" > foo.txt
$ echo "hello from standard input" | ruby argf.rb foo.txt
```

we'll see only the output:

```
hello from a file
```

This is because `ARGF` actually behaves as follows:

```
if ARGV.length > 0
  # Read from the files specified on the command line
else
  # Read from standard input
end
```

That is, if the script has been passed some arguments on the command line, treat them as files and read from those files; otherwise, read from standard input.

In practice, this is exactly how we generally want our scripts to behave. We're using them either with files or with standard input in pipelines, not both, so this behavior makes sense.

ARGF-specific Methods

Although ARGF is a stream and behaves similarly to $stdin, it has some methods of its own. These are of particular use when ARGF is reading from files, allowing you to interact with or obtain more information about those files, but they can also offer more general information.

Two methods allow you to find out more information about the file you're processing. The first method is ARGF.filename, which returns the name of the file that's currently being read. The second is ARGF.file, which returns a File object pointing to that file.

Let's put these methods to use. We'll write a script that outputs the contents of the files we pass to it, and at the start of each file outputs the name of the file and its size:

argf-features.rb

```
ARGF.each do |line|
  if ARGF.filename != "-" && ARGF.file.lineno == 1
    puts "\n#{ARGF.filename} (#{ARGF.file.size} bytes):\n\n"
  end

  puts line
end
```

First, we check that ARGF.filename isn't -. If it is, that means we're processing standard input, and this functionality is not needed. Then, we check ARGF.file.lineno to get the number of the current line in the current file. At the start of a file this will naturally be 1, so we know that we've moved to a new file. That's our cue to output the extra information we want to display.

If we wanted to get the number of the *overall* line that we're processing, not the line within the file, we can use ARGF.lineno. ARGF maintains its own count, starting at 1, from the first line of the first file to the last line of the last. So if we wanted to number the lines of input that we receive, we could:

argf-lineno.rb

```
ARGF.each do |line|
  puts "#{ARGF.lineno}: #{line}"
end
```

Unlike the filename and file methods, which naturally only work when we're using ARGF to process files, we can use the lineno method when we're processing standard input, too.

Not all of ARGF's own methods are about getting information, though. If you'd like *not* to process a file, ARGF has you covered, too: just call ARGF.skip. This is useful if you want to process only files of a certain type, or you want to stop processing partway through a file (once you've got what you need, for example):

argf-skip.rb
```
ARGF.each do |line|
  unless ARGF.filename.end_with? ".txt"
    ARGF.skip
    next
  end

  puts line
end
```

In this example, we check whether the filename ends with .txt—that is, whether the file we're processing is a plain text file. If it's not, then we tell ARGF to skip to the next file, and then use next to skip the rest of our block. If it is, we output the line of text. There's other behavior that this facilitates, though:

argf-skip2.rb
```
ARGF.each do |line|
  case ARGF.file.lineno
  when 1
    puts "\n#{ARGF.filename}\n\n"
  when 6
    ARGF.skip
    next
  end

  puts line
end
```

In this example, we output only the first five lines of each file before skipping to the next. This gives us a summary of each file passed to us, but no more than that.

With these extra methods, ARGF becomes a bit more powerful and further justifies its use over just processing files or just processing standard input.

Modifying Files

Until now we've only dealt with using ARGF to read input. When we're dealing with files, though, it's common that we might also want to make modifications to them. With its *in-place mode*, Ruby offers a simple way to do this. This is useful if you're running a filter across many different files—a find-and-replace task, for example.

We can invoke this mode by passing the -i flag to Ruby. For example, if we wanted to work across a set of files and change the spelling of a word across them all—the British *tranquillity* to the U.S. *tranquility*, for example—we could write the following simple script:

argf-sub.rb

```
ARGF.each do |line|
  puts line.gsub("tranquillity", "tranquility")
end
```

We can run the script in the same way as we've seen in previous examples in this chapter:

```
$ echo "tranquillity" > file.txt
$ ruby argf-sub.rb file.txt
tranquility
```

By doing so, we see written to standard output the contents of file.txt, with the spelling changed as we wanted. But we could also invoke the script as follows, passing the -i option to the Ruby interpreter:

```
$ echo "tranquillity" > file.txt
$ ruby -i argf-sub.rb file.txt
```

As we can see, there's no output from our script this time. Instead, our puts wrote to the file itself, modifying it in place. Like other uses of ARGF, this doesn't work with just one file. We could pass in hundreds of files, and all of them would be modified—very handy.

Handy, yes, but also quite destructive. We didn't receive a prompt or confirmation. The original contents of the file were lost. Imagine running this over many files and then discovering that we'd made a mistake—we'd have lost all our data!

Thankfully, the -i option accepts a value. If we pass one, instead of writing to the same file and discarding the original, Ruby will back up the original file by adding whatever we pass to -i as a suffix. Let's change our example to see it in action:

```
$ echo "tranquillity" > file.txt
$ ruby -i'.bak' argf-sub.rb file.txt
$ cat file.txt
tranquility
$ cat file.txt.bak
tranquillity
```

As in the first example, file.txt has been modified and contains the new content. Unlike that example, though, the original contents of the file have been preserved in file.txt.bak. We might then compare the two files to make sure that the changes are as we expected, and then safely delete the backup file once we're sure everything went well.

Manipulating ARGV

If we pass arguments to our Ruby script on the command line, then the ARGV array will contain those arguments as values. In this case, as we've seen, ARGF will assume that these command-line arguments refer to files, so it will try to read from them.

So far, all we've done with this knowledge is to pass files on the command line. But ARGV isn't a fixed proposition. It's something that you can modify, adding or removing elements to either pretend something was passed on the command line or pretend that it wasn't.

This comes in useful in two different scenarios. First, when the actual arguments passed on the command line contain things that aren't files, which you likely want ARGF to ignore rather than attempt to read. And second, when you want to make ARGF think that a particular file was passed on the command line even when it wasn't.

Deleting Elements

The most common example of the first scenario—wanting to allow non-file arguments to be passed as well as file arguments—is to to allow options to be passed to your script. These typically start with -; things like -v for *verbose mode* or -f for *file*, and so on. You don't want to consider these arguments as files. In other words, if your script is invoked as script -v foo.txt bar.txt, you want to end up with ARGF processing foo.txt and bar.txt, and not trying and failing to read a file called -v.

If we were to use ARGF normally:

argv1.rb

```
ARGF.each do |line|
  puts line
end
```

we'd get the following error:

```
$ ruby argv1.rb -v foo.txt bar.txt
argv1.rb:1:in `each': No such file or directory @ rb_sysopen - -v (Errno::ENOENT)
from argv1.rb:1:in `<main>'
```

Ruby is trying to read from a file called -v and failing because such a file doesn't exist. We can handle this by removing things from ARGV that aren't supposed to be interpreted as files:

argv2.rb
```
options = { v: false }

ARGV.delete_if do |a|
  a.start_with?("-") &&
    options[a.sub(/^-/, "").to_sym] = true
end

ARGF.each do |line|
  puts line
end
```

This might seem complex at first, but it breaks down into simple parts. First, we initialize a hash to store our options, and set the default value of our -v option to false. Then, we loop over the arguments passed to the script. For any argument that starts with a hyphen, we simultaneously delete it from ARGV and set the option with the same name to true, to indicate that this option has been passed.

By the time we call ARGF, then, the -v value that was causing us problems has been deleted from ARGV, and so Ruby won't attempt to read it like a file. We've now gained the ability to pass things that aren't files along with things that are, while still seeing the benefits of using ARGF.

Once you want to accept more than a couple of command-line options, or perhaps want to do more complex arguments (ones with default values, or that take values), then handling this manually might become a bit tedious. Luckily, the standard library comes with the OptionParser library,[1] which can handle these more complex tasks. Libraries like Main[2] and Thor[3] go even further, allowing you to create full-blown command-line applications with different modes and many different complex arguments. Helpfully, these libraries will also remove the options from ARGV for you, so you'll be able to use ARGF the same way as you could if you handled everything manually. But for simple scripts, with just one or two arguments, it can be simpler to do this yourself.

Adding Elements

In our second scenario, we wanted to add elements to ARGV. There are likely to be two different scenarios for this: that we want to prepend our extra

1. http://ruby-doc.org/stdlib-2.1.5/libdoc/optparse/rdoc/OptionParser.html
2. https://github.com/ahoward/main
3. https://github.com/erikhuda/thor

files—that is, process them first—or that we want to append them, to process them last.

Either way, the task is simple. We just treat ARGV like the array that it is and use unshift to add files at the start and push to add them at the end.

For example, let's imagine a script invoked in the following way:

```
$ ruby script.rb bar.txt
```

...with the following content:

```
ARGV # => ["bar.txt"]
ARGV.unshift("foo.txt") # => ["foo.txt", "bar.txt"]
ARGV.push("baz.txt") # => ["foo.txt", "bar.txt", "baz.txt"]
```

If we now do something with ARGF, it will operate on three files, even though only one was passed on the command line. It will also process them in the exact order we've specified.

Wrapping Up

We looked at how, for a certain type of text processing utility—a filter, in essence—ARGF makes handling both standard input and files easy. We looked at how we can process ARGF as a stream, reading lines sequentially without caring where they come from. Next we modified files in place, giving us the ability to write find-and-replace types of utilities that work across many files. Finally, we saw how we could manipulate ARGV either to skip certain arguments and not process them as files, or to add to the list of arguments and process files that weren't passed on the command line.

ARGF neatly combines the previous chapters in this section. We can now get text into our program from standard input and from files, and we know how to write flexible command-line filters that can accept input from both. But much of the data we encounter in the real world isn't just plain text, it's wrapped up in structure, in delimited formats such as CSV files. So, let's look at how we can extract text from these more troublesome formats.

CHAPTER 5

Delimited Data

So far we've worked only with unstructured, plain-text input. But in the real world, input typically has a structure that reflects the data stored within it. We've seen glimpses of this—separating parts of a line by whitespace, for example—but we haven't delved deep into the idea of representing the structure of our data within our programs, so that we can transform and manipulate it however we like.

The simplest structured data is stored in so-called *delimited files*. You may well have encountered files with the extensions CSV (*comma-separated values*) or TSV (*tab-separated values*). Both of these are delimited file formats.

The structure that these file formats introduces is centered around the concepts of *records* and *fields*. A file contains many records, and each record has many fields. Perhaps the easiest way to translate this is to think of a spreadsheet, where records are rows and fields are columns.

A delimited file format typically has two delimiters. The first separates one record from another, and the second separates fields within a record. In a TSV file, then, records are separated by newlines, and fields are separated from one another with a tab character.

Even though you might encounter many different types of delimiters, and many different types of delimited files, the same principles apply when parsing the files into Ruby data structures.

In this chapter, we'll take a look first at how to parse arbitrary formats, looking especially at TSV files since they're perhaps the simplest formats you might encounter in the real world. Then we'll look at a more complex, but much more common, sort of delimited file: the CSV, which has become, for better or for worse, the universal format for data interchange. If you want to handle data exported from spreadsheets, databases, and web services, being able to process CSVs will be essential.

Parsing a TSV

Let's imagine we have a spreadsheet that represents our personal expenditures. We want to keep track of what we buy, how much it costs, and where we bought it. So we set up a spreadsheet in which each row (or record) represents a purchase, and in which the columns (or fields) represent the item name, the price, and the retailer from which it was bought.

We happily record our data, and all is well. But the list soon becomes unwieldy, and it's difficult to analyze the data. We might want to find out our most expensive ever item, for example, or calculate the average cost of an item from a particular retailer. If we get the data into Ruby, these calculations will be straightforward, so let's find out how to do that.

Our first step is to export our data as a TSV file, something most spreadsheet software can do. It will look something like this:

data/shopping.tsv
```
White Bread	£1.20	Baker
Whole Milk	£0.80	Corner Shop
Gorgonzola	£10.20	Cheese Shop
Mature Cheddar	£5.20	Cheese Shop
Limburger	£6.35	Cheese Shop
Newspaper	£1.20	Corner Shop
Ilchester	£3.99	Cheese Shop
```

We can see that in the TSV format, each record is separated by a newline, and each field is separated by a tab. One of the nice things about the TSV format is that it visually tends to resemble a table: the tabs that separate the fields typically cause them to line up, and they look much like the spreadsheet they came from. Our job is to split the file up into records, and then split each record up into its constituent fields.

Splitting the File into Records

Our first task is to split the file into records, so that each row is its own value. As we saw when we explored processing text from files, Ruby offers many methods for getting a line of text: `gets`, `readline`, `each_line`, and so on—they all allow us to process our input one line at a time.

For our TSV example, this behavior is fine. Our records are separated by newlines, so if we call `each_line` on our file, we'll be able to loop over its records:

tsv-each.rb

```
File.open("data/shopping.tsv") do |file|
  file.each_line do |record|
    record
    # => "White Bread\t£1.20\tBaker\n"
    #    , "Whole Milk\t£0.80\tCorner Shop\n"
    #    , "Gorgonzola\t£10.20\tCheese Shop\n"
    #    , "Mature Cheddar\t£5.20\tCheese Shop\n"
    #    , "Limburger\t£6.35\tCheese Shop\n"
    #    , "Newspaper\t£1.20\tCorner Shop\n"
    #    , "Ilchester\t£3.99\tCheese Shop\n"
  end
end
```

But what if our records aren't separated by newlines? It would be a shame if we lost the benefit of all these existing methods and had to implement our own splitting logic. Luckily, that's not the case. These methods don't actually have to work in the context of lines at all, and they only do so because of Ruby's `$/` variable—the *input record separator.*

The default input record separator is `\n`, which is why these methods work line-wise. But we can change that. Whatever we set `$/` to will be the new delimiter used by `gets`, `readline`, and other similar methods.

Let's assume we have a file called `foo.txt` with the following content:

```
this is line one
this is line two
```

If we open the file as normal, each call to `gets` will return a line from the file until the end of the file is reached, at which point it will return `nil`:

```
file = File.open("foo.txt")

file.gets
# => "this is line one\n"
file.gets
# => "this is line two\n"
file.gets
# => nil
```

Now let's try changing the input record separator and see how the behavior changes:

```
file = File.open("foo.txt")
$/ = " "

file.gets
# => "this "
file.gets
```

```
# => "is "
file.gets
# => "line "
```

We can see that, as we instructed it to, gets is now separating records by spaces rather than by newlines. By manipulating Ruby's built-in variables, we don't need to implement any logic to actually split the string up ourselves; we can leave that to Ruby. While manipulating the input record separator isn't necessary to parse our TSV file, it's important to know.

Splitting Records into Fields

Having split up our file into its individual records, we now need to split each record into the fields it's made up of.

For this, we'll reach for the split method of the String class, used to separate a string into individual chunks by separating on a specific character. So, if we wanted to split a paragraph of text into words, we could split on " ":

```
paragraph = "This is a paragraph of text."
words = paragraph.split(" ")
# => ["This", "is", "a", "paragraph", "of", "text."]
```

If we don't pass anything to split, though, we achieve the same effect:

```
paragraph = "This is a paragraph of text."
words = paragraph.split
# => ["This", "is", "a", "paragraph", "of", "text."]
```

In much the same way as we saw that File's each method has a default value, the input record separator, so too does split. If you don't pass an argument to it, it checks the value of $;, the *input record separator*. If there is one, it splits on that character; if there isn't one—which there isn't by default—then it splits on whitespace.

So, we can continue our TSV parsing script by explicitly splitting on tabs:

tsv-split.rb

```
File.open("data/shopping.tsv") do |file|
  file.each do |record|
    record.chomp.split("\t")
    # => ["White Bread", "£1.20", "Baker"]
    #    , ["Whole Milk", "£0.80", "Corner Shop"]
    #    , ["Gorgonzola", "£10.20", "Cheese Shop"]
    #    , ["Mature Cheddar", "£5.20", "Cheese Shop"]
    #    , ["Limburger", "£6.35", "Cheese Shop"]
    #    , ["Newspaper", "£1.20", "Corner Shop"]
    #    , ["Ilchester", "£3.99", "Cheese Shop"]
  end
end
```

This works fine. As you can see, each record is split into an array, each element of which is one of the fields in our record. If we wanted to state our intent at the outset of our script, though, we could explicitly state the separators we planned to use. This would allow us to use the implicit split on our records:

tsv-implicit-split.rb
```
$/ = "\n"
$; = "\t"

File.open("data/shopping.tsv") do |file|
  file.each do |record|
    record.chomp.split
    # => ["White Bread", "£1.20", "Baker"]
    #    , ["Whole Milk", "£0.80", "Corner Shop"]
    #    , ["Gorgonzola", "£10.20", "Cheese Shop"]
    #    , ["Mature Cheddar", "£5.20", "Cheese Shop"]
    #    , ["Limburger", "£6.35", "Cheese Shop"]
    #    , ["Newspaper", "£1.20", "Corner Shop"]
    #    , ["Ilchester", "£3.99", "Cheese Shop"]
  end
end
```

Whether it's wise to redefine these globals depends on our application. What might be acceptable in a throwaway, single-use script is not going to be acceptable in a library that has to play nicely with others' code.

We've now done all that's necessary to parse a TSV file into a data structure within our script. We're looping over all of the records and have broken each record into fields. This is enough for us to begin performing analysis or calculations on the data within.

Performing a Calculation with the Data

Once we've parsed the file and have a representation of its data in our Ruby script, we can start to do the calculations that we wanted to in the first place. This is where Ruby can really flex its muscles as a general-purpose programming language and where we see the benefit of representing the structure of the data in our program. Doing so will make it easy to perform tasks that would be far too difficult in a spreadsheet or on the command line.

One useful thing to know would be how much we've spent in total at the cheese shop. Breaking this into steps, we need first to select only those records where the retailer is Cheese Shop. Then we need to get the price of each item. Finally, we need to add these prices together to obtain the total.

Thanks to Ruby's Enumerable module, these tasks are straightforward:

tsv-total.rb

```
File.open("data/shopping.tsv") do |file|
  cheese_total = file.each_line
    .map         { |line| line.chomp.split("\t") }
    .select      { |_, _, shop| shop == "Cheese Shop" }
    .map         { |_, price, _| price }
    .reduce(0.0) { |total, price| total + price[1..-1].to_f }
    .round(2)

  puts "£#{cheese_total}"
end
# >> £25.74
```

In the first two lines of the block, we split the file into lines with each_line. But instead of passing a block to it, we run map over the result. This allows us to construct an array of all of the records—so an array-of-arrays—without having to store an array of all the fields as strings first. The logic for splitting the record into fields is the same as we've used in previous examples.

Next, we use select to select only those records where the shop field's value is Cheese Shop. Rather than access cryptic references like record[2], which say nothing about what the field actually represents, we take advantage of Ruby's destructuring of block arguments to give these values readable names. For fields that we're not using, we use the name _, which signifies an unused value.

Then we use map again to take only the prices, since that's what we'll be calculating with. Finally, we use reduce to sum the prices, rounding the end result to two decimal places.

Although straightforward in Ruby, this sort of processing would be painstaking or impossible in other systems. Ruby's powerful collections and wealth of methods in its Enumerable module make these sorts of filtering tasks easy and expressive. Hopefully you can imagine many other things to do with this data: displaying the most popular item, for example, or the most popular shop; finding the most expensive product we've ever bought; and so on.

Delimited Data and the Command Line

Not all of our processing of delimited data will be quite so formal as reading from TSV-formatted files on our disk, though. Sometimes, text is delimited in a more casual way: pipe symbols that separate two different values in the output of a command, for example, or even just the spaces that separate words in any passage of text.

In Chapter 3, *Shell One-Liners*, on page 29, we discovered how to use Ruby in ad hoc, write-once pipelines to filter and transform text. We can do the same with delimited data, too, and just like with plain text Ruby offers some helpful shortcuts that make doing so easy.

The first way that we can get Ruby to help us when processing delimited text is by passing the -F option to the Ruby interpreter. This automatically sets the field separator ($;) to whatever we pass to the -F option. So if we pass a -F value of :, the input record separator will be set to that:

```
$ ruby -F: -e 'p $;'
/:/
```

Any calls to split in the code passed to Ruby would then split on : characters. That's slightly useful, perhaps. But it becomes much more powerful when we pair it with another option passable to the Ruby interpreter: the -a, or *autosplit*, option.

If we pass -a as well as -F, Ruby will populate the global variable $F with the contents of $_.split—that is, it will automatically split every line in the input.

Let's go back to our expenditure example to see how these options can be useful. We had the following TSV file:

data/shopping.tsv

```
White Bread     £1.20   Baker
Whole Milk      £0.80   Corner Shop
Gorgonzola      £10.20  Cheese Shop
Mature Cheddar  £5.20   Cheese Shop
Limburger       £6.35   Cheese Shop
Newspaper       £1.20   Corner Shop
Ilchester       £3.99   Cheese Shop
```

If we wanted to output the price of every item—just the price, no other information—then we could, without needing to write a script, invoke Ruby as follows:

```
$ ruby -F'\t' -ane 'puts $F[1]' shopping.tsv
```

Here we tell Ruby that we'd like to split fields on the tab character by passing -F'\t'. We then, by passing -a, say that we'd like to automatically split input, and then with -n that we'd like to loop over all the lines in the input. Then we pass in the code to execute with -e. This code tells Ruby simply to puts the second field of each line ($F[0] being the first, $F[1] being the second, and so on). Finally, we tell Ruby to read its input from a file called shopping.tsv.

This can come in really handy for removing the need to use cut in our pipeline chains. Imagine we wanted to list the home directory of every user on our system. One way we could do that would be by looking in our passwd file.

This file is a list of all the users on our system, among other things. It's usually stored in the /etc directory on Unix systems, and it looks something like this:

```
# User Database
adent:x:1001:1000:Arthur Dent:/bin/zsh
fprefect:x:1002:1000:Ford Prefect:/bin/bash
zbeeblebrox:x:1003:1000:Zaphod Beeblebrox:/bin/tcsh
```

Lines starting with a # symbol are comments. Otherwise, lines are colon-delimited structures, the first field of which is the username of each user on our system—and that's all we're interested in. It's not necessary to write a full-blown script to extract these fields. We can do it with a Ruby one-liner:

```
$ ruby -F: -ane 'puts File.expand_path("~" + $F[0]) unless /^#/' /etc/passwd
```

Here we tell Ruby to separate on the colon character with -F: and then pass the now-familiar -ane options to tell Ruby to automatically split lines, to loop over input, and to execute the code we pass to it on the command line. The code we pass simply takes the first field in each line and uses the File class to look up the home directory of that user, but only if the line doesn't start with a comment. (That's what the unless /^#/ does: executes the code unless the current line of input has a hash at the start of it.)

Just like we saw when processing unstructured text using one-liners, using the -a and -F flags enables all sorts of ad hoc text processing. They allow us to construct complex text processing pipelines on the fly, and allow us to see the intermediary steps of the solution as we're writing them. Both of these things serve to shorten the feedback loop between writing and executing our code, which means that we spend less time heading down rabbit holes and more time progressing toward solving our problem.

The CSV Format

It's for good reason that the example file we started with was the humble TSV file. It's probably the simplest sort of delimited data we're likely to encounter. However, the most *common* format by far is the *comma-separated values* (CSV) file. It is, for better or for worse, the standard file format for exporting data from and importing data to websites, databases, spreadsheets, and pretty much any other data store. If you haven't encountered CSV files in your development so far, you're virtually guaranteed to at some point.

Initially, it might seem like a simple proposition to parse CSV files. You might think that you can set your field separator to , rather than a tab character, and then generally proceed as you did for TSV files.

For a whole host of reasons, technical and historical, the CSV format is a little hairier than that. For a start, the chosen delimiter is incredibly common—commas occur frequently in the text that we typically want to include in a field. So, it's generally necessary to quote fields by surrounding them in double quotes ("). Otherwise, it wouldn't be clear whether the comma was within a field or was separating two different fields.

However, double quotes are *also* fairly common in text. So the quoting of fields simply creates another problem: what to do when we want to include a double quote inside our field. Well, we need to escape them. The problem with *that* is that there are two competing standards for how they should be escaped. The first, used by Microsoft Excel, says to precede them with a backslash (\"); the second, technically the standard but less common in the real world, says to double them ("").

For all these reasons and more—we haven't even gotten into the mind-bending issue of what to do with newlines in fields—parsing CSV files is a complicated business, best left to geniuses and masochists. Thankfully, James Edward Grey II, who is undoubtedly the former but possibly also the latter, has put an enormous amount of hard work into solving this problem. His FasterCSV library was included in the Ruby standard library in Ruby 1.9.2 and does all of the complicated parsing work for you.

To use Ruby's CSV library, you simply need to `require` it:

```
require "csv"
```

Let's take a look at what it can do. For consistency, let's use the same shopping list as we did in the previous, TSV-based examples. Its CSV representation looks like this:

data/shopping.csv

```
"White Bread","£1.20","Baker"
"Whole Milk","£0.80","Corner Shop"
"Gorgonzola","£10.20","Cheese Shop"
"Mature Cheddar","£5.20","Cheese Shop"
"Limburger","£6.35","Cheese Shop"
"Newspaper","£1.20","Corner Shop"
"Ilchester","£3.99","Cheese Shop"
```

We'll be using this data throughout this section as we explore Ruby's CSV library and its features.

Parsing an Entire File

If you've been following the entire book, the interface to CSV will feel very familiar. Its API is modeled closely on the IO class that underpins File and standard input, so interacting with CSV files feels very similar to processing these other forms of input.

And so, just like we can use File.read to load an entire file into a string, we can use CSV.read to load an entire CSV file into an array of arrays:

csv-read.rb
```
require "csv"

CSV.read("data/shopping.csv")
# => [["White Bread", "£1.20", "Baker"],
#     ["Whole Milk", "£0.80", "Corner Shop"],
#     ["Gorgonzola", "£10.20", "Cheese Shop"],
#     ["Mature Cheddar", "£5.20", "Cheese Shop"],
#     ["Limburger", "£6.35", "Cheese Shop"],
#     ["Newspaper", "£1.20", "Corner Shop"],
#     ["Ilchester", "£3.99", "Cheese Shop"]]
```

For small CSV files, this might be fine. But we soon run into the same problems we would with regular files: it's typically wasteful, and often impossible, to read the whole file into memory when we're normally working on only small parts of it at a time. The ideal arrangement would be a method to process a CSV file one record at a time, the same thing we can do by calling each_line on a file object or by using File.foreach. Thankfully, Ruby's CSV library offers us this functionality.

Streaming a File Record by Record

Just as we have File.foreach, which iterates over the lines of a file, we have CSV.foreach. As with read, we'll get back an array of fields for each record in the file:

csv-foreach.rb
```
require "csv"

CSV.foreach("data/shopping.csv") do |record|
  record
  # => ["Bread", "£1.20", "Baker"]
  #    , ["Milk", "£0.80", "Corner Shop"]
  #    , ["Cheese", "£10.20", "Fromagerie"]
end
```

The block we pass to foreach will be executed once per record in the file and will have that row's values passed into it as an array. Only one line will be read into memory at a time, so there's no need to worry about memory usage even when reading large files.

Nine times out of ten, when parsing CSV files, foreach will do everything you need. It streams, so it works with even the biggest files. It's fast. And it gives us a simple and straightforward representation of each record: an array with an element for each field.

Header Rows

A common idiom in CSV files, especially ones exported from spreadsheets and databases, is for the first row to contain information about the fields themselves. For example, in our shopping list example, we might label our fields as follows:

data/shopping-with-header.csv

```
"Item","Price","Shop"
"White Bread","£1.20","Baker"
"Whole Milk","£0.80","Corner Shop"
"Gorgonzola","£10.20","Cheese Shop"
"Mature Cheddar","£5.20","Cheese Shop"
"Limburger","£6.35","Cheese Shop"
"Newspaper","£1.20","Corner Shop"
"Ilchester","£3.99","Cheese Shop"
```

If we just used the CSV library as normal, then this won't quite work as we hope it will. The CSV library has no idea whether the first row is a header—it just looks like normal data to it—and so the first row we process will contain the values "Item," "Price," and "Shop."

If we set the :headers option to true when creating our CSV object, however, the result is something a little more logical. If we try it out on the previous example, we can see that the object returned for each of the rows has changed from being a simple array of values to being a CSV::Row object:

csv-header.rb

```
require "csv"

CSV.foreach("data/shopping-with-header.csv", headers: true) do |record|
  record
# => #<CSV::Row "Item":"White Bread" "Price":"£1.20" "Shop":"Baker">
# , #<CSV::Row "Item":"Whole Milk" "Price":"£0.80" "Shop":"Corner Shop">
# , #<CSV::Row "Item":"Gorgonzola" "Price":"£10.20" "Shop":"Cheese Shop">
# , #<CSV::Row "Item":"Mature Cheddar" "Price":"£5.20" "Shop":"Cheese Shop">
# , #<CSV::Row "Item":"Limburger" "Price":"£6.35" "Shop":"Cheese Shop">
# , #<CSV::Row "Item":"Newspaper" "Price":"£1.20" "Shop":"Corner Shop">
# , #<CSV::Row "Item":"Ilchester" "Price":"£3.99" "Shop":"Cheese Shop">
end
```

These objects behave rather like hashes. In particular, we can use the [], or *subscript*, operator to access individual fields:

csv-row-objects.rb
```
require "csv"

CSV.foreach("data/shopping-with-header.csv", headers: true) do |record|
  record["Price"]
  # => "£1.20"
  #    , "£0.80"
  #    , "£10.20"
  #    , "£5.20"
  #    , "£6.35"
  #    , "£1.20"
  #    , "£3.99"
end
```

There are some subtle differences between CSV::Row objects and normal hashes, the main one being that a CSV::Row can have multiple values with the same name, but they are fairly similar in practical terms.

Wrapping Up

In the real world, most of the plain-text files we'll encounter won't be chaotic and unstructured. Delimited files, like CSVs, are far more common. Practically every database, spreadsheet program, or web service imports data from or exports data to CSV format, so parsing it is essential. We explored how to parse these structures ourselves for simple formats like TSV, but also how to use Ruby's built-in CSV library to take the hard work out of processing the more complex CSV format.

We also saw how we could adapt our shell one-liners to delimited data by passing the -F and -a options to the Ruby interpreter, allowing us to explore delimited data in ad hoc scripts from the command line.

The next step in our processing journey increases the complexity of the structure of our text significantly: we'll be looking at extracting information from HTML web pages.

CHAPTER 6

Scraping HTML

As developers, the text that we process isn't always readily available in an easy-to-read plain-text format. It's not always available as the searchable, easy-to-digest result of some well-designed third-party API. Sometimes, it exists only on web pages, buried among a tangle of messy HTML. Extracting it can seem a daunting task: how do we cut through the clutter and get to just the information that we want?

Luckily, Ruby—with its good HTTP support and powerful text-processing capabilities—is a great choice for doing this sort of task, known as *screen scraping* or *web scraping*. Let's look at how.

The Right Tool for the Job: Nokogiri

Often novices—and experts, too—approach the problem of extracting HTML with regular expressions. (If you're not familiar with regular expressions, we'll be covering them in detail in Part II.) This is a truly terrible idea, and one that generally leads to a level of pain that can make people avoid scraping HTML again—a great shame, since knowing how to extract information from web pages is of huge practical benefit. But the fact remains: attempting to parse HTML with regular expressions is an awful idea.

The right tool to use is an HTML parser, which will parse the document into a tree and allow you to search and manipulate the nodes within that tree. A few libraries are available, but one called Nokogiri[1] is the most popular among Rubyists, and with good reason: it's fast, stable, and powerful.

An HTML parser works by taking the HTML that we give it and constructing a document tree from it. This is the same thing your web browser does when it reads a web page, and if you've ever used JavaScript you've likely worked

1. http://nokogiri.org

with your browser's representation of a document structure. It's called the Document Object Model (DOM), and it makes it easy to target specific elements and modify them, or add new elements.

Nokogiri does exactly the same thing under the hood: given some HTML, it provides us with a DOM-like interface to that HTML, allowing us to read it and manipulate it. Just like in JavaScript, we can modify and remove elements, but since we're looking at scraping we're going to focus on searching through the document to match particular elements we're interested in, and then extracting their content.

Nokogiri is packaged as a Ruby Gem, so installing it is as easy as:

```
$ gem install nokogiri
```

Now we just `require "nokogiri"`, and we're all set to begin parsing web pages.

If we require the `open-uri` library, part of the Ruby standard library, we can simply use `open` to fetch a web page, passing the result into Nokogiri's `HTML` method to create a document object:

```
require "nokogiri"
require "open-uri"

doc = Nokogiri::HTML(open("http://example.com/some/page.html"))
```

`open-uri` will take care of making the request for us. What it returns is an IO object containing the HTML from the web page. Nokogiri is happy with either a string containing HTML or an IO object, such as a file, so it will happily parse the result of `open` for us.

The next step is to actually do something with this document: we can search through it for elements that match particular criteria, for example, or to modify the structure. Let's take a look at how.

Searching the Document

When we're scraping a web page, we're generally interested in a small part of it. But a document contains so much information that we need some way of telling Nokogiri which particular bit of the page we're interested in. As humans, we do this in a visual way. We might look at a page and see a table, grasping its contents from the title above it. We'd scan down the rows to see the particular record we're interested in, and then across the columns to find the particular data value we were looking for. At no point do we have anything more than a vague appreciation for the *structure* of the page we're viewing; it doesn't matter to us what how the document is represented in HTML.

But, predictably, that's not how a computer sees the page. If we wanted to achieve the same result in a script—extracting a particular data value from a table—we need to understand the page's structure. We need to tell Nokogiri exactly which table within the page to look at, how the body rows are structured separately from the headers, how to identify the particular column that we want rather than the other data values, and so on.

The tricky part of this searching process is excluding the 99 percent of the page that we're not interested in, and honing in on the 1 percent that we are. Not only that, the ideal solution does so in a way that's flexible and that stands the best chance of continuing to work even if parts of the page change their structure. The web is, after all, a living thing, constantly changing and forever being updated.

Nokogiri gives us two techniques with which to trim complex documents down to size, each with strengths and weaknesses: XPath selectors and CSS selectors. Although they have their differences, there are some key similarities between them, primarily in the types of selectors that they offer. Let's take a look at these different types of selectors, and how we can use them in both XPath and CSS queries.

Writing Selectors

Originally developed for searching XML documents (hence the X in the name), XPath is a language in itself that's incredibly powerful. The basic syntax, though, is quite straightforward.

XPath selectors are, fundamentally, a representation of a hierarchy. We can think of them like a path to a file on our hard disk: we start at the root (/) and then walk down into directories, separated with slashes. XPath is just the same: we start at the root of the document and then walk down through the tags, each one separated with a slash.

The other method that Nokogiri offers for searching documents will be familiar to developers who've written CSS before or who've used the JavaScript library jQuery. CSS selectors are exactly as they sound: they're the same selectors you'd use to target elements in a CSS stylesheet. It's likely that they'll be more familiar to you than XPath selectors if you're from a web development background.

Throughout this section we'll be using this simple HTML document as an example:

nokogiri/sample-document.html

```
<!DOCTYPE html>
<html>
<head>
  <title>A sample document</title>
</head>
<body>
  <div class="container">
    <article>
      <h1>A sample document</h1>
      <div class="content">
        <p>
          This is a sample document.
          <img src="example.jpg" alt="A sample image">
        </p>
      </div>
    </article>
    <aside>
      <p>
        <img src="aside.jpg" alt="An aside" class="aside">
      </p>
    </aside>
  </div>
</body>
</html>
```

It should contain enough complexity to explore different selectors without being too complex to actually read.

You can search the document with XPath using the `xpath` method on a document and search it with CSS selectors using the `css` method. Each of these methods returns a `NodeSet`, which is a fragment of the document. It might represent a single continuous chunk of the document—everything under the `body`, for example. Or it might represent many discontinuous nodes—such as every image in the document, regardless of where they appear. These `NodeSets` behave a bit like arrays: you can loop over them with `each`, index into them with `[]`, and so on.

Let's have a look at some different types of selectors and how we can use them to target elements within a document.

Types of Selectors

There are four basic types of selectors, which allows you to select elements based on their type, their attributes, or their position in the hierarchy of the document. Each of these basic selectors can be written in either XPath or CSS, so there's no particular advantage of one over the other when selecting elements in this way.

Selecting by Element Type

Selecting by the type of element—in other words, by the name of a particular tag—is one of the simplest ways to select elements. Used alone, this will select all elements of a particular type; all the images on a page, for example, or all the paragraphs.

In both XPath and CSS selectors, we can target elements by their type by simply typing the element name. For example, to target the initial html element in our document, we could use the following selector in either XPath or CSS:

```
html
```

So, for example, these two methods return the same NodeSet, in each case containing a single Node:

```
doc.xpath("html")
doc.css("html")
```

The difference between XPath and CSS in this case is in their treatment of hierarchy. This XPath selector will match an html element only at the root of the document, not one nested deep within the document. As a CSS selector, it will match an html element regardless of its position in the document hierarchy. In this case that doesn't matter, because the html element is always at the root, but it's worth keeping in mind.

Child Selectors

In XPath, child selectors aren't significantly more complex than element type selectors, and are especially intuitive if you consider the filesystem inspiration of XPath. To select a child element we simply write the parent element, then a slash, then the child element. We can do this as many times as we like to build up a hierarchy of arbitrary depth.

If we wanted to target the article tag in the previous document, we could use the following XPath:

```
/html/body/div/article
```

Just like a filesystem path, we start at the root—the html element—and then get progressively deeper into the document as we go.

You might find it easier to think of the selector backwards: that is, that we're looking for any article tag, as long as it's the child of a div tag, which is the child of a body tag, which is the child of an html tag, which is at the root of the document. Whew!

In CSS, child selectors can be expressed with the > sign. So to select the article element, we'd use the following CSS selector:

```
html > body > div > article
```

Specifying the entire hierarchy of the page like this, though, is not only verbose but also brittle. It would be better if we could search for an article element regardless of where it appeared in the document.

Descendant Selectors

The selectors we wrote previously, which walk down the whole document from the root html tag eventually to an article, were quite verbose. It might possibly work for our unrealistically simple document, but it's not going to cut it in the real world. We'd end up with selectors a mile long, sore hands from typing, and an end result that is enormously brittle—any change to the structure of the document would be highly likely to break our selector.

Thankfully, we can do two things to cut down on the length of selectors: first, we can not start from the root; and second, we can not always to refer to direct children. We achieve both of those things using descendant selectors.

Revisiting the same HTML document as in the previous example, let's imagine that we wanted to match the img tag in the article, but not the one in the aside. If we stuck to our child selectors working from the root of the document, we'd end up with something like this:

```
/html/body/div/article/div/p/img
```

Those html, body, and div tags are pretty redundant, though. Everything we match in this document is likely to be below this level, so it can safely be skipped. We can do this by using a descendant selector at the start of the path:

```
//article/div/p/img
```

In other words, look for an img tag that's the child of a p tag, that's the child of a div, that's the child of an article that occurs anywhere in the document. This small change removes the need to tie our selector right back to the root of the document, which in HTML documents (that always have html and body elements) can cut them down significantly.

But that div might also give us pause, having as it does no real meaning in the structure of the fragment we're dealing with. If the document structure changes, and that div ceases to exist, our script will break. It's not just the div, though: if for some reason there's some nesting inside the content—a p inside a blockquote for example—then it will also break. It feels like we might have written something that's brittle, something that will break if the document structure changes even slightly. Given how often things change on the web, that's something we want to avoid if we can.

We're not limited to using descendant selectors at the start of a path—we can use them anywhere. So we could adapt our path to remove the div, like this:

```
//article//p/img
```

Now we're matching an img that's the child of a p, that's the descendant of an article that occurs anywhere in the document. It doesn't matter whether the p is the child, grandchild, or great-great-great-great-grandchild of the article; as long as it's nested below the article, the p will be matched.

This makes things a lot more flexible. If an extra wrapper is introduced, something gets nested that wasn't nested before, or any number of other changes are made to the document structure, our selector will still match. We've reduced the selector to just the essential elements and found that sweet spot between too general and too specific.

In CSS, as we saw when looking at element type selectors, descendant selectors are actually the default. We build up a hierarchy of descendants simply by listing the tags in order. The previous XPath example in CSS, then, would be:

```
article p > img
```

The downside of this descendant-by-default approach is that if we want to restrict a selector to the root, we can only do so implicitly. In web pages, though, the html element is at the root, so defining something relative to html will achieve the same behavior as the default XPath behavior.

Attribute Selectors

Previously we've only matched using the types of elements and their place in the hierarchy: match an img, for example, or match a p that's the child of an article. But in real life, that's often too general. There are lots of images in a document, lots of divs, lots of everything. To narrow things down, we probably want to match on other parts of the tag: its class, for example, or its ID, or any other attribute.

XPath supports this in a very straightforward way: you can put the attribute you want to match on in square brackets, prefixed with a @. Let's imagine we wanted to match the container in the previous document; it's a div with a class of container. We can do that:

```
//div[@class="container"]
```

This allows us to match any attribute we want—src, href, anything. We're not just limited to exact matches, either—we can match attributes that start with a particular value or that contain a particular value. For example, we could match our container example with all of these selectors:

```
//div[starts-with(@class, "container")]
//div[starts-with(@class, "con")]
//div[starts-with(@class, "c")]
//div[contains(@class, "container")]
//div[contains(@class, "ontainer")]
//div[contains(@class, "ntai")]
```

Attribute selectors are also possible with CSS selectors, and the syntax is similar to in XPath. To test for the presence of an attribute, just put the name of the attribute in square brackets:

```
img[src]
```

To test for exact values, we just write the attribute as we would in HTML, with an equals sign and the value in quotes:

```
img[src="example.jpg"]
```

We can also do the same "starts with" and "contains" selectors as we can in XPath. To match our container div, like we did with XPath selectors, we could use any of the following:

```
div[class="container"]
div[class^="container"]
div[class^="con"]
div[class^="c"]
div[class*="container"]
div[class*="ontainer"]
div[class*="ntai"]
```

CSS also adds a few more attribute selectors. We can match something at the end of a string with $=:

```
div[class$="ainer"]
```

We can also work with whitespace-separated values. In HTML, some attributes accept multiple values by separating them with spaces. We can give an element multiple classes, for example, by writing class="foo bar baz". We can check for the presence of one of these with the ~= selector:

```
div[class~="container"]
```

This would match our div even if it had other classes apart from container.

In practice, though, we wouldn't select classes this way. Just like when writing CSS, we can use `.` as a shortcut:

```
div.container
```

This is a lot simpler and clearer. CSS selectors offer a similar shortcut for `id` attributes:

```
div#main
```

When scraping web pages, these two shortcuts turn out to be incredibly useful and are the main reason why CSS selectors are typically shorter than their XPath equivalents.

Multiple Selectors

Sometimes there are elements accessible by two different selectors that you nevertheless want to treat in the same way. In these cases, we can combine two or more selectors.

So if we wanted to select all `img` elements that were children of either paragraph tags or list items, we could use the following XPath:

```
//p/img | //li/img
```

The pipe symbol is known as the *union operator*. In CSS, simply separate the selectors with a comma:

```
p > img, li > img
```

Using multiple selectors in this way often allows for a good compromise between specificity and reusability. It's often hard to write a single selector that targets exactly the elements you want, no more and no less; with multiple selectors, that task becomes easier. It's possible to write a selector that targets the general case and some more selectors that cover edge cases, and then the combination of those selectors returns exactly the elements that you're looking for.

Whether you use CSS or XPath selectors is entirely up to you. You don't have to make a strict choice between them; you can combine them in the same script, and a `NodeSet` returned by one will be identical to a `NodeSet` returned by the other. You can even chain them with each other, so all of these will return the same `NodeSet`:

```
doc.xpath("//p//img")
doc.css("p img")
doc.xpath("//p").css("img")
```

If one offers an easier way of doing something than another or can do something that the other can't, then go ahead and use it. There's value in knowing both ways of selecting elements.

Working with Elements

Once we've selected the elements that are appropriate for the task at hand, using either XPath or CSS selectors, our job is most likely only half done. We typically want to actually do something with the elements we've matched.

There are two types of things we might want to do with the elements. The first set of tasks involves extracting information—either the text of elements within the set or the contents of attributes on those elements. Exactly where the information is stored depends both on the elements we're dealing with and what we're trying to do. If we've matched an image, the interesting part might be the `src` attribute, specifying the URL of the image; if we've matched a paragraph, then we're likely to be interested in the text within the element.

The second set of tasks involves navigating the document from the position we've reached. Since the document is a tree, we can navigate up, down, and across it from a given position. This is useful when we want to do something with all of a particular element's children, for example, or to go up a level to a parent and then proceed again.

Let's look at the various methods on `Nodes` and `NodeSets`, and how we can use them to achieve these tasks.

Extracting Information from Elements

There are generally three pieces of information to extract from an element: its own text contents, the contents of an attribute, and the name of the element. There are three useful methods provided on Nokogiri nodes for extracting these three types of information.

Reading an Element's Text

To extract the text of an element, we can use the `text` method. So to extract all of the level-two headings in a document and print their text, we could use the following Nokogiri code:

nokogiri/h2-text.rb
```
require "nokogiri"

doc = Nokogiri::HTML(<<-DOC)
<html>
<body>
```

```
  <h2>This is a heading</h2>
  <p>This is a paragraph</p>

  <h2>This is also a heading</h2>
  <p>This is also a paragraph</p>
</body>
</html>
DOC

doc.css("h2").each do |heading|
  heading.text
  # => "This is a heading"
  #    , "This is also a heading"
end
```

However, this might not behave exactly as we expect: it actually selects the text of this node *and all of its descendants*. For something like an h2, which typically has no descendants apart from the text content of the heading, this works fine. But if we ran it on something like a div, for example—something with many descendants—then it might produce unexpected results. For example, suppose we used the same document but asked for the text of the body:

nokogiri/body-text.rb

```
require "nokogiri"

doc = Nokogiri::HTML(<<-DOC)
<html>
<body>
  Some body text

  <p>Some paragraph text</p>
</body>
</html>
DOC

doc.at_css("body").text
 # => "\n  Some body text\n\n  Some paragraph text\n"
```

We can see that we get the text not just of the body tag itself, but of the paragraph, too. It's as though we stripped all of the HTML tags and are left with what remains. If we're interested only in the text of the current node, though, we need to target not the node but a child of it: the text() node. To revise the previous example, then:

nokogiri/body-text-node.rb

```
doc.at_css("body text()").text
 # => "\n  Some body text\n\n  "
```

Rather than request the text of the body itself, we select the text node within the body. That gets us the results we're looking for.

We can target this text node using either XPath or CSS selectors; the previous example in XPath would simply be body/text().

Reading an Element's Attributes

Reading attributes is also achieved by calling a method on the node. In this case, that method is attr. So to output the source URL of every image in a document, we could use the following:

```
doc.css("img").each do |image|
  puts image.attr("src")
end
```

Nokogiri provides a shortcut to attr, since it's something that's used so frequently: we can use the subscript operator ([]) on a node, passing it the name of the attribute. So we could rewrite the last example as:

```
doc.css("img").each do |image|
  puts image["src"]
end
```

Reading an Element's Name

Rounding out the three most useful methods is name, which allows us to check what type of element we're dealing with. In the previous example, then:

```
doc.css("img").each do |image|
  image.name
  # => "img"
end
```

We can see we get back img, since it's img elements that we've asked for in our selector. This might be useful when our selector matches multiple types of elements and we want to do something slightly different for each—extracting the src attribute of a script tag but the href tag of a stylesheet link, for example.

Between these three methods, we can generally extract any information in a web page. After all, if it's not the content of an element, stored in an attribute of an element, or reflected in the name of the element itself, there are few other places it could be on a page.

Navigating from Nodes

We don't just use nodes for extracting information; we can also use them to navigate through our document. Imagine we've targeted items in a list, where we might want to get a reference to the list itself. Or we could imagine the reverse situation, where we have a reference to the list itself and we want to do something with its children.

In both cases, we want to navigate the hierarchy of the document. In the former case, we want to navigate upward, to an element's *parent*; and in the latter case we want to navigate downward, to an element's *children*. Here's an example of doing both:

nokogiri/hierarchy.rb

```
require "nokogiri"

doc = Nokogiri::HTML(<<-DOC)
<html>
<body>
  <ul><li>List item one</li>
    <li>List item two</li></ul>
</body>
</html>
DOC

list = doc.at_css("ul")

list_item = list.children.first
list_item.name                    # => "li"

list_item.parent.name             # => "ul"
```

First we select the ul. Then we access the first list item by requesting the children of the list and then taking the first child. Then we return to the list itself by requesting the parent of the list item.

We can move arbitrarily up and down the hierarchy as we please using just these two methods. That's the nature of the tree structure that all HTML documents fundamentally are. But we can move across the hierarchy, too. Just as nodes have parents and possibly also children, we can speak of them having *siblings* too.

Revisiting the list example:

nokogiri/siblings.rb

```
require "nokogiri"

doc = Nokogiri::HTML(<<-DOC)
<html>
<body>
  <ul><li>List item one</li><li>List item two</li></ul>
</body>
</html>
DOC
```

```
first_li = doc.at_css("li")

second_li = first_li.next_sibling
second_li.text
# => "List item two"

first_li = second_li.previous_sibling
first_li.text
# => "List item one"
```

Again, we're able to arbitrarily and repeatedly move between elements, this time by using the next_sibling and previous_sibling methods. This can come in handy if we're interested in one element in particular, but we want to alter our behavior based on what's around it. For example, we might want to extract captions from images, but only where they existed:

nokogiri/figcaption.rb

```
require "nokogiri"

doc = Nokogiri::HTML(<<-DOC)
<html>
<body>
  <figure>
    <img src="example.jpg"><figcaption>This image has a caption</figcaption>
  </figure>

  <figure>
    <img src="example-2.jpg">
  </figure>
</body>
</html>
DOC

Image = Struct.new(:file, :caption)

doc.css("img").each do |img|
  file = img["src"]

  caption = if img.next_sibling.name == "figcaption"
              img.next_sibling.text
            else
              "No caption"
            end

  Image.new(file, caption)
  # => #<struct Image file="example.jpg", caption="This image has a caption">
  #    , #<struct Image file="example-2.jpg", caption="No caption">
end
```

To recap, we now know how to search through an HTML document for the tags we're looking for, then extract information from those tags. That's all the elements of Nokogiri that we need to know in order to scrape web pages; we have enough tools to extract all the information we could want. But we've learned how to find something that we're looking for specifically, not necessarily how to discover what that specific thing might be.

There's a first step missing here: we know how to write selectors to target elements, but we don't know how to figure out what selectors we need to write or what logic needs to surround them. Luckily, we can use Nokogiri for this exploratory step, too.

Exploring a Page

The important first step in scraping information from a web page is to explore the page, figuring out how to extract information from it, understanding its structure and how to translate our idea of what we want ("the title of the latest post," "the price of the most expensive product") into that structure.

It doesn't make sense to leap straight into writing a script at this point—we're just exploring, after all. There are two different ways to do this exploration without writing a script, and both are useful. The first is to look at the page in a web browser, using the browser's inspection tools to explore the structure of the document. The second uses Nokogiri, but from the command line, to bridge the divide between exploring a page in the browser and actually writing a script.

General Principles

We should keep in mind some principles when exploring the page—things we should be looking for that will help us when it comes to writing our selectors and searching the document.

The first is the problem of specificity—that is, of trying to narrow down our search to the specific part of the page that's relevant. We want to target an image, for example, but only a particular one—not the many other irrelevant images that will invariably be on the page. In essence, this is about developing abstractions, identifying the qualities that are unique to the types of thing we want to match and that aren't present in others. Our selectors should be as broad and as general as they possibly can be without matching information that we're not looking for.

Trying to find a parent element with something unique about it that allows us to home in on what we're looking for is a helpful step. An `id` attribute is great for this, since they're (supposed to be) unique within a page. So if we're trying to extract information from a certain cell of a certain table, discovering that the table has a unique ID is perfect. It immediately lets us restrict our search for the table cell to only the table that we're interested in, removing the possibility of our matching the wrong cell.

That's often not possible, so we end up matching according to the structure of the element. "The image we're interested in is always inside a `figure` tag," we might notice, "but others aren't." That would be enough to go on. But we must be careful with such rules, because they have a tendency to be brittle. If the site changes its structure or design, our previously steadfast rule might no longer match.

The leads us neatly onto our second principle: robustness. Once we've found an anchor that narrows down the broad area of our search, we should try to think of a way to target the elements we're interested in, such that changes to the markup of the page stand the smallest chance of affecting our selectors. When matching a table we probably shouldn't, for example, select "the third row" or "the fifth column." If we do, as soon as new information is added to the table our selector will be out of date. Where possible, we shouldn't rely on specific element types, either. A `div` might become an `article` in a tweaking of the page structure, and it would be nice if our code didn't break as a result.

Again, the existence of IDs or at least classes here is a saving grace: if we're looking for a table cell containing the GDP of Burkina Faso, that table cell having a class of `gdp-burkina-faso` would be amazing. Unfortunately, we're unlikely to be so lucky in the real world, but the principle remains. We should try to write selectors that are flexible, not ones that are tied to a specific markup structure. We should try to match on content, rather than position. And we should try to use classes and IDs that we have a good hunch will remain even if the markup is altered.

Now that we know what we're looking for, let's look at the practicalities of exploring a web page.

Using a Web Browser

Our first port of call when exploring a site should be the web browser. Apart from feeling fairly natural, there are many advantages to exploring the page using a browser, the main one being that we can see the website visually. It's easy to pick out the elements we want to extract if we can see them as we normally would when browsing the website.

Using an inspection tool—such tools are included in the Google Chrome, Firefox, and Safari browsers—we can look at the structure of the page and discover what elements are necessary to pick out the section of the page we're looking for.

Open up the web inspector and target the element that you ultimately want to extract information from. Keeping the principles of good selectors in mind, think about the qualities of the element: its attributes, its classes, and its id if it has them. Consider its place in the hierarchy of the page. Think about what the most general selector could be that targeted this element and no others. Thinking about all these things will start to give us an idea of the best way to target the element or elements we want in a specific and robust way.

We can even use the inspector to test out selectors. In the console part of the inspector, pass a CSS selector to document.querySelectorAll:

```
> document.querySelectorAll('a.image > img')
[
  <img src="example.jpg">,
  <img src="example-2.jpg">
]
```

Once we've got a feel in the browser for how we're going to target our particular elements, we can move on to figuring out how to implement that targeting in Nokogiri. But that still doesn't mean writing a full-blown script. Nokogiri has a further trick for us—its ability to be used from the command line in a *read–evaluate–print loop*, or REPL.

Nokogiri from the Command Line

Nokogiri ships with a little-known but incredibly useful command-line interface, allowing us to experiment with selectors without actually writing a full-blown script. This interface takes the form of a read–evaluate–print loop, or *REPL*; this is the same prompt that you'll have seen if you've ever used IRB, Pry, or the Rails console. We type some Ruby code into the prompt and hit Enter, the code is executed, the result of the code is printed for us, and we're returned to the prompt. (Read, evaluate, print, loop—the four steps.)

If you have the Nokogiri Gem installed, which hopefully you do by now, you can invoke it by passing a URL to the nokogiri command:

```
$ nokogiri http://example.com
```

If you run this with a real URL, you should see something like the following:

```
Your document is stored in @doc...
2.1.5 :001 >
```

We're now in an IRB session. This is an ordinary Ruby REPL, like the one we'd get if we typed `irb` at the command line, but—just like the intro text says—there's one difference: we have a variable called `@doc` that contains a reference to a Nokogiri document. Nokogiri has helpfully downloaded the web page we passed on the command line and created a Nokogiri document from its HTML. Now we can begin experimenting.

It works exactly as we've seen in our previous use of Nokogiri. So we can make inquiries of Nokogiri, such as discovering how many images there are on the page:

```
2.2.0 :001 > @doc.css('img').length
=> 62
```

This command-line version of Nokogiri also supports an `-e` option, just like the Ruby interpreter does. This allows us to write Nokogiri one-liners, just like the Ruby one-liners we saw in Chapter 3, *Shell One-Liners*, on page 29. So we could write the previous example as:

```
$ nokogiri http://example.com -e 'puts @doc.css('img').length'
```

If the task and selectors are simple enough, this might remove the need to write a script at all. We could simply call our one-liner from the shell or from a shell script (or a cron job, or anywhere else) and extract the information we need. This way of using Nokogiri also slots neatly into pipeline chains, allowing us to use Nokogiri to extract some text from a page and then pipe that text into other utilities for further processing.

Example: Reading a League Table

Until now we've danced around the practicalities of scraping, discussing the theory, the tools we'll be using, and how to approach things. Now let's try to apply that knowledge and extract some information from a site.

For this example, I'm going to extract the names and point totals of the teams in the Premier League, the highest football (that's soccer in the US) league in England. This information is available on a page on the BBC website.[2]

The league table, as visitors to the website see it (as of February 2015), looks like this:

2. http://www.bbc.co.uk/sport/football/premier-league/table

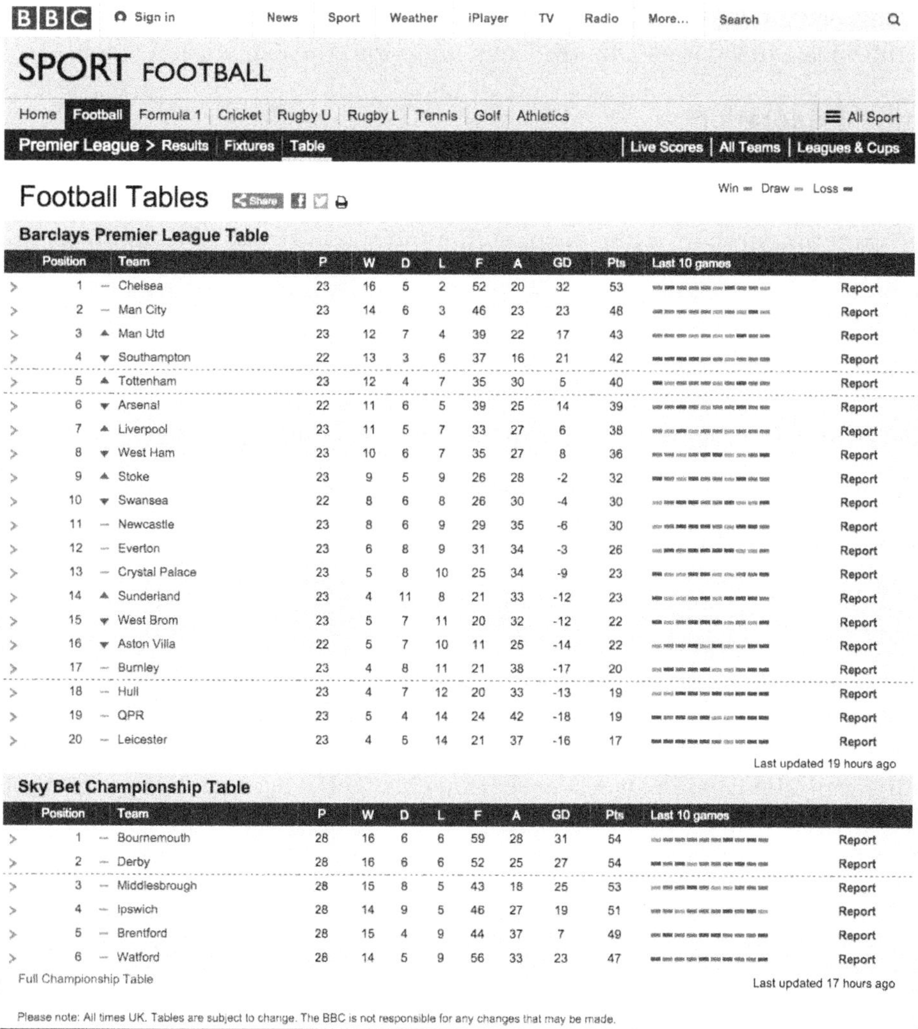

BBC Sign in News Sport Weather iPlayer TV Radio More... Search

SPORT FOOTBALL

Home Football Formula 1 Cricket Rugby U Rugby L Tennis Golf Athletics All Sport

Premier League > Results Fixtures Table | Live Scores | All Teams | Leagues & Cups

Football Tables

Win Draw Loss

Barclays Premier League Table

Position		Team	P	W	D	L	F	A	GD	Pts	Last 10 games	
1	—	Chelsea	23	16	5	2	52	20	32	53		Report
2	—	Man City	23	14	6	3	46	23	23	48		Report
3	▲	Man Utd	23	12	7	4	39	22	17	43		Report
4	▼	Southampton	22	13	3	6	37	16	21	42		Report
5	▲	Tottenham	23	12	4	7	35	30	5	40		Report
6	▼	Arsenal	22	11	6	5	39	25	14	39		Report
7	▲	Liverpool	23	11	5	7	33	27	6	38		Report
8	▼	West Ham	23	10	6	7	35	27	8	36		Report
9	▲	Stoke	23	9	5	9	26	28	-2	32		Report
10	▼	Swansea	22	8	6	8	26	30	-4	30		Report
11	—	Newcastle	23	8	6	9	29	35	-6	30		Report
12	—	Everton	23	6	8	9	31	34	-3	26		Report
13	—	Crystal Palace	23	5	8	10	25	34	-9	23		Report
14	▲	Sunderland	23	4	11	8	21	33	-12	23		Report
15	▼	West Brom	23	5	7	11	20	32	-12	22		Report
16	▼	Aston Villa	22	5	7	10	11	25	-14	22		Report
17	—	Burnley	23	4	8	11	21	38	-17	20		Report
18	—	Hull	23	4	7	12	20	33	-13	19		Report
19	—	QPR	23	5	4	14	24	42	-18	19		Report
20	—	Leicester	23	4	5	14	21	37	-16	17		Report

Last updated 19 hours ago

Sky Bet Championship Table

Position		Team	P	W	D	L	F	A	GD	Pts	Last 10 games	
1	—	Bournemouth	28	16	6	6	59	28	31	54		Report
2	—	Derby	28	16	6	6	52	25	27	54		Report
3	—	Middlesbrough	28	15	8	5	43	18	25	53		Report
4	—	Ipswich	28	14	9	5	46	27	19	51		Report
5	—	Brentford	28	15	4	9	44	37	7	49		Report
6	—	Watford	28	14	5	9	56	33	23	47		Report

Full Championship Table

Last updated 17 hours ago

Please note: All times UK. Tables are subject to change. The BBC is not responsible for any changes that may be made.

It's presented in a pretty table, but that's not much use to us in our scripts. Our goal is to convert this table, intended for people to read, into a Ruby data structure that we can then use in a script. A natural data structure for this would be an array of hashes. Each element in the array will represent a team, and the hash will contain that team's position in the table, its name, and its point total.

```
[
  { position: 1, team: "Chelsea", points: 53 },
  { position: 2, team: "Man City", points: 48 },
  # ...snip...
]
```

In this section we'll write a script that takes the HTML page and transforms it into this Ruby data structure. Let's jump into the exploration stage.

Initial Exploration

The first thing to do is to fire up our web browser and take a look at the page's source. We're looking for an element that isolates the area of the page that we want to search in, while keeping in mind the principle of robustness.

In this case, it seems sensible to limit our search to the table element that contains the league table. But since there are two league tables on the page (it also shows the top teams in the division below), let's look to see if there's anything unique about the first table that will enable us to target just it. The markup for the first table is:

```
<table class="table-stats" id="comp-118996114-CFBB82013S1R1">
```

And for the second, it's:

```
<table class="table-stats" id="comp-118996115-CFBB102013S1R1">
```

They both have IDs that are unique. It might be perfectly sensible to use the ID to target the table, but something doesn't feel quite right about using it in this case. It feels machine-generated, rather than something with universal meaning, so we might be worried that it will change in the future and break our script. (Imagine the worst case, that this ID changes each time the table is generated—that would be disastrous! Our script would work for only a few days.)

It might be sensible just to look for the first table in the document that has a class of table-stats. Although this might also change in the future, that class name feels like something that will probably survive a change to the document in the future, and it seems fairly reasonable that the league table we're interested in will be first on the page.

We've now isolated our search to just the area of the page we want. Then we need to figure out what the next part of the selector will be and loop over the positions. Each is in a row in the table, so that's easy enough, and the headers are helpfully isolated in a thead, so we don't need to write some logic to ignore them.

After that we need to extract the positions, team names, and point totals. Again, we open our inspector and take a look to see whether there's anything there that will allow us to extract them. Here's the markup for a row:

```
<tr id="team-138824012" class="team first">
  <td class="statistics"><button>Arsenal team statistics</button></td>
```

```
  <td class="position">
    <span class="no-movement">No movement</span>
    <span class="position-number">1</span>
  </td>

  <td class="team-name">
    <a href="/sport/football/teams/arsenal">Arsenal</a>
  </td>
  <td class="played">22</td>

  <td class="won"><span>11</span></td>
  <td class="drawn">6</td>
  <td class="lost">5</td>
  <td class="for">39</td>
  <td class="against">25</td>

  <td class="goal-difference">14</td>
  <td class="points">39</td>
</tr>
```

In this case, the markup is well written, and we can see that extracting the values will be straightforward. The position is a `span` with a class of `position-number`; the team name is contained within a `td` with a class of `team-name`, and the point total is in a `td` with a class of `points`. It couldn't be much more straightforward!

Experimentation

Now that we've got a picture of how we're going to write our scraping script, we can open up Nokogiri and figure out how this abstract idea translates to Nokogiri calls.

The first thing we want to do is target the table. That should require just one selector, so let's target the tables that have the `table-stats` class:

```
> tables = @doc.css('table.table-stats')
 => [#<Nokogiri::XML::Element:0x3ffd24c7a180 name="table"...
> tables.length
 => 2
```

Here, we query for the tables and check how many elements we were returned (just to sense-check our selector). In this case, we got two, which matches our expectations. It's surprising how often we'll find that more elements match our selector than we expected. Sometimes elements are hidden in the structure of the document, and sometimes names are just more generic than we might think.

We can get the first table by calling the `first` method on the `NodeSet` we have:

```
> table = tables.first
 => #<Nokogiri::XML::Element:0x3ff7989232fc name="table"...
```

We've managed to isolate our league table, then. The next step is to extract the teams from it. We can do this by taking the rows of the table and again using length to sense-check the result—we're expecting 20 teams:

```
> rows = table.css('tr')
 => [#<Nokogiri::XML::Element:0x3ffd24c73e0c name="tr"...
> rows.length
 => 22
```

Immediately, we see a problem: we're getting 22 rows back, not the 20 we expected. The issue is that we haven't been specific enough. Our query is returning not just the rows containing teams, but also the header rows. Let's refine our search to look only for rows in the table body and see whether that gets us there:

```
> rows = tables.first.css('tbody tr')
 => [#<Nokogiri::XML::Element:0x3ffd24c73e0c name="tr"...
> rows.length
 => 20
```

Perfect. Now the only experiment is to try to extract the other values. In the real script we'll do this in a loop, but for now let's just try to extract the first one and match it visually against the values we expect. As we saw earlier, the columns have class names that make isolating them straightforward:

```
> rows.first.at_css('span.position-number').text
 => "1"
> rows.first.at_css('td.team-name').text
 => "Chelsea"
> rows.first.at_css('td.points').text
 => "53"
```

Bingo. It looks like this will be fairly straightforward. We might make a note here that the values we get back from text are always strings, so we'll need to convert them to numeric values later, but otherwise we've figured out the logic of our script.

Writing the Script

We've got all the information we need to write our script now, and we've done a lot of the experimentation that we might otherwise have done while writing the script. We should be able to write something that works the first time (famous last words).

First, we need to include our libraries. We'll also create a class to hold our functionality:

nokogiri/league-table.rb
```
require "open-uri"
require "nokogiri"

class LeagueTable
```

We inject our URLs into the class using the constructor, so calling code can request a different URL if it likes. (This logic might work fine for other league tables on the same site, for example.)

```
def initialize(url = nil)
  @url ||= "http://www.bbc.co.uk/sport/football/premier-league/table"
  parse(html)
end
```

We fetch and parse the document immediately, so let's write those methods. The first one should fetch the HTML, and the second should construct a Nokogiri document from it:

```
def html
  @html ||= open(@url)
end

def parse(html)
  @doc ||= Nokogiri::HTML(html)
end
```

We memorize both of the methods by storing their result in an instance variable, so that repeated calls won't fetch or parse the page over and over again but instead will return the content of the variable.

That's our boilerplate done with. Now let's think about how to extract the information in the league table. The calling code is probably going to expect a `teams` method that returns information about the teams. So, let's write that:

```
def teams
  @teams ||= rows.map { |row| Team.from_html(row) }
end

def each(*args, &block)
  teams.each(&block)
end
include Enumerable
```

This method just calls other methods to assemble a data structure that represents our league table. We assume that there's a method called `rows` that returns the rows in the table, and that for each of them we can create a `Team` object from the HTML using Team.from_html. We also define a method called each, which just calls each on the array of teams. This allows us to include the Enumerable module, which means users of our code will be able to call things like table.select { |t| t[:points] > 50 } to select all teams with more than 50 points, or table.find { |t| t[:name] =~ /^M/ } to find the highest-placed team beginning with M, and so on.

Next we define the methods that actually do the work of parsing the HTML. In this case, we're looking to do two things: first, to extract the rows of the table, so that we can loop over the teams in it; and second, to extract information from each of these rows. So we create a class to represent a team, which has attributes for a name, a position, and a points total. This class has a method to parse these values from a row in the table—the method we called in our teams method:

```
  private
  def rows
    @doc.at_css('table.table-stats').css('tbody tr')
  end
end

class Team < Struct.new(:position, :name, :points)
  def self.from_html(row)
    new(
      row.at_css('span.position-number').text.to_i,
      row.at_css('td.team-name').text,
      row.at_css('td.points').text.to_i
    )
  end
end
```

That's it. Here it is all together:

nokogiri/league-table.rb

```
require "open-uri"
require "nokogiri"

class LeagueTable
  def initialize(url = nil)
    @url ||= "http://www.bbc.co.uk/sport/football/premier-league/table"
    parse(html)
  end

  def html
    @html ||= open(@url)
  end
```

```
  def parse(html)
    @doc ||= Nokogiri::HTML(html)
  end

  def teams
    @teams ||= rows.map { |row| Team.from_html(row) }
  end

  def each(*args, &block)
    teams.each(&block)
  end
  include Enumerable

  private
  def rows
    @doc.at_css('table.table-stats').css('tbody tr')
  end
end

class Team < Struct.new(:position, :name, :points)
  def self.from_html(row)
    new(
      row.at_css('span.position-number').text.to_i,
      row.at_css('td.team-name').text,
      row.at_css('td.points').text.to_i
    )
  end
end
```

Here's a sample of how we could use it. In this case, we use printf to output a neatly aligned, text-only version of the table, but we could of course do anything with the result:

nokogiri/league-table.rb

```
table = LeagueTable.new
table.each do |team|
  printf "%2s. %-14s %3d pts\n", team.position, team.name, team.points
end
```

If we run this script we should see output that looks something like this (depending on how the football games have gone):

```
 1. Chelsea         64 pts
 2. Man City        58 pts
 3. Arsenal         57 pts
 4. Man Utd         56 pts
 :    :              :
18. Burnley         25 pts
19. QPR             22 pts
20. Leicester       19 pts
```

Ta-da! Using a bit of common sense and plenty of help from Nokogiri, we've extracted useful information from a mountain of HTML. There was no API, no nice system to query—just solid markup. The solution we have, though, feels pretty solid and dependable. Code that calls our LeagueTable class will feel like it's doing something logical and sensible. Calling code isn't dependent on the source of the data; we could swap it out for data scraped from another site, and the calling code would be none the wiser. And now that we have the information in a structure that actually makes sense to our script, we can do what we like with it: present the information to our user, store it in a database, or process it further.

Hopefully, this simple example shows you the power of scraping websites and you how easy it can be to write an elegant scraper in Ruby and Nokogiri. Try it yourself: think of some information that's trapped on a website somewhere, that you've always wanted to manipulate or just extract. Go ahead: write a scraper for it!

Wrapping Up

This chapter had a lot to take in. You learned the basics of Nokogiri and how you can use both CSS and XPath queries to search for elements within the document. We looked at what we can do with elements once we got a hold of them, accessing their attributes and their inner text. But we also learned some principles about what makes a good selector and what we should be looking for when we're exploring a page.

Finally, though, we saw how to translate this all into the real world, writing a robust script that queries information from a web page and translates it into a Ruby data structure. This illustrates how powerful scraping can be. The information we wanted wasn't intended for machine consumption at all. No API existed, but we were still able to consume the data and get it into a format where we could then run further queries on it or manipulate it in whatever way we wanted.

We've almost reached the end of our exploration of the "extract" stage of text processing. There's just one more subject left to tackle, but it's a tricky one: the issue of character encodings.

CHAPTER 7

Encodings

It's sometimes easy to forget, ensconced as many of us are in an English-speaking bubble, that the world is a multilingual place. It has different languages, different alphabets, and different sets of symbols—not just English with its 26 letters, simple punctuation, and handful of symbols.

Even if we're not trying to work directly in one of these many different languages, though, it doesn't take very long when working with text in our scripts and programs to encounter the frustration of character-encoding issues. Output littered with boxes and question marks, odd characters showing up unexpectedly (seeing Ã¶ instead of ö, for example), the dreaded "invalid byte sequence" error—these are all character-encoding issues, and they can be one of the biggest sources of frustration for those trying to process text.

Dealing with these issues is a tricky subject. Character encoding cuts across programming at several levels, from the lowest—the fundamentals of how strings are stored as bytes—right up to the highest. Although it's certainly possible to get by without a clear understanding of how character encoding works, working with text will become a lot easier and a lot less frustrating if you develop at least a practical understanding of this admittedly broad subject.

The subject is also tricky for how far it reaches back into the annals of computing history. The specifics of how text is encoded today have their roots in decisions made in the 1960s, where the main consideration was how text was used in teleprinters, not personal computers. So while some decisions might seem baffling at first, it's important to understand their historical contexts and the constraints that the original designers were under.

A final layer of trickiness comes from the sheer variety of different character encodings that exist and that you'll encounter. Although the world has largely decided in recent years that UTF-8 should be a standard character set, this transition is far from universal, and perhaps will never be. As a result, it's still common to have to deal with text in less widely used character sets or to encounter situations where text from different sources is encoded in different ways. In these situations, it's important to know how to detect encodings, deal with multiple encodings in one program, convert text from one encoding to another, and deal with invalid characters and sequences.

Fortunately, the topic isn't nearly as daunting to wrap your head around as it might seem at first blush. And fortunately, Ruby, especially in recent versions, has robust ways to handle all of the problems you're likely to encounter—whether you want to ignore problems with character encodings or whether you want to intelligently convert them.

But we're getting ahead of ourselves. First, let's look at what character encodings actually are at a relatively low level—only then can we move on to some Ruby specifics.

A Brief Introduction to Character Encodings

Historically, strings in programming languages were just collections of bytes—that is, binary numbers. In these collections of bytes, each byte corresponded neatly to one character. A standard system, known as ASCII, was created; it mapped these raw bytes to human-readable characters. So it was decided that, for example, `65` would be an uppercase `A`, `119` would be a lowercase `w`, and so on. The string `abc123`, then, would be composed of the following bytes:

```
97, 98, 99, 49, 50, 51
```

This simple one-to-one mapping from bytes to characters was convenient. Operations that from a programmer's perspective worked with characters could, under the hood, work with bytes. "Give me the first character of this string" in this system translated easily to "give me the first byte of this array of bytes."

The only problem with this system is that representing characters as a single octet (eight bits, or what's now universally known as a byte) gives a possible $2^8 = 256$ characters. That's fine when you're dealing only with English letters and numbers, with a few punctuation and control characters thrown in, as early computer scientists inevitably were. And so ASCII specified a mere 128 characters, from bytes 0 to 127.

But soon it became apparent that there would be problems with this approach. What about French or German, with their additional diacritics? What about

Russian, with its entirely different Cyrillic alphabet? What about Mandarin, which even in its simplified form has 2,000 characters?

The first response to this problem was simply to extend ASCII. Since it specified only 128 characters, and an octet gave the possibility of 256, the rest of the space was filled up in different ways. So a character encoding called ISO-8859-1 was created, aimed at covering Western Europe. It specified, for example, that `163` corresponded to the British pound sign (£). But there was also ISO-8859-2 for Eastern Europe, in which `163` wasn't a pound sign at all, but instead the Polish letter Ł. And in ISO-8859-5, for Cyrillic alphabets, `163` was something else again: the letter Ѓ.

Although this solved the problem of representing characters other than those used in English, it also created two problems. First, it was impossible to use characters from multiple encodings in a single string. You had to pick and then work around any problems that arose. So German speakers forced to use ASCII might substitute `ae` for the unavailable ä; Croatians, unable to use Đ in an ISO-8859-1 string, might instead use `Dj`.

Second, you had to know exactly what character encoding to display a string in. Otherwise, you'd end up with nonsensical substitutions—like expressing prices to a British person with a Ł character rather than a £, or showing a Croatian a ¹ instead of a š.

This madness persisted for years and abated only relatively recently, with the advent of Unicode. Its creators looked at the landscape of multiple, conflicting character encodings and decided that the only way to avoid this nightmare was to create a single character encoding that included all possible characters, ending once and for all the question of "Which character encoding should I use?"

But how could this be done, when as we've seen a byte can only have 256 different values? The answer was to abandon the idea that a single character mapped neatly to a single byte. UTF is what's known as *multi-byte encoding*, where letters are created with sequences of multiple bytes. It's also a *variable-width encoding*, where some characters are expressed in only one byte, while others take up more. The most common UTF encoding is UTF-8, which can use up to six bytes per character. This allows for a staggering 1,112,064 different *code points*—enough for all the world's alphabets many times over, with room to spare for dingbats, control characters, and plenty more besides.

So that pesky Polish Ł, which was `163` in the Eastern European character set but which wasn't expressible at all in the Western European one, is made up of two bytes in UTF-8: `197 129`. GThe Croatian š has one place in UTF-8 where it can be found: 197 161. And so, in UTF-8 text, we can use that Polish character next to the Croatian one, but also next to a Russian Cyrillic one, and next to that an Arabic character, and next to that a Mandarin character. All in perfect harmony.

This does create some complications, though. For example, we can no longer operate on a string at the byte level and assume that we're operating on the character level, too. This can cause problems: imagine you're writing a method to split a string into characters. With a single-byte encoding, you can just split the string into bytes and be sure that you're splitting it by characters. With UTF-8, you have to know about how "wide" characters are (how many bytes they're formed from) to make sure you don't split the string in the middle of a character. But these complexities are generally considered to be a trade-off well worth making, in exchange for being able to represent every character we could ever wish to. After all, they're primarily concerns for language implementers, not for end users like us.

As an added bonus, the first 127 characters in UTF-8 are represented as single bytes and correspond exactly to ASCII. This brilliant decision—to make UTF-8 a super-set of ASCII—means that all ASCII text is instantly valid UTF-8, without any need for conversion. It's perhaps this factor more than any other that spurred on the adoption of UTF-8 and that makes it infinitely more straightforward to work with. Sometimes, the computing gods smile on us.

So if UTF-8 has made the "what character set" question a thing of the past, why do we still have to deal with character sets at all? Well, unfortunately, UTF-8 hasn't conquered the world quite yet. There are still many sources of data that will give you text in ASCII, ISO-8859-1, Mac Roman, and plenty of other character sets besides. Sooner or later, knowing how to convert these into something your program is able to work with will become essential as you work with text in Ruby.

Ruby's Support for Character Encodings

Ruby's support for character encodings has progressed slowly but surely in recent versions. Explaining its support for encodings in the latest version is best done by taking a journey from Ruby 1.8, which had no support for any character encodings apart from US-ASCII, to the rather robust support you can find in the latest version of Ruby.

Ruby 1.8

In Ruby 1.8, released in 2003, there was essentially no support for character encodings at all. Source files were always interpreted as US-ASCII, and methods that operated on strings would often get confused when they encountered multi-byte characters. For example, look at the following code when run using Ruby 1.8:

```
"Hellø".reverse # => "\270\303lleH"
```

Instead of seeing `ølleH`, as we might expect, Ruby is blindly treating the string as a collection of bytes—six in this case—and reversing each of them, splitting up our `ø` character and making the whole thing nonsensical.

Although there were some workarounds, such as the `iconv` library, it's fair to say in general that working with UTF-8 text in Ruby 1.8 was unpleasant at best and impossible at worst.

Ruby 1.9

Ruby 1.9, released in December 2007, added two important encoding-related capabilities. The first was the ability to specify an encoding for source code files, and the second was the ability to have different encodings for individual strings within a program.

File Encodings

The first important change in Ruby 1.9 was the ability to tell the Ruby interpreter what the encoding of your file was, allowing for the first time source files written in UTF-8 or other character encodings.

This was done by way of a so-called *magic comment* at the top of your file, specifying the encoding. Without the magic comment, files continued to be assumed to be US-ASCII. And so in Ruby 1.9 the following file:

```
puts "Hëlló Wôrld"
```

produces, as it would in Ruby 1.8, an "invalid multibyte char" error. This is because the file is interpreted in US-ASCII by default, and none of these characters is valid ASCII. But if we use a magic comment to tell Ruby that our source file is in UTF-8:

```
# encoding: utf-8
puts "Hëlló Wôrld"
```

we get no error, and things work as we expect. Suddenly, we've gained the ability to write programs in different character sets.

String-Specific Encodings

The second important addition in Ruby 1.9 was the ability to store the encoding of individual strings. This important change allowed us to juggle strings of different types in the same program, and to convert strings from one encoding to another. This allowed what's known as *multilingualization*, or the ability to have multiple languages and character sets in the same program.

So from Ruby 1.9 onward, we can ask a string for its encoding:

```
# encoding: utf-8
puts "Hello world".encoding # => UTF-8
```

By default, strings are created with the same encoding as the file they're created in. But a key aspect of multilingualization is the ability to change the encoding of a string. So Ruby 1.9 also added the `encode` method to strings, which allows us to transcode a string from one encoding to another.

Let's imagine that we're dealing with UTF-8—encoded strings. But we want to store them somewhere else that supports only ASCII, not the extended goodness of UTF. Before we do whatever we're going to do with the string, we can convert it into ASCII format:

encoding-remove-undefined.rb

```
# encoding: utf-8
string = "Hëlló Wôrld".encode("US-ASCII", undef: :replace, replace: "")

string.encoding # => #<Encoding:US-ASCII>
string # => "Hll Wrld"
```

Here we take a string encoded as UTF-8 (we know it's UTF-8 because our file is encoded as UTF-8). We then use the `encode` method to convert it into one encoded as US-ASCII. This returns a new string, leaving the original untouched.

In the options we pass to `encode`, we tell Ruby that characters that are undefined (`undef`) should be replaced and that they should be replaced with a blank string (in other words, that they should be stripped). The result is a string encoded as ASCII that has had any characters that are invalid ASCII stripped from it.

If we know that the string we have is in a specific format, we can tell Ruby to use that character encoding without performing any kind of conversion at all, using another String method added in Ruby 1.9: `force_encoding`.

This can be illustrated in the following example. Let's create a string that has some valid UTF-8 code-points in it. For this we can go back to our trusty Polish Ł, which we know is composed of the bytes 197 and 129 in decimal (and therefore 0xC5 0x82 in hexadecimal). If we create a string containing those bytes in ISO-8859-1 encoding and then again in UTF-8, we can see how some normal string methods behave differently:

```
# encoding: ISO-8859-1
string = "\xC5\x82"
puts string.length, string[0]
# => 2, ?

string = string.force_encoding("UTF-8")
puts string.length, string[0]
# => 1, Ł
```

In the first section of code, the string is created in the ISO-8859-1 character encoding. In that particular encoding, these series of bytes have no meaning, and so Ruby interprets the string as being two characters long. If we ask it for the first character of the string, it gives us the "unknown character" character—normally an empty box or a question mark.

But in the second example, we tell Ruby that we know the string we're dealing with contains UTF-8 text. force_encoding is our way of telling Ruby: "I know that this is UTF-8 already. Treat it as such without doing any kind of conversion."

After we force the encoding to UTF-8, things work as we would expect. Ruby tells us that the string is one character long, and when we ask it for the first character we get back exactly what we expect: that trusty Polish Ł.

This often occurs when you know the character encoding of a source of data, and you know that it's different from the one you're working with in your program. By using force_encoding, you can juggle the two character sets without a problem.

External Encodings

Linked to both the previous additions is the addition of character encodings to IO. In previous versions of Ruby, reading from a file, socket, or other IO object would return strings in the same encoding as the Ruby script—that is, US-ASCII. Reading a file that was stored in UTF-8, for example, would result in the file being interpreted as US-ASCII regardless, potentially causing encoding issues.

Ruby 1.9 introduced the concept of an *external encoding*, allowing us to specify what the encoding of the file (or socket, or other IO source) is at the point we open it. So, we could open a file stored as ISO-8859-1 Western European in a UTF-8 script in the following way:

western-european.rb
```
# encoding: utf-8
File.open("western-european.txt", "r:iso-8859-1") do |file|
  file.external_encoding # => #<Encoding:ISO-8859-1>
  contents = file.read # => "This file contains some ISO-8859-1 text.\n"
  contents.encoding # => #<Encoding:ISO-8859-1>
end
```

We specify the encoding in which we'd like to open the file by appending it to the mode at the point of opening. Rather than a plain "r", for read-only, we pass in "r:iso-8859-1" to specify read-only and an encoding of ISO-8859-1. The File object itself has an external_encoding method that we can query to find out the encoding of the IO stream. In this case, we see that it's ISO-8859-1 as we requested. When we read from the file, the string we get back is, correctly, set to the ISO-8859-1 encoding.

This allows us to read from files stored in any encoding at all, regardless of what encoding our own script is. There's one more neat feature to external encodings, though: we can use them to convert from one encoding to another. So, let's adapt our previous example to convert the file from ISO-8859-1 to the same UTF-8 encoding we're using in our script:

western-european-convert.rb
```
# encoding: utf-8
File.open("western-european.txt", "r:iso-8859-1:utf-8") do |file|
  file.external_encoding # => #<Encoding:ISO-8859-1>
  contents = file.read # => "This file contains some ISO-8859-1 text.\n"
  contents.encoding # => #<Encoding:UTF-8>
end
```

Here we see that, although the file has an external encoding of ISO-8859-1 as we specified, reading the contents of the file gives us a string that's been automatically converted to UTF-8.

With the additions made in version 1.9, Ruby became for the first time a truly capable language when it comes to dealing with multiple character encodings. So if you're stuck on Ruby 1.8 for some reason, try as hard as possible to upgrade; your life will become instantly easier.

Ruby 2.0

In Ruby 2.0, the default encoding for Ruby files was changed to UTF-8. This welcome change removed the need for most magic comments, since in Ruby

1.9 most people used them to specify a UTF-8 encoding. For this reason, it's now relatively uncommon to see magic comments in the wild.

Ruby 2.1

In Ruby 2.1, released at the end of 2013, one minor change was made: strings gained a scrub method. This method makes for an easy way to strip invalid byte sequences out of a string.

Invalid byte sequences can be symptomatic of an underlying problem—for example, that your text is being wrongly encoded somewhere along the process, possibly multiple times. However, sometimes there's nothing to be done about that; the text is what it is. When you just need to use the text and are happy to strip malformed sequences of bytes, scrub is what you're after.

Here's an example. We define a string of valid UTF-8, but on the end we append a mangled sequence of totally invalid UTF-8:

```
string = "Hëllø wôrld\xFE\xFF"
```

The final two bytes in this string, fe and ff in hex, are invalid anywhere in a UTF-8 string. If we try to print this string, things don't break entirely. We'd see the expected string, followed by two invalid character symbols. If, however, we try to actually process the string, for example to split it into words:

```
string = "Hëllø wôrld\xFE\xFF"
string.split
```

then we'll see the dreaded ArgumentError: invalid byte sequence in UTF-8.

Running the string through scrub will help us. If we don't specify an argument to scrub, then the invalid characters will be replaced by the "replacement character"—in UTF-8's case, the question mark in a diamond:

```
string = "Hëllø wôrld\xFE\xFF"
string.scrub.split # => ["Hëllø", "wôrld��"]
```

This can sometimes be useful, because it still alerts us to a potential problem with our text but will still allow us to process it. If we want to ignore invalid byte sequences entirely, scrub accepts an argument—just like those passed to encode—that allows us to specify what character will be used for replacement. If we pass it an empty string, invalid byte sequences will be completely stripped:

```
string = "Hëllø wôrld\xFE\xFF"
string.scrub("").split # => ["Hëllø", "wôrld"]
```

It's frustratingly common to encounter invalid byte sequences in text. It's especially common when the flow of text is, for example, from a user's computer, to a web browser, into a web application, into a database, back out into a CSV file or other export, and then into our program. Each one of those steps is an opportunity for encoding mistakes to creep in, and scrub is useful when we just want to process the text without worrying too much about trying to correct the mistakes.

Detecting Encodings

We've only looked at the issue of known character formats: that is, of converting text from one particular format to another when we know what both those formats are. But sometimes we don't know exactly what we're dealing with: in those cases, we must resort to guessing the character encodings in question.

Ideally, we'd want to be able to follow a general logic of guessing what the character encoding of the text is and, if the answer is anything other than UTF-8, converting the text into UTF-8.

This is definitely possible, but it will always be a guess, so it isn't going to work 100 percent of the time. But often a guess is all we need or all we can do, so it's definitely worth exploring.

In Ruby, we can do this guessing with a library called Charlock Holmes,[1] developed by Brian Marino, that wraps the mature International Components for Unicode (ICU) library.

Charlock Holmes can be installed like any other Ruby gem; its gem name is charlock_holmes. Once you've installed it and the ICU library that it depends upon, using it is straightforward. Although it offers a general interface, I find myself more often than not using the methods that it adds to the String class. Let's take a look at them:

```
require "charlock_holmes/string"

string = "H\xC3\xABll\xC3\xB8 w\xC3\xB4rld"
string.detect_encoding
# => {:type=>:text, :encoding=>"UTF-8", :confidence=>80}
```

Here we require the Charlock Holmes library. By requiring charlock_holmes/string, rather than just charlock_holmes, the library will add its helper methods to String for us.

1. https://github.com/brianmario/charlock_holmes

Next, we define a string. In this case, it contains some UTF-8 code points, but Ruby doesn't know that—it just sees them as some bytes. Finally, we call Charlock Holmes's detect_encoding method. It tells us that it has guessed, with 80 percent confidence, that the string is UTF-8—bingo, correct answer.

If we want to both detect the encoding and also change Ruby's internal encoding of the string—in other words, to also call force_encoding on the string—we can do so with the detect_encoding method. To see how this works, let's try the previous example but with the Ruby script set to US-ASCII encoding:

```
# encoding: US-ASCII
require "charlock_holmes/string"

string = "H\xC3\xABll\xC3\xB8 w\xC3\xB4rld"
string.encoding # => US-ASCII
string.detect_encoding!
string.encoding # => UTF-8
```

We can see that the string is created as US-ASCII by default. As is, the string would be unusable, since it contains so many characters that are invalid ASCII. After calling detect_encoding!, though, Charlock Holmes changes the encoding of the string to UTF-8. At this point, the string and all its methods should be entirely usable.

One thing to note is that since Charlock Holmes is using a heuristic to guess what encoding the text is, it's more accurate the more data it has to work with. On small strings like the one in this example, you're much more likely to run into false positives. Run it on a file of several kilobytes, and it's almost certain to get a match. And somewhere in between the performance is likely to be, well, somewhere in between.

Wrapping Up

Encodings can be a tricky issue. But generally, the landscape is better than it was a few years ago. The world is slowly but surely moving to UTF-8, and as we inch closer to that point we also approach the point where we no longer have to worry about character encoding for the vast majority of our programs.

Before that point, though, knowing how to recover from invalidly encoded strings without losing data is an important string to have in your bow.

Thankfully, Ruby too is moving in the right direction. From being unable to support anything but ASCII text in version 1.8, it now boasts among the best multilingualization support of any programming language. We can handle infinitely different string encodings in our scripts all at once, we can write our scripts in any encoding we like, and we can perform many tasks of encoding detection and conversion.

We've now completed the first part of our journey, understanding how to get text into our Ruby scripts. You should now be able to perform the important first step of getting text into your program, ready for processing, whether that text is in files or comes from other processes, whether it's freeform or in some delimited format, whether it's on a web page or on your local filesystem, and whatever character encoding it might be stored in.

That's an impressive set of skills—and useful, too. But once we've got that text into our program, we generally want to do something with it—manipulate it in some way or extract something from it. We'll be looking at these skills in Part II.

Part II

Transform: Modifying and Manipulating Text

Now that we've figured out how to read text from various sources, we need to figure out the things we can do with text once we've got it into a script. Generally, this means either extracting some data from it or transforming it into a different format.

We'll look at a variety of techniques, each useful in different scenarios. First, we'll look at regular expressions, which will come in useful almost everywhere that we process text. Then we'll learn how to write parsers for handling more formally structured text. Finally, we'll take a whistle-stop tour of natural language processing, a broad but exciting topic.

CHAPTER 8

Regular Expressions Basics

We've looked now at a variety of ways that you can get text into your Ruby programs: from the user, from a pipe, from files. The next step, naturally, is to actually do something with that input.

When processing text, our aims can generally be split into three broad categories: testing, where we check whether the data matches a particular pattern; extraction, where we try to pull interesting information out of the data; and transformation, where we convert the data from one format to another. Often, we'll want to do some combination of all three of these things: checking for particular formats, extracting key pieces of information, and then transforming them (converting them to a different text format, perhaps, or calculating an average, or converting them from a certain set of units to another).

Programmers of every sort, whether they're programming in object-oriented or functional languages, whether they're working with powerful servers or humble desktop machines, will often—too often, perhaps—reach for *regular expressions* as a tool of first resort for both extraction and transformation of text. There's good reason for this: regular expressions are enormously powerful, and a relatively standard syntax for them has grown up, which means that once you've learned them in one language, there's not a great deal of adjustment when working with them in another.

But what exactly are they? Well, in layman's terms at least, a regular expression (almost always abbreviated to *regex*) is a way of describing a pattern in text, which can then be used to extract or replace text that matches those patterns.

So you might have a regular expression that matches the format of a URL. You could use that pattern to check whether a given string was a valid URL (matching). You could use it to extract all the URLs in a given piece of text (extraction). And you could use that same pattern in a replacement—for example, to make all the URLs in the text into HTML links so that they can be clicked on (transformation).

It has to be said that few topics in programming are as feared by new programmers as regular expressions. Their power, combined with their frighteningly terse syntax, makes them seem impenetrable and mysterious. Writing them can often seem closer to incanting a magical spell than to programming.

But it needn't be like this. If you're processing text, then regular expressions are your friend, and the quicker you dive into them the better.

A Gentle Introduction

Even if you haven't used regular expressions before, you might have used wildcards. On the command line, for example, we can use patterns like `dog-*.jpg` to match many files (in this case, matching things like dog-jumping.jpg, dog-2.jpg, dog-large.jpg, and so on for infinitely more files).

These wildcards work because the `*` character is understood to have a special meaning. It doesn't represent the literal `*`, but instead represents *any and all* characters.

Regular expressions work in exactly the same way. The difference is that they extend the list of these special characters significantly, allowing you greater power and flexibility. Wildcards allow you to say "I want to match this specific character" and "I want to match any character at all," with nothing in between those two extremes. With regular expressions you can say, "I want to match this set of characters but no others," or "I want to match exactly `X` or exactly `Y`, but nothing else," or "I want to match `Z` but only if it's immediately preceded by `A`," and so on.

Simply put, then, a regular expression is a *description of a pattern of text*. That pattern might be something simple, like "the letter `a`, followed by the letter `b`, followed by the letter `c`." Or it might be more complex, such as "the word `http`, followed optionally by an `s`, then `://`, then a series of alphanumeric characters, then a `.` character, then `com`."

As you can see from describing these patterns in English, they get very verbose very quickly—and these aren't particularly complex patterns. For that reason, the syntax of regular expressions has been deliberately crafted to be as short as possible. That latter example, describing a URL, can be expressed as `/https?://[a-z0-9]+\.com/`—significantly shorter. This ability to describe complex patterns in few characters is what lends regular expressions both their power and their intimidating reputation.

Pattern Syntax

It's beyond the scope of this book to teach regular expressions in their entirety. But it's not necessary to learn anything close to the entirety of regular expressions to productively use them to process text. In the rest of this chapter, we'll take a tour of the fundamentals of regular expressions—that 20 percent of functionality that allows you to perform 80 percent of the tasks you'll encounter.

Regular expression syntax is, as we've discussed, famously terse. This terseness makes it relatively unintuitive. There's sometimes no astoundingly logical reason why a particular special character represents a particular pattern, apart from that it hadn't already been used for something else. But this terseness brings great power, so making the effort to remember the special characters and their roles is worth it in the long run.

Matching Characters

We've mentioned that, like wildcards, regular expressions use special characters to represent particular patterns. But more fundamentally, the first thing to note about them is that characters other than these special characters don't do anything special at all: they just match themselves. So to write a regular expression that matched the string `abc` anywhere in the text, we'd simply write `/abc/`; to write one that matched `hello, world`, we'd write `/hello, world/`; and so on.

At the other extreme, we can match any character at all using a dot (`.`). So the regex `/h.llo/` would match `hello`, `hallo`, `hullo`, `h_llo`, and so on. There can be absolutely any character in that second position, provided there's actually a second character.

Somewhere between these two extremes are *character classes*, which match specific lists of characters. So if we wanted to limit our earlier expression to only match `hello`, `hallo`, and `hullo`, we could use the pattern `/h[eau]llo/`. Similarly, to match both the British and US spellings of "initialise," we could use the pattern `/initiali[sz]e/`.

We can also use *ranges* in character classes: so, for any lowercase letter we could use `[a-z]`, and for any number we could use `[0-9]`. Ranges can be arbitrary, of course; we can limit ourselves to just the numbers 4–9 with `[4-9]` or just the letters f–t with `[f-t]`.

As well as character classes, there are some shortcuts for common character types. There's \d for any digit (equivalent to [0-9]), \w for any "word character" (equivalent to [a-zA-Z0-9_]), and \s for any whitespace character.

These also have negative forms, each of which is just the uppercase version of the same letter. So \D matches any character except a digit, \W matches any character except a word character, and \S matches any non-whitespace character.

You can make negative character classes yourself, too: simply start the class with a ^ character. So to match any character apart from vowels, we could use [^aeiou]; to match any character except uppercase letters, we could use [^A-Z].

Quantifiers

So far we've written patterns that match only single characters. What do we do if we want to match more than one instance of the same pattern? We could match two numbers in a row with /\d\d/, for example, but what if we want to match an arbitrary number? That's where *quantifiers* come in: they let us say how many times a pattern can repeat while still matching.

The simplest quantifier is *. This matches *zero or more* instances of the preceding pattern. This often trips people up: zero or more is an important concept, since it matches, well, anything. /n*/ ("zero or more n characters"), to make things a bit more concrete, matches both "hand" and "spanner," as you might expect (they contain one and two n's, respectively). But it also matches "trowel." And "beeblebrox." And any other string of characters, regardless of whether any of them is an "n."

* is more useful in the middle of a pattern, of course, where it does restrict the characters that can appear. For example, /hello\s*world/ will match "helloworld" and "hello world," but not "hello, world." (You'll often see this \s* pattern, where whitespace is optional and is likely being ignored.)

Maybe we don't want to allow for arbitrary repetitions; we just want a character or pattern to be optional. In that case, we can use ?. It counts *zero or one* repetitions but doesn't allow any more than that. So to match both the US and British spellings of "tranquillity" (it's spelled "tranquillity" in British English and "tranquility" in the US), we could write /tranquill?ity/; this matches both correct spellings, but not the obviously incorrect "tranquilllity."

To go in the other direction, if we want to match *one or more* (but not zero) repetitions of a pattern, we can use the + quantifier. This ensures that the preceding pattern occurs at least once but allows for an arbitrary number of repetitions. If we wanted to match the exclamations "great," "greeeat," and "greeeeeeeeat," then we could use /gre+at/. This lets us be as much like Tony the Tiger as we like, but doesn't match the nonsensical "grat" like * would.

Finally, if we want to match specific numbers of repetitions, we can do that, too, by using braces. So, to match four repetitions, we use {4}; to match between one and four, we use {1,4}. This allows us to write, for example, /ste{1,2}p/, a pattern that would match both "step" and "steep," but not "stp" or "steeep." We can leave the second value blank, too, so to match five or more repetitions, we could write {5,}.

Anchors

We've thus far only written patterns that can occur anywhere in a string. But in reality, we often want to either test that the whole string matches a pattern—when validating input, for example. Or we might want to check that a string starts or ends in a certain way, or that a pattern occurs at the start or end of a line.

We can do this using *anchors*. Let's imagine we have the regex /\d+/, which matches a sequence of one or more numbers. It will match 12345, as we'd expect, but it would also match "abc12345def." In other words, it's checking that the string *contains* a sequence of one or more numbers, not that the string *is* a sequence of one or more numbers. But if we use \A to anchor to the start of the text and \z to anchor to the end, we can make sure the text consists entirely of digits: /\A\d+\z/.

If we'd just like to ensure that a line matches a particular format, we can use the ^ (start of line) and $ (end of line) anchors. It's important to know that, unlike many other regular expression engines, Ruby doesn't use these to anchor the start and the end of the string. Many people will write a regex like /^\d+$/ and expect it to match only if a string consists entirely of numbers. However, it will also match the input:

```
not a number
12345
also not a number
```

If you're using this kind of validation for security, then this can lead to vulnerabilities. If you're expecting to match the whole text, use \A and \z instead.

Capture Groups

The final element of basic regex syntax is the ability to group segments of your match. Let's say that you wanted to match a British telephone number. These are in the format of a five-digit area code and then a six-digit number. But you want to capture the area code and the phone number separately, because you want to distinguish between these two parts that make up the whole phone number.

To match a number in this format, you could write: `/\d{5}\s*\d{6}/`. Five digits, followed by optional whitespace, followed by six digits. To group the elements of the match, all you need to do is put them into parentheses: `/(\d{5})\s*(\d{6})/`. After matching these in Ruby, you can then access the two different elements individually. (We'll look at exactly how to do that shortly.)

Grouping in this way results in numbered capture groups (the area code in 1, the phone number in 2). But we can also name them, with the `?<name>` syntax. The previous example with named groups would look like this:

```
/(?<area_code>\d{5})\s*(?<number>\d{6})/
```

This can make the code after the match clearer; it reveals our intentions more clearly. Accessing `match[:area_code]` and `match[:number]` is much more obvious than `match[0]` and `match[1]`.

A secondary feature of capture groups is the ability to perform alternation: that is, to match one string of characters or another. So to match two greetings, "hello there" and "hi there," we can use the expression `/(hello|hi) there/`.

We can also use alternation in the whole pattern; for example, to match text that contains either "this" or "that," we can write the pattern `/this|that/`, without the need for capture groups.

And with that, we've covered the fundamentals of regular expression syntax. By composing these special characters together in different ways, we can create limitless combinations of patterns that allow us to match anything we might find ourselves needing to. The next question, then, is a practical one: how does this actually translate to Ruby?

Regular Expressions in Ruby

In Ruby, regular expressions are a first-class construct. Literal regexes have their own syntax (`//`), and regular expressions are taken as arguments by countless methods in the standard library. This is particularly true of the `String` class, but regular expressions are also used in other, perhaps less obvious, places—Enumerable#grep, for example. They're definitely not an afterthought; they are as fundamental to the language as strings or numbers.

Let's take a look at how we can define regular expressions in Ruby so that we can use our newfound knowledge.

Defining Regular Expressions

Regular expressions in Ruby are instances of the Regexp class. Technically, you can create one by passing a string to Regexp.new, but this never happens in practice. Instead, we use the // literal:

```
regex = /^[a-z]{1,2}[0-9]+$/
```

Anything inside the slashes will be interpreted as the pattern, while options are passed after the slash. For example, we can make a regular expression case insensitive by adding the i option after the final slash:

```
regex = /^[a-z]{1,2}[0-9]+$/i
```

There's also a %r literal that achieves the same result:

```
regex = %r{^[a-z]{1,2}[0-9]+$}
```

The percent literal is generally used if the pattern that you're writing contains a lot of forward slashes; many people consider that there's an improvement in readability with this syntax:

```
%r{^http://}
```

versus:

```
/^http:\/\//
```

Regexes in Ruby are just like any other object. So, you can use them as arguments to methods, assign them to variables and constants, and so on:

```
URL = /https?:\/\/\S+/
URL.match("http://www.example.com")
# => #<MatchData "http://www.example.com">
```

Like string literals, they support interpolation, so you can use the values of variables or the return values of method calls when constructing expressions:

```
letters = "A-Za-z"
numbers = "0-9"
pattern = /[#{letters}#{numbers}]/
```

Pattern Modifiers

Regular expressions have default behaviors, things they do unless you tell them otherwise. They're case-sensitive, for example, and whitespace is counted as part of the pattern to match. But, as in other languages, Ruby allows us to override these options. We do so by passing a pattern modifier when defining the regular expression. These modifiers are letters that go after the final slash. So, to use all of the possible modifiers, we'd write:

```
/foo/imox
```

Or with the alternative regular expression literal:

```
%r{foo}imox
```

Let's dig into what each of these four modifiers does.

Case-insensitive Matching (i)

Probably the most common option is `i`, which tells the regular expression engine to ignore the case of the string being matched against. Perhaps an example is the best way to illustrate this:

```
text = "The British Broadcasting Corporation (BBC)"

text.match(/bbc/)
# => nil

text.match(/bbc/i)
# => #<MatchData "BBC">
```

We can see that the first, case-sensitive regular expression failed to match, whereas the second, case-insensitive version did, because `/bbc/` matches "BBC" only if we ignore case.

Multiline Mode (m)

The `.` character, in an ordinary regular expression, is often translated as "match any character." But that's not quite accurate. Let's look at an example where this isn't the case.

If we assume that `.` matches any character, then we might expect the expression `/(.*)/` to match the entire string we give it, putting the whole string in capture group one. Let's try it and see what happens:

```
text = <<TEXT
This is line one
This is line two
TEXT
```

```
text.match(/(.*)/) do |match|
  puts match[1]
end
```

If you run this script, you'll see that it outputs `This is line one`. Our dot character isn't matching any character; it's only matching any character in the first line. What gives?

Strictly speaking, `.` matches any character *except newlines*. Normally, that's likely to be the behavior that you want, especially if you're using the `^` and `$` anchors to match the start and end of a line. But sometimes it's not what we're after, if we want to match patterns that span multiple lines.

If we want this behavior, we can use the `m` or "multiline" modifier. Let's revisit the previous example, but this time use `m`:

```
text = <<TEXT
This is line one
This is line two
TEXT

text.match(/(.*)/m) do |match|
  puts match[1]
end
# => This is line one
# => This is line two
```

This is the output that we expected.

Substitute Once (o)

As we've seen, we can use interpolation to place the values of variables or method calls into patterns:

```
letters = "A-Za-z"
numbers = "0-9"
"A1".match(/[#{letters}#{numbers}]/)
```

This is generally perfectly acceptable to do. But let's make two changes to this scenario. First, let's imagine that the matching is happening in a loop, so it may happen hundreds or even thousands of times. Second, let's imagine that instead of just interpolating a variable, as in the previous example, we're using the result of a method call that might involve an expensive calculation. Here's an example of what this might look like:

```
def letters
  puts "letters() called"
  sleep 1
  "A-Za-z"
end
```

```
words = %w[the quick brown fox jumped over the lazy dog]
words.each do |word|
  puts "Matches!" if word.match(/\A[#{letters}]+\z/)
end
```

Let's take a minute to step through this example.

First, we're defining a method called letters. It just returns the same as our variable did earlier, but we can imagine that such a method might involve a database lookup or another such expensive calculation. We've simulated this slowness by sleeping for one second, to make sure we notice the delay.

Then we're looping over some words in a sentence and outputting "Matches!" if the string matches a regular expression—in this case, checking whether the word consists entirely of letters.

If we were to run this script, we'd see the following output:

```
letters() called
Matches!
letters() called
Matches!
letters() called
Matches!
letters() called
Matches!
letters() called
Matches!
letters() called
Matches!
letters() called
Matches!
letters() called
Matches!
letters() called
Matches!
letters() called
```

We'd also notice that it was slow—very slow, in fact. That's because every time we ran match, the interpolation was being recalculated—meaning that our letters method was being called every time too, with its one second of overhead. Using the time utility can confirm that this is indeed a slow way to do things:

```
$ time ruby o-modifier.rb
letters() called
Matches!
:   :
letters() called
Matches!
```

```
real	0m9.040s
user	0m0.027s
sys	0m0.006s
```

Nine seconds! That's pretty wasteful.

Luckily, the o modifier can help us in situations like this. Suppose we change our code so that the match call uses this modifier:

```
words.each do |word|
  puts "Matches!" if word.match(/\A[#{letters}]+\z/o)
end
```

Then, when running the script with time, we'll see the following output:

```
$ time ruby o-modifier.rb
letters() called
Matches!
Matches!
Matches!
Matches!
Matches!
Matches!
Matches!
Matches!
Matches!

real	0m1.031s
user	0m0.024s
sys	0m0.005s
```

We can see from the output that the letters method was called only once—when the first word was matched—and then not again. This resulted in the script taking just over one second to execute, rather than the previous nine seconds.

Of course, this is a rather extreme example; it's rare that you'll find yourself needing to interpolate the result of a calculation that takes this long into a regular expression, and on top of that to be doing it inside a loop. But if you do, it's worth remembering the o modifier.

Extended Expressions (x)

The final pattern modifier is x, which enables "extended" regular expressions. This allows you to do two things: first, you can add whitespace into your regular expressions to improve readability, without that whitespace actually being a part of the pattern; and second, you can add comments with the # character just as you would in Ruby itself.

Let's compare a regular expression with and without the x modifier, to see how it can improve readability. In this case, we'll use a regular expression that matches UK postcodes, somewhat notorious for their complexity:

```
uk_postcode = /(([A-Z]{1,2}[0-9]{1,2}[A-Z]?)\s?([0-9][A-Z]{2})|(GIR)\s?(0AA))/

uk_postcode = /
(                     # Capture the whole postcode in $1
  (                   # Capture outward postcode part in $2
    [A-Z]{1,2}        # The postcode area (e.g. L => Liverpool)
    [0-9]{1,2}        # The postcode district
    [A-Z]?            # Some postcode districts have a trailing
                      # letter (e.g. London W1A)
  )                   # End capture group $2

  \s?                 # Although a space between parts is
                      # technically mandatory, in practice
                      # it's widely omitted

  (                   # Capture inward postcode part in $3
    [0-9]             # Sector within this district
    [A-Z]{2}          # Unit within this sector
  )                   # End capture group $3
  |
  (GIR)\s?(0AA)       # GiroBank has a unique postcode that
                      # doesn't fit the usual format
)                     # End capture group $1
/x
```

Although it's much, much more verbose, the second example is also infinitely clearer. What was a dense jumble of letters and numbers is now clearly explained. Granted, this is an extreme example. In practice, you probably wouldn't want to explain the format of a UK postcode, since it's clear enough from the variable name what pattern the actual regex is matching. But if you're matching something complex that wouldn't immediately be grasped by the average reader, consider using an extended regex.

Wrapping Up

We looked at what regular expressions are and how we can use them to describe patterns of text. We looked at how to define basic patterns, including quantifiers, anchors, character classes, and more. And we looked at how we can use pattern modifiers to alter the behavior of our regexes—for example, to make them case-insensitive.

Now that you've learned about the patterns themselves, it's time to learn how you can actually put them to use in processing text.

CHAPTER 9

Extraction and Substitution with Regular Expressions

Now that we know what regular expressions are and how to define them, let's look at how we actually use them to do something practical.

The use of regular expressions generally falls into two categories: matching (both to check whether a string matches a pattern and to extract matches from it) and substitution (replacing patterns with other text). Let's look first at matching.

Matching Against Patterns

If we want to check whether two strings are identical, we can of course use the equality operator:

```
if "something else" == "something"
  # we'll never get here
end
```

To check whether a string matches a regular expression, Ruby offers the =~ operator. Some people call it the "matches" operator, or the "is like" operator. If the string matches the pattern defined in the regular expression, it returns a truthy value, which means we can use it in an `if` check. If we wanted to check whether a URL was an `https` one rather than `http`, we could use =~:

```
url = "https://example.com/"

if url =~ /\Ahttps:/
  puts "The URL is https"
else
  puts "The URL is not https"
end
```

We can also use the match method for this. It exists on both String and Regexp, so we can call either:

```
url.match(/\Ahttps:/)
```

or:

```
/\Ahttps:/.match(url)
```

If the string doesn't match the regular expression, match will return nil, so you can use it in an if statement just like =~. If it does match, match will return a MatchData object containing information about the match. MatchData objects behave like collections, so you can access named or numbered capture groups with [], check the number of matches with .length, and so on.

Let's write a pattern to match the protocol and hostname of a given URL. That means that, given the URL https://example.com/, we'd like to extract https as the protocol and example.com as the hostname. We can use match for this:

regex/matchdata.rb

```
url = "https://example.com"

matches = url.match(/([a-z]+):\/\/([\w\.]+)/)
# => #<MatchData "https://example.com" 1:"https" 2:"example.com">
if matches
  puts matches[0]
  puts matches[1]
  puts matches[2]
end
# >> https://example.com
# >> https
# >> example.com
```

Our pattern has two capture groups. The first matches a sequence of letters followed by a colon, therefore capturing the protocol. (We're not just restricting our pattern to either http or https; we'll match any URL protocol.) The second group matches a sequence of word characters or periods, and so captures our hostname. Between the two is the ://, which we don't capture.

Accessing the zeroth element of the match data returns for us the whole string that was matched by the pattern. In this case, that's the whole string, but that's not necessarily always the case; we might only be matching a tiny portion of it. The first element is the first capture group—in this case, our protocol—and the second is the second capture group.

The match method also accepts a block, which is executed only if the string matches the expression. The block is passed the MatchData as an argument. This is especially useful because it means you can avoid checking whether the pattern actually matched, and therefore whether the return value from match was nil:

regex/matchdata-block.rb
```
url = "https://example.com"

url.match(/([a-z]+):\/\/([\w\.]+)/) do |matches|
  puts matches[0]
  puts matches[1]
  puts matches[2]
end
# >> https://example.com
# >> https
# >> example.com
```

Here we avoid the if, which makes things a little neater.

Global Match Variables

Until now we've been calling the match method and using its return value, or the arguments passed to its block, to discover information about the matched text. But data from the last match is also available, after the match has occurred, in a series of global variables. They're a little more cryptic, compared to referencing the MatchData directly, but can come in handy—especially when writing Ruby in the shell.

Each one of these global variables contains a different piece of information about the match—things like the specific text that was matched, the contents of any subgroups within the expression, and so on. Let's explore each one and what it can be used for.

$~

The first global is $~, which contains the entire MatchData of the last match. This is the same data that's returned from the match method, and that means you can access match data even if you didn't call match explicitly or capture its return value—for example, when using the =~ comparison operator:

regex/globals/tilde.rb
```
url = "https://example.com"

if url =~ /^https:/
  $~
  # => #<MatchData "https:">
end
```

This means that we can achieve the same things using the =~ operator as we could if we use match.

$1, $2, $3 up to $9

These contain the values of the capture groups from the last match—those sections of the match grouped in parentheses. For example:

regex/globals/numbers.rb
```
"hello world".match(/(\w+) (\w+)/)

puts $1   # >> hello
puts $2   # >> world
puts $3   # >>
```

We can see that there were two capture groups in the pattern, each matching a word. The first capture group goes into $1, and the second goes into $2. $3 is nil because there wasn't a third group in the pattern.

These global variables are the most commonly used regex-related globals in Ruby, since they're a lot shorter than other ways of accessing the same data. We don't need to assign the result of match to a variable or pass in a block. We can just match a pattern and then directly access the capture groups.

$&

$& contains the whole match as a string. It's the equivalent of accessing the zeroth element of the MatchData. That is, it contains the entire section of the original string that matched the pattern:

regex/globals/ampersand.rb
```
matches = "hello world".match(/\w+\s\w+/)

puts $&             # >> hello world
puts matches[0]     # >> hello world
```

This is probably the next most useful global; again, it's a handy shortcut.

$+

$+ contains the final capture group of the most recent match—equivalent to $~.captures.last. If there were no capture groups, it returns nil:

regex/globals/plus.rb
```
"hello world".match(/(\w+)\s(\w+)/)
last_match = $+       # => "world"

"hello world".match(/\w+\s\w+/)
last_match = $+       # => nil
```

This can be particularly useful if our expression has a lot of groups—for alternation using |, for example—but we're only interested in the final one.

$` and $'

$` (a dollar and a backtick) contains the string from the beginning up to the start of the match; conversely, $' (a dollar and an apostrophe) contains the string from the end of the match to the end of the string. They're the equivalent of $~.pre_match and $~.post_match, respectively. Here's an example:

regex/globals/backtick.rb

```
"hello world".match(/lo wo/)

p $`           # => "hel"
p $'           # => "rld"
```

So, if we wanted to, we could reconstruct the original string:

regex/globals/backtick-dollar.rb

```
"hello world".match(/lo wo/)

string = $` + $& + $'       # => "hello world"
```

These are actually quite handy. If we want to simultaneously test for a prefix while discarding it, for example, we could write:

```
"name: Rob Miller".match(/name: /)

name = $'         # => "Rob Miller"
```

We don't have to bother with capture groups or with knowing what characters are allowed in the name; we can just slurp up everything after the name.

These globals are certainly not always appropriate, and many people frown on them, finding them too obscure or too cryptic. But their terseness, like that of regular expressions themselves, can often be useful.

Extracting Multiple Matches

You've seen how we can use match to check whether a string matches a pattern and to extract capture groups within that pattern. Let's take a look now at how we can use a pattern to extract many values from within a piece of text, a common requirement of text processing tasks. This will enable us to define a pattern once and then match arbitrary occurrences of it.

In these examples we're going to work with the following block of text:

```
Here are the top ten countries by population, as of 2013 when the
world population was 7 billion.

China:         1,361,540,000
India:         1,237,510,000
United States: 317,234,000
```

```
Indonesia:     237,641,326
Brazil:        201,032,714
Pakistan:      185,028,000
Nigeria:       173,615,000
Bangladesh:    152,518,015
Russia:        143,600,000
Japan:         127,290,000

The total population of these most populous ten countries is
4,137,009,055.
```

At the moment, this is just a passage of text as it might be written in an article for people to read. But using regular expressions, we can extract the data stored within that text and bring it into a script. Let's take a look.

Creating a Pattern

Let's imagine that we wanted to extract the names of the countries in the top ten. The key part in doing this is to identify a pattern, figuring out what the data we're looking for have in common.

In this case, the countries all start at the beginning of the line. They all have a colon after them, too. In fact, in this example at least, that's all we need to distinguish them from other elements in the text. So let's write a regex to match text that fits this pattern.

The first element of the pattern is, as we mentioned, that the country names are at the start of the line. To match this, as we saw in the last chapter, we can use the caret character (^):

```
countries = /^/
```

Next, we need something that will match the countries themselves. They consist of only letters and space characters, so to match multiple characters in this way, we can use a character class and tell it the list of characters we'd like to accept. So, extending the regex, we'd get:

```
countries = /^[a-zA-Z ]/
```

But we don't want to match just one character: we want to match one *or more*. For that, if you remember, we use the + quantifier:

```
countries = /^[a-zA-Z ]+/
```

We're almost there! At the moment, though, we're going to match more than we need. If you think of the first line of this passage of text, we're going to match right up to the comma after "population," since before that there's only lowercase letters, uppercase letters, and spaces.

Thinking back to how we originally thought of our pattern, we can get around this by including the colon; doing so will limit our matches to just the country names.

```
countries = /^[a-zA-Z ]+:/
```

So now we've got a pattern that matches, from the start of the line, one or more letters and spaces, provided they're followed by a colon.

Extracting the Matched Text

Our regular expression seems like it's complete. Now we need a way to run it across the string and extract all of the text that matches the pattern. Earlier we used match to check whether a string matches a pattern, but that only gives us the first match. In this case, we want all of them. Instead of match, we can use String's scan method:

```
matches = text.scan(/^[a-zA-Z ]+:/)
```

scan returns for us a nice array of the countries in the text:

```
["China:",
"India:",
"United States:",
"Indonesia:",
"Brazil:",
"Pakistan:",
"Nigeria:",
"Bangladesh:",
"Russia:",
"Japan:"]
```

We're almost there, but the country names all end in colons. Let's get rid of them.

Lookaheads

We've extracted the country names from the text, including the colon at the end of each of them. We could just loop over the countries, removing the colon manually from each one:

```
matches = text.scan(/^[a-zA-Z ]+:/)
matches = matches.map { |country| country.chomp ":" }
```

But this isn't a particularly nice solution. It would be better if there was a way, when defining our pattern, to say that while we wanted to use the colon as part of the matching, we didn't actually want to include it in the returned match data.

Regular expressions allow us to do this using something called a positive lookahead. In technical terms, the lookahead is a *zero-width assertion*. This means that while it's an *assertion* (it asserts that the character or pattern is present), it's also *zero-width* (it doesn't include the character in the final match data). This allows us to match something without capturing it, which is exactly what we want to do in this case.

So we can adapt our regular expression to:

```
matches = text.scan(/^[a-zA-Z ]+(?=:)/)
```

And, as if by magic, the countries we get back no longer have colons:

```
["China",
"India",
"United States",
"Indonesia",
"Brazil",
"Pakistan",
"Nigeria",
"Bangladesh",
"Russia",
"Japan"]
```

There's a lot to take in here, and it's worth taking some time to play with some real data to see it in action. But the basic principles—of breaking the text we're trying to extract into a pattern, building a regular expression that matches that pattern, and then using `scan` to extract the matches—will remain constant. It's a process that scales well with the complexity of our matches.

Transforming Text

We've dealt with merely matching patterns in text, but that's only half of what regular expressions can do. We can also use them to perform substitutions, transforming text that matches patterns into something else entirely.

We can do this in fairly simple ways, replacing a pattern with a fixed string. Or we can do more complex replacements, using capture groups to include information from the pattern we're matching in the replacement.

Two methods are used to perform the majority of regex-based substitutions in Ruby. Let's look at them next.

sub and gsub

Even if you're not familiar with regular expressions, you might have used the `sub` and `gsub`—*substitute* and *global substitute*—methods to perform replacements on text.

Both methods take either a string or a regular expression as their first argument, and a string as their second. The first argument defines a pattern to match, and the second is the text that replaces this match. For example:

```
"hello".sub(/[aeiou]/, "")
```

You might expect the return value here to be "hll"; that is, "hello" with *all* of its vowels removed. But instead what we get is "hllo"—only the first vowel has been replaced. That's because `sub` replaces only the first match it finds. If we'd like to replace them all, we need to use `gsub` instead.

`gsub` operates in exactly the same way as `sub`, taking a search pattern as either a regular expression or string as its first argument, and a replacement string as its second argument. The only difference is that if there are multiple matches of the search pattern, all of them will be replaced rather than only the first. So we can update our vowel-replacement example with:

```
"hello".gsub(/[aeiou]/, "")
```

And, as expected, we get back the string "hll."

Both methods have bang versions—`sub!` and `gsub!`—that modify the string directly, rather than returning a new string with the replacements made:

regex/gsub-bang.rb

```
text = "hello, world"
text.gsub(/[aeiou]/, "")
puts text
# >> hello, world
text.gsub!(/[aeiou]/, "")
puts text
# >> hll, wrld
```

Pattern-Based Replacements

As we've seen, we can use capture groups in regular expressions to group subsections of a match. This allows us to extract multiple parts of a pattern in one go. But we can use these capture groups in replacements, too.

Let's say we had the following text, listing the discography of a band:

```
1994 - Zopilote Machine
1995 - Sweden
1996 - Nothing for Juice
1997 - Full Force Galesburg
2000 - The Coroner's Gambit
2002 - All Hail West Texas
2002 - Tallahassee
2004 - We Shall All Be Healed
2005 - The Sunset Tree
```

```
2006 - Get Lonely
2008 - Heretic Pride
2009 - The Life of the World to Come
2011 - All Eternals Deck
2012 - Transcendental Youth
2015 - Beat the Champ
```

If we wanted to extract the years and titles of these albums separately, we could do so with a relatively simple pattern:

regex/discography-scan.rb

```
discography.scan(/^([0-9]{4}) - (.+)$/)
# => [["1994", "Zopilote Machine"],
#      ["1995", "Sweden"],
          :         :           :
#      ["2012", "Transcendental Youth"],
#      ["2015", "Beat the Champ"]]
```

Let's imagine that we don't really want to extract this information, though; we just want to reformat it so that the album titles go first—"Tallahassee (2002)," for example.

We could loop over the results of the scan and build up a new string, but that would be silly. Instead, we can do this with a pattern-based replacement, which allows us to use the values of capture groups in the replacement string.

We can do this by using a single-quoted replacement string and by using a backslash to refer to the numbers of the capture group we require. In this case, we want \1 for the year and \2 to get the name of the album, so our replacement is as simple as this:

regex/discography-gsub.rb

```
puts discography.gsub(/^([0-9]{4}) - (.+)$/, '\2 (\1)')

# >> Zopilote Machine (1994)
# >> Sweden (1995)
  :        :        :
# >> Transcendental Youth (2012)
# >> Beat the Champ (2015)
```

What if we wanted to use named capture groups, though? They'd certainly improve the clarity of the regex. In this case, instead of backslash and a number, we can use \k to refer to a named group:

regex/discography-gsub-named.rb

```
puts discography.gsub(
  /^(?<year>[0-9]{4}) - (?<album>.+)$/,
  '\k<album> \k<year>'
)
```

```
# >> Zopilote Machine 1994
# >> Sweden 1995
  :       :       :
# >> Transcendental Youth 2012
# >> Beat the Champ 2015
```

This is clearer than the numbered version, at the expense of being slightly longer. That's often, but not always, the correct trade-off to make.

Replacement Blocks

You don't necessarily have to pass a string to sub or gsub to define the replacement. You can pass a block instead. Somewhat confusingly, and unlike when you pass a block to match, the argument given to the block isn't the MatchData, but is instead just the matched string. So if you want to access this match data, you need to use the $~ global (or any of the other regex globals mentioned earlier).

This allows you to perform more complex logic on the replacement string—running another substitution, for example, or even something much more complicated, such as querying a database for a particular piece of data and then using that in the replacement.

Sticking with our discography example, we might want to display relative years rather than absolute ones. That is, rather than displaying something like 2002, we'd like to display 13 years ago. By passing a block to gsub, we could do just that:

regex/discography-gsub-block.rb

```
  discography.gsub(/^(?<year>[0-9]{4}) - (?<album>.+)$/) do |match|
    album_year = $~[:year].to_i
    years_ago = Date.today.year - album_year
    title = $~[:album]

    "#{title} (#{years_ago} years ago)"
  end

puts discography

# >> Zopilote Machine (21 years ago)
# >> Sweden (20 years ago)
  :       :       :
# >> Transcendental Youth (3 years ago)
# >> Beat the Champ (0 years ago)
```

Here we take the album's year and convert it to an integer. Subtracting it from the current year tells us how many years ago the album was released. And that's it! The string that we return from the block will be used as the replacement, so we just need to format our text as we'd like it to appear—the album title followed by the relative age in parentheses.

Wrapping Up

We started this chapter by using the `match` method both to check whether a string matched a particular pattern and to extract capture groups from within that pattern. Then we explored the `scan` method on strings, and how we could use it to extract many different patterns from within a string.

As well as simply matching patterns, we discovered how to use `sub` and `gsub` to take portions of text that match a pattern and replace them with something else. We also covered `gsub`'s ability to take a block, and we used that to perform some further processing of the matched text before replacing it.

Next up, we'll be looking at an alternative technique to regular expressions—parsers—and when they can be useful.

CHAPTER 10

Writing Parsers

Sometimes regular expressions can get a little hairy. Once you begin using lots of lookahead assertions, have many capture groups, and generally have a regular expression that's getting a bit scary to look at, it's probably a sign that you're trying to do too much in a single expression. Some problems are also just plain impossible to solve with a regular expression, so an alternative isn't only desirable, but is also actually necessary. We saw one such example in Chapter 6, *Scraping HTML*, on page 63, when thinking about how to handle HTML.

In that case and many others, the best approach is to write a parser. A parser generally steps through a piece of text bit by bit, building up information as it goes and deciding what action to perform based on the text that it encounters—and the surrounding context. This ability to take different paths based on the input encountered is a key strength of parsers.

Another important distinction versus a regular expression is that parsers are able easily to *recurse*. This allows us to define things in terms of themselves: an example of this would be HTML, where an element can contain an element (which can contain an element, which can contain an element...and so on *ad infinitum*). Creating a parser makes matching such infinitely nested structures straightforward.

Perhaps the most common uses of a parser that you'll have encountered is when writing computer programs. Here, a parser translates the source code, written by a human, into something understandable by a computer. Sometimes this involves two steps: *lexing*, to transform each part of the source code into a *token* (for example, *function* or *number* or *operator*); then *parsing*, to transform these tokens into a *syntax tree*. For simplicity's sake, we'll consider both of these things to be parsing, since they have much in common.

The question of whether to use a regular expression or to write a parser is a difficult one. Its answer has to do with the nature of the problem (whether it's one that naturally lends itself to parsing), but also with the complexity of the problem (whether, if you solve the problem with a regular expression, you'll still understand your solution in 24 hours, let alone 24 months).

If the problem you're dealing with is suited to parsing, Ruby comes with a fantastic library that makes writing simple parsers trivial. It's called StringScanner, and we'll take a look at it in this chapter.

After StringScanner, we'll look at creating more powerful parsers that can easily parse completely flexible text. Using a library called Parslet, you'll learn how to create a *grammar* that describes rules of the text you want to parse, and then a *transformation* that does something useful with the parsed result.

First, though, we'll look at writing a simple parser using StringScanner.

Simple Parsers with StringScanner

The essence of StringScanner is in its name. It lets you scan through a string, moving through it as you capture information, always knowing where in the string you are. Unlike with a regular expression, at any point in our scanning through the string we can stop and make decisions. We can look ahead to see what's coming next, and take a different course of action depending on the answer. We can use recursion, too, to match nested constructs.

StringScanner manages this scanning process by maintaining a *scan pointer*. This behaves in effectively the same way as a cursor in a text editor does, indicating what part of the string we've moved past and what part is yet to come. We can then use varying methods to advance that pointer through the string, either capturing or discarding portions of the string as we pass through.

We won't be discarding our newly gained regular expression knowledge. At a low level, when deciding what part of the string ahead to consume, we'll be using regular expressions. This gives us the power to consume, say, the next word—or string of numbers, or piece of punctuation, or anything else we'd care to define.

StringScanner is part of the standard library, so there's no need to install a gem. Simply require "strscan" in scripts when you'd like to use its functionality.

We start using it by passing a string to its constructor:

```
require "strscan"

scanner = StringScanner.new("The quick brown fox jumped over the lazy dog.")
```

We now have a scanner object that will keep track of our progress through the string.

Scanning

Once we've initialized the scanner, we can begin to use it. Its methods can generally be split into two main categories. The first is query methods, which tell you information about where you are in the string—what's behind you and what's in front of you. The second is scanning methods, which allow you either to advance or to retreat the scan pointer throughout the string.

To continue our previous example, let's look at one method from each category. The first query method is pos, which tell us our position in the string in terms of characters, and the first scanning method is the aptly named scan.

```
require "strscan"

scanner = StringScanner.new("The quick brown fox jumped over the lazy dog.")
# => #<StringScanner 0/45 @ "The q...">
  scanner.pos # => 0
  scanner.scan(/The/) # => "The"
  scanner.pos # => 3
  scanner.scan(/The/) # => nil
  scanner.pos # => 3
```

This small snippet illustrates much of the major functionality of StringScanner. After initializing our scanner object, we check the position of the string. We start, as we might expect, at position zero, before the first character.

Then, we scan for the expression /The/. This matches, so the scan method returns the matching string. When we check the position now, we see we've advanced three characters—the three that were returned—and so our position is 3. In this sense, scan can be said to *consume* the string that it matches.

If we now call scan with the same pattern, we no longer get a match. If scan doesn't find text matching the pattern we give it, it will return nil. Since we haven't matched anything, we also haven't advanced through the string, so pos still returns 3.

At this point, we could make a decision about what to do, given that we haven't had a match. We could try to match something else, for example, or we could abort our processing. This is the point where we begin to diverge in capability from using regular expressions.

Checking, Peeking, and Skipping

As we've seen, the scan method advances the scan pointer if the expression matches. In this way, we can think of it as consuming the text that it matches; we get the matched text and then move on past it. But sometimes we don't want to do that. We just want to see what's coming up and make a decision about what next to do based on that.

To do this, we can use the check method. It returns exactly what scan would return (so the matching text if there's a match, and nil if there isn't), but it won't advance the scan pointer in either case. We'll remain exactly where we are.

This behavior can come in handy during a loop. Let's imagine we've got a comma-separated list, and we want to extract all of the items within it:

```
Eggs, cheese, onion, potato, peas
```

By using check within a loop, we can skip through items until we run out of commas, at which point we can break out of our loop:

strscan/list.rb

```
require "strscan"

text = "Eggs, cheese, onion, potato, peas"
scanner = StringScanner.new(text)

items = []
loop do
  items << scanner.scan(/\w+/)
  if scanner.check(/,/)
    scanner.skip(/,\s*/)
  else
    break
  end
end

items
# => ["Eggs", "cheese", "onion", "potato", "peas"]
```

Here we saw another method used: skip. As we might guess, it advances the pointer past the given pattern without capturing it. In this case, we don't want to capture the commas or any whitespace after them, so we use skip to ignore them. If skip doesn't match, it will do nothing.

Consuming Arbitrary Text

So far we've just looked at consuming (or checking, or skipping) the portion of the string immediately after the scan pointer. In doing so, we've always known what we'd like to match at that point—a word, a number, and so on. But what if we're not quite sure what's immediately after the pointer, or we just want to match up until some arbitrary future point?

As an example, we might be parsing a large chunk of text and want to do something with all of the text within parentheses inside this passage of text. If it's in parentheses, we care about it regardless of what it is; if it's not in parentheses, we don't care about it at all.

So outside the parentheses, we want to skip all of the text until we encounter an opening parenthesis, and then inside the parentheses, we want to consume all of the text until we find a closing one. We don't care what that text might be; we just care about matching everything up to a certain point.

With just scan, skip, and check, we'd have to either know what we were matching before the parentheses or write something ugly like .*\(to match anything followed by an opening parenthesis. Thankfully, though, sibling methods will give us what we're after: scan_until, skip_until, and check_until.

They behave like their shorter-named cousins, except instead of matching just a pattern, they'll match everything *up to and including* that pattern.

So for our parentheses example, we might write something like:

```
parentheticals = []
scanner = StringScanner.new(
"'Hello,' he (the man) said. (To no one in particular.) 'How are you?'"
)
until scanner.eos? || scanner.check_until(/\(/).nil?
scanner.skip_until(/\(/)
parentheticals << scanner.scan_until(/(?=\))/)
end

p parentheticals
# => ["the man", "To no one in particular."]
```

Here, we loop over the string either until we reach the end or until there are no more parenthetical statements to match (in which case check_until will return nil). Then we skip within the text to the opening parenthesis and consume up to and including the final parenthesis to capture what's inside. Because scan_until will include everything up to *and including* the match, we're using a zero-width lookahead to make sure we don't include the bracket in the text that's returned.

Again, this is an example that we'd probably use String#scan for in real life, but it hopefully illustrates the power of the *_until methods.

Example: Parsing a Config File

We've seen the various parts of StringScanner in action, but to get an appreciation for how they work in concert it would be useful to see a slightly broader example.

One situation where you might write a parser is when encountering a new file format, one for which there isn't a ready-made library that can be used to parse its content. As an example, let's take the following fictional file format, which in this case stores the configuration of a website:

strscan/config.txt

```
name = "Alice's website"
description = "Alice's personal blog"
url = "http://alice.example.com/"
public = "true"
version = "24"
```

It's pretty simple, as file formats go. The name of each configuration variable is at the start of the line; there's then an equals sign, and the values—enclosed in quotes—are on the right-hand side.

Let's imagine we want to take this config file and parse it so that we have access to its contents as a hash in a Ruby script, so that we easily access the config variables.

First, let's do some setup. It would be good to have a class, Config, that represented a config file and handled its parsing, so let's do that. We also need to require StringScanner:

strscan/config.rb

```
require "strscan"

class Config
  def initialize(config_file)
    @config_data = File.read(config_file)
    @config = {}
    parse_file
  end

  def [](name)
    @config[name]
  end

  private
```

Here our initialize method does three things: it reads the config file passed to it, it creates an empty hash that will later be populated with the values from the config file, and it calls the parse_file method. We also create a [], which will allow users of our class to access individual config values.

That's our boilerplate dispensed with. We now need to implement the parse_file method and its logic for parsing the file. First, let's create a new StringScanner object and pass in our config data:

strscan/config.rb
```
def parse_file
  @scanner = StringScanner.new(@config_data)
```

Next we need to begin scanning through the file. We want to parse the entire file, so it makes sense to continue until we reach the end of the string. We can do this by looping until the eos? method of our scanner returns true. Until that happens, we'll continually try to parse the file's items:

strscan/config.rb
```
until @scanner.eos?
  @line += 1
  parse_item
end
```

We're storing the number of the line that we're parsing here, so that we can reference it in any syntax errors that we raise. The next step is to define a method for raising such errors:

strscan/config.rb
```
class SyntaxError < StandardError; end

def syntax_error
  SyntaxError.new("Syntax error on line #{@line} (pos. #{@scanner.pos})")
end
```

Here we define a SyntaxError exception class, then create a helper method for creating these errors. This method simply includes the current line number and overall character position in the error message.

Now we need to write our parse_item method, the bit that actually does the heavy lifting. First, though, let's define some aspects of what we're parsing: first, the allowed characters in a config name, and second what we're considering to be whitespace:

strscan/config.rb
```
NAME = /[a-z]+/
WHITESPACE = /\s+/
```

Within the parse_item method, we return to familiar ground. We first extract the name and raise a SyntaxError exception if we can't parse it:

strscan/config.rb
```
def parse_item
  name = @scanner.scan(NAME)
  fail syntax_error unless name
```

At this point we've consumed the first part of the line—the name of the configuration value being set on this line—and have stored it in a variable called name. We now need to deal with the actual assignment. We want to verify that the equals sign exists, but we don't actually care about its value, so we can call scan without storing its result anywhere:

strscan/config.rb
```
@scanner.skip(WHITESPACE)
fail syntax_error unless @scanner.scan(/=/)
@scanner.skip(WHITESPACE)
```

On either side of the equals we skip any whitespace that might exist, since it's optional. After this the only part that remains is the value, enclosed in quotes. We want to verify that the quote exists, consuming it, and then scan until the end quote:

strscan/config.rb
```
quote = @scanner.scan(/"|'/)
fail syntax_error unless quote

value = @scanner.scan_until(/(?=#{quote})/)
fail syntax_error unless value

@scanner.scan(/#{quote}/)
```

There are a couple of things going on here. First, we raise another SyntaxError if a quote isn't present. We allow both a double or a single quote here, storing whichever it is in a variable called quote.

Next, we extract the value. Since scan_until scans up to *and including* the pattern we pass to it, we use a positive lookahead. This will scan up to but not including the quote character, since the quote won't be returned as part of the match.

Finally, we scan for and consume the terminating quote character.

At this point we have both the name of the config value—from the left-hand side of the assignment—and its value—from the right-hand side—inside the quotes. All that remains is to store these two things and then we can move on:

strscan/config.rb
```
@config[name] = value

@scanner.skip(WHITESPACE)
```

Here we store the value in the hash that we created earlier and skip whitespace to move on. This will consume any whitespace at the end of the line, including the newline character itself, and also any whitespace at the start of the next line. After that, we'll be ready to parse another item—which is just what we'll do, since parse_item is being called in a loop.

Let's look at the code in action, using the example file from the start of this section:

strscan/config.rb
```
config = Config.new("config.txt")
config["name"]
# => "Alice's website"
config["url"]
# => "http://alice.example.com/"
```

That's it; we've written a parser for this type of file. Anything that matches this grammar—a name, followed by an equals sign, followed by a quoted value—will be parsable by our script. We can add new config variables, or any kinds of quoted values, and the parser will accept them.

Of course, it would be possible to do this with regular expressions alone. But the parser example feels more robust and is certainly easier to reason about. It also has the advantage of better error reporting for its end users; if there's a parsing error, they'll get an exception with the line and character at which the error occurred, potentially helping them to fix their configuration file.

Next, though, we'll look at things that we couldn't parse with regular expressions even if we wanted to. For these, we'll need to create a full-blown *parsing expression grammar*.

Rule-Based Parsers

Stepping above the simple StringScanner-based parsers that we've looked at thus far requires us to enter a heady and complex world. Parsing is studied by both computer scientists and linguists, and its techniques are the subject of much research. Major advancements continue to be made, and the field is an active one.

But as with most such fields, it's possible to reap the advantages of this active research without having to study for a doctorate, and one relatively recent development that will be useful to us is the *parsing expression grammar* (PEG).

A grammar is essentially a way of defining the rules that govern a particular *language*. Using a grammar, a parser can then discern the meaning of text written in that language. PEGs are simply one way to describe such grammars—but a way that makes for intuitive code.

PEGs offer an intuitive way of describing languages. As Ruby developers, we're lucky: the most popular library for creating and parsing PEGs is brilliantly designed and wonderfully intuitive. It's called Parslet, and we'll be using it for the rest of this chapter.

Let's take a look at how we can use Parslet to parse some simple languages. We'll define and compose simple rules that describe a language, and Parslet creates the parser. Indeed, Parslet is what's known as a *parser generator*. It takes a grammar as input and creates a parser for that grammar for us, saving us lots of manual effort. Let's try it out.

The Basics

Parslet is available from RubyGems, so it can be installed with a simple `gem install parslet` on the command line. After that we can `require` it to begin:

```
require "parslet"
```

There are two things you'll generally create when using Parslet. The first is a *parser*, which translates the source text into an *intermediate tree*. The output of this first step is a nested hash, with each element of the source text tagged with the sort of thing it is. For a programming language, those things might be *functions* or *strings* or *numbers* or anything else that has meaning in the language. Naturally, these vary wildly according to what it is you're parsing.

The second thing you'll create is generally a *transformation*, which takes a tree generated by a parser and performs some processing on it. Again, what this is depends on what you're parsing. It might be something small, such as converting parsed numbers from strings to actual numbers; or it might be more substantial, such as actually evaluating a whole programming language.

In this section, we'll be parsing the same config file format that we saw in the previous section. It looks like this:

```
name = "Alice's website"
description = "Alice's personal blog"
url = "http://alice.example.com/"
public = "true"
version = "24"
```

Let's take a look at how we can write a parser for files in this format.

Creating a Parser

The first thing we need to do, after requiring the Parslet library, is to create a parser class. This will contain the description of the language that we're parsing:

parslet/parser.rb
```
require "parslet"

class ConfigParser < Parslet::Parser
```

In Parslet, a parser is simply a class that extends Parslet::Parser. Next, we need to define the rules that govern the language we're parsing. We do this by defining *atoms*—the individual elements that make up the language. These might be something as simple as "a space" or "a sequence of digits," or they might be something more complex, even something that is itself composed of other atoms.

In this config file example, the first atom that we'll need to define is the config names—the bits on the left-hand side of the assignment. These can only contain word characters, so let's go ahead and define a rule for this:

parslet/parser.rb
```
rule(:name) { match("\\w").repeat(1).as(:name) }
```

Here, we define a new rule and call it :name, since that's what we're describing. We use the match method to define a regular expression—in this case, one matching word characters (\w). We specify that a name matches a repeated string of at least one such character, and using as we specify that it should be tagged as a :name in the tree that our parser will output.

The next part of our file format is an assignment. Again, we define a new rule for this atom:

parslet/parser.rb
```
rule(:whitespace) { match("[ \\t]").repeat(1) }
rule(:assignment) { whitespace.maybe >> str("=") >> whitespace.maybe }
```

In this case, we're actually defining two rules. The first matches one or more whitespace characters. The second matches an assignment, which we're defining as optional whitespace, followed by an equals sign, followed by more optional whitespace.

There are four new concepts here. First, we can join together atoms using the >> operator, thereby specifying that one follows the other. Second, we can use the str method to specify an exact string to match—rather than the regular expression that we defined using match. Third, we can compose atoms together, in this case specifying that an assignment can be made up of whitespace plus something else. And finally, we can use maybe to specify that a particular part of an atom is optional (in other words, that it can appear *zero or one* times).

The next atom we need to define is the value that comes on the right-hand side of the assignment. These are just quote-enclosed strings, so let's specify that:

parslet/parser.rb
```
rule(:newline) { str("\n") | str("\r\n") }
rule(:value) {
  str('"') >>
  (str('"').absent? >> any).repeat.as(:string) >>
  str('"')
}
```

This simple matcher looks for a quote character, followed by zero or more non-quote characters, followed by a quote character. We tag the non-quote characters using as, so that we can access the contents of the quoted string in the final output. In this case, we specify that the string should be tagged as a :string. This will allow us to perform processing on these strings later.

We've now got all of the elements that make up an item within the file. But that's not enough to parse the whole file. We need to make it clear that these three things are related to each other, that together they define a config item. We can create a new rule for that:

parslet/parser.rb
```
rule(:item) { name >> assignment >> value.as(:value) >> newline }
```

This atom consists exclusively of the other atoms that we've defined. It specifies that each item within the config file is made up of a name, then the assignment operator, then a value. We then allow for whitespace at the end of the line, followed by a newline character. We capture the value as a token called :value, leaving us with a :name and :value pair in the final tree.

We can now match a single item. Our final step is therefore to specify that a document is made up of many items:

parslet/parser.rb
```
rule(:document) { (item.repeat).as(:document) >> newline.repeat }

root :document
```

We define a document as zero or more items repeated, followed by zero or more newline characters (to allow for blank lines at the end of the file). We capture this as a :document, giving us a single root node in our tree. Then we use the root method to tell Parslet that it should begin by trying to parse the document. It will then drill into and recurse through the elements that we've said make up a document.

Here's what the parser looks like in full:

parslet/parser.rb

```
require "parslet"

class ConfigParser < Parslet::Parser
  rule(:name) { match("\\w").repeat(1).as(:name) }

  rule(:whitespace) { match("[ \\t]").repeat(1) }
  rule(:assignment) { whitespace.maybe >> str("=") >> whitespace.maybe }

  rule(:newline) { str("\n") | str("\r\n") }
  rule(:value) {
    str('"') >>
    (str('"').absent? >> any).repeat.as(:string) >>
    str('"')
  }

  rule(:item) { name >> assignment >> value.as(:value) >> newline }

  rule(:document) { (item.repeat).as(:document) >> newline.repeat }

  root :document
end
```

As you can see, we started with the lowest level of items: the leaves on our tree, in essence. We then progressed further upward, eventually arriving at the very root—the document as a whole.

If we run this parser over the example config file, you'll see that it produces a representation of the file that looks exactly like that tree:

parslet/parser.rb

```
config = ConfigParser.new.parse(File.read("config.txt"))
# => {:document=>
#      [{:name=>"name"@0, :value=>{:string=>"Alice's website"@8}},
#       {:name=>"description"@25,
#        :value=>{:string=>"Alice's personal blog"@40}},
#       {:name=>"url"@63, :value=>{:string=>"http://alice.example.com/"@70}},
#       {:name=>"public"@97, :value=>{:string=>"true"@107}},
#       {:name=>"version"@113, :value=>{:string=>"24"@124}}]}
```

In this case, because the file format is so simple, the tree isn't very deep; there isn't much nesting in this type of file. But we can see that there is an array of config items, with each part of the config item tagged correctly: the name and the value.

If we wanted to, we could use this tree as it was. To get the value of a particular config item, we'd index into the hash:

```
puts config[:document][0][:value][:string]
```

But that's awfully clunky. The problem is that this intermediate tree isn't quite in the format we want, and it contains information from the parsing that isn't relevant to the end user of the data. For a start, we could reduce the data to a simple hash, with the key as the name of the config item so that we can easily look up values. But there are other things, too: for example, the Boolean value true is still a string, as is the version—which should clearly be a number. To correct these issues, we'll need to perform the second step of the process: a *transformation*.

Creating a Transformation

As a result of the parsing operation, we now have what Parslet calls an *intermediate tree*. Occasionally, that might be all we want. But more likely is the situation where we'd like to perform some sort of transformation on the parsed structure.

These transformations might take the tree and completely transform it, the end result unrecognizable compared to the input. Or they might perform a very slight change, outputting a slightly modified tree that could then be fed into another transformation.

In this case, we want the former. We need to transform our parsed tree into a simple hash, where each item is represented with its name as a key and its quoted-string value a value.

Just as parsers subclass Parslet::Parser, transformations in Parslet inherit from Parslet::Transformation:

parslet/parser.rb

```
class ConfigToHash < Parslet::Transform
```

There are further similarities. Just as we built up our parser by writing rules, we do the same with our transformation. And just as we started from the leaves of our tree when thinking of rules, we'll do likewise when writing a transformation, working from the deepest (and by extension simplest) leaves of the tree upward to the root.

In this case, the deepest leaves on our parsed tree are the string values of each config item. (From the root, they're accessible as :document[n][:value][:string].) We tagged them as being something called a :string, so we can tell Parslet what to do with anything of that type.

Our first rule, then, looks something like this:

parslet/parser.rb

```
rule(string: simple(:s)) {
  case s
  when "true"
    true
  when "false"
    false
  when /\A[0-9]+\z/
    Integer(s)
  else
    String(s)
  end
}
```

The argument to the rule method specifies what we'd like to match. In this case we're looking for something with a key of :string that has a simple value. Simple values are ones that don't extend any deeper into the tree. In other words, they allow us to match *leaves* rather than *branches*.

The value of the matched element will be passed into our block. In this case, we're using a case statement to do a few different things depending on what that value is: if it looks like a Boolean value, we return either true or false as appropriate; if it consists entirely of numbers, we coerce the string to an integer; otherwise, we coerce the value to a string. (We need to do this final step because the value that we're actually passed is a Parslet::Slice, an object that stores some more information about the parsed structure than a simple string does—but we want to discard this information at this point.)

Our next and as it turns out the final step is to transform the hash into a simple one, with the names of each config item as the keys. This requires us to write two rules. The first is to process the items themselves, and the second is to transform the overall document. Here's the first:

parslet/parser.rb

```
rule(name: simple(:n), value: simple(:v)) { [String(n), v] }
```

This rule looks for branches of the tree that have a name and a value, and transforms them into a two-element array. So a value like:

```
{ :name => "name", :value => "Alice's website" }
```

will be transformed into:

```
[ "name", "Alice’s website" ]
```

After these first two rules have been applied, the tree looks like this:

```
{
  :document => [
    [ "name", "Alice’s website" ],
    [ "description", "Alice’s personal blog" ],
    [ "url", "http://alice.example.com/" ],
    [ "public", true ],
    [ "version", 24 ]
  ]
}
```

The final rule, then, acts on a :document and converts the array of arrays into a hash:

parslet/parser.rb

```
rule(document: subtree(:i)) { i.to_h }
```

Since the value of the document is an array, we need to match a subtree here rather than a simple value as we did with our previous rules. Then we can call to_h, a method defined on all arrays that converts them to a hash.

That’s all there is to our transformation. Our parser had a parse method for performing the parsing, and the equivalent for a transformation is apply, which accepts a single argument containing a parse tree—which is typically going to be the output of a parser.

Let’s wrap these two things up into a method and see what output we get:

parslet/parser.rb

```
def parse_config(config_file)
  parsed = ConfigParser.new.parse(File.read(config_file))
  config = ConfigToHash.new.apply(parsed)

  config
end

config = parse_config("config.txt")
# => {"name"=>"Alice’s website",
#     "description"=>"Alice's personal blog",
#     "url"=>"http://alice.example.com/",
#     "public"=>true,
#     "version"=>24}
```

Bingo! The transformation outputs a simple hash, and we can easily access individual elements of the config. Because we’ve separated the two steps of parsing and transforming, though, we're not limited to this particular interpretation. We could easily write a transformation that converts the file to a different format such as JSON, for example. It's also possible to combine multiple transformations, breaking up functionality into different independent transformations that can be composed and combined.

Now we've looked at how to write a parser and transformation for a simple file format, let's take a look at a real-world problem that's a bit more complex. For this, we'll look at the parsing RTF files, a formatted text format that can be output from word processing software.

Example: Parsing RTF Files

Rich-Text Format (RTF) files have long and storied history. First introduced in 1987 with Microsoft Word 3, RTF became the default file format of many word processors in the intervening years. It's still the default format of TextEdit in Mac OS X, for example, almost thirty years after its introduction. Since it allows for a wide variety of formatting and is a standard, well-understood, and lightweight file format, it's still common to find data stored in RTF format.

While these files are admittedly less common in the wild than, say, .doc files, their structure is also much simpler. It's fundamentally a plain text format, peppered with the occasional instruction to define some element of the text's formatting—its color, whether it's bold, what its alignment is, and so on. And that means that it's something we can write a parser for without melting our brains—hopefully!

Let's dig in to the format and explore how we could use Parslet to write a parser for it. We'll first look at simply parsing RTF documents into a syntax tree, and then we'll explore some simple transformations that will allow us to do something useful with our parsed representation of RTF files—in this case, transform them to basic HTML.

The File Format

The simplest possible RTF document is the traditional *Hello World* example:

rtf/hello-world.rtf

```
{\rtf1\ansi\deff0
Hello, World
}
```

The content of the file begins with an opening curly brace and ends with a closing one. Everything within these braces will be interpreted as RTF. The first part of the file is a header. In this case, the header specifies that this file is an RTF file that's compliant with version 1 of the RTF specification (\rtf1). It states that the encoding of the file is ANSI (\ansi). And it specifies that the font used should be the application's default (\deff0). All three of these elements of the header are required, but many more might be present—tables of fonts, lists of revisions to the file, and so on.

After the header comes the body of the document. Unless we specify otherwise, text here is unformatted. So our *Hello World* will be displayed in the default font and the default color (black on white).

Text within RTF files is formatted using *control words*. These begin with a backslash and can be used to specify things like whether text is normal weight or bold, whether it's italicized, or what its foreground and background colors are.

Let's take a look at a document with some control words in it:

rtf/bold.rtf
```
{\rtf1\ansi\deff0
\b Hello\b0, World
}
```

Here two control words have been added to our first example. The first control word, \b, specifies the start of bold formatting, and the second, \b0, specifies the end of bold formatting. So this example produces a document with the same *Hello World* text as the first example, but with the *Hello* bolded.

For the final example, let's look at how RTF deals with colors. It does this using a *group* within the header that defines a *color table*—the list of colors used in the document. These colors can then be referred to using the \cf (*color foreground*) control words. \cf1 will format text in the first color in the color table, \cf2 in the second, and so on. Here's a file that uses colors:

rtf/colors.rtf
```
{\rtf1\ansi\deff0
{\colortbl;\red0\green0\blue0;\red255\green0\blue0;}
This is some normal text, formatted in black.\line
\cf2
This is some more text, but this time it's colored red.\line
\cf1
Finally, this text is back to the normal color, but is \b bold\b0.
}
```

We see on the second line the definition of the color table. As a group, it's enclosed in braces (just like the whole document, which is itself a group). The group starts with the \colortbl control word and then defines each color in terms of the proportion of red, green, and blue in it. In this case, we set the first color to pure black and the second color to pure red.

We then use the \cf1 and \cf2 control words to set the first line to black, set the second to red, and then reset the final line to black once more. (Note the use of the \line control word, which specifies a line break; this allows us to wrap the text in our RTF files if we want to without those line breaks showing up in the output.) For good measure, we throw in some bold text on the last line.

Although there's a great deal more to the full RTF spec than this, there's quite a lot going on in this example, so let's use it as the sample file for our RTF parser. Successfully parsing it will involve handling headers, color tables, control words, and freeform text. If we can parse it, then we'll be able to parse a large portion of real RTF files.

Parsing the File

Just like in our simple example, we'll be defining a new subclass of Parslet::Parser, and just like in our simple example we'll work from the leaves toward the root when writing the rules for it. One thing that will make our rules easier to read is if we define some initial rules for characters, or sequences of characters, that we'll be parsing often:

rtf/parser.rb

```
require "parslet"

class Rtf < Parslet::Parser
  rule(:space)           { str(" ") }
  rule(:hyphen)          { str("-") }
  rule(:integer)         { match["0-9"].repeat(1) }
  rule(:newline)         { str("\n") }
  rule(:slash)           { str("\\") }
  rule(:letter_sequence) { match["a-z"].repeat }

  rule(:special_chars)   { match["\\\\{}"] }
```

These rules have two advantages. First, when referring to these characters later on, we'll be using descriptive names; it's easier to decipher integer at a glance than match["0-9"].repeat(1). But second, they're helping us avoid repetition. If we decide later on that we want to change the semantics of newlines, for example, then we have to do that in only one place.

The final rule, which ultimately matches a backslash followed by braces, is worth talking about simply because of the unwieldy number of backslashes. We want to match a backslash, but in a regular expression—which this rule ultimately is—we must escape backslashes, so each backslash becomes \\. But we must also escape backslashes in Ruby strings, so each of those two backslashes must be escaped further, and the string becomes \\\\. Thankfully the escaping ends here, and we don't continue on forever.

With these rules in place, we can begin writing rules for the elements of RTF files. The easiest of these is unformatted text, since this is simply text that doesn't contain any special characters.

rtf/parser.rb

```
rule(:unformatted_text) {
  ( special_chars.absent? >> any ).repeat(1).as(:text)
}
```

The absent? method is something we haven't seen before, and it's worth exploring. It functions essentially as a *negative lookahead*. Following it with any, which matches any string, allows us to say that we want to match anything that doesn't contain special characters. We allow this to repeat at least once, and tag the match as :text.

The next type of content we need to match is control words: those slash-beginning structures that set formatting and other functions:

rtf/parser.rb

```
rule(:control_word) {
  (
    slash >>
      letter_sequence.as(:word) >>
      control_delimiter.maybe.as(:delimiter)
  ).as(:control_word)
}
rule(:control_delimiter) { space | ( hyphen.maybe >> integer ) | str(";") }
```

We define a control word as a slash, followed by a letter sequence (which we tag as a :word in the parse output), followed by one of the characters that are allowed as delimiters of control words. This delimiter is optional, as specified by maybe.

In the delimiter definition, we're introduced to another new concept: alternation. By using the pipe symbol, we can tell Parslet that there are multiple acceptable values. In this case, a delimiter can be either a space, a number (including an optional hyphen, to allow for negative numbers), or a semicolon.

The other thing that can be part of text in an RTF file is a group. But a group is actually a recursive structure: groups can contain content like unformatted text and control words, but they can also include other groups (which in turn can contain other groups, and so on to a potentially infinite depth). That means we need two rules: one to define a group itself, and one to define its content. The first rule is fairly straightforward:

rtf/parser.rb

```
rule(:group) {
  (
    str("{") >>
    newline.maybe >>
    content >>
    newline.maybe >>
    str("}") >>
```

The meat of the rule here is that a group starts with an opening brace character, contains some `content` (which we'll define in our next rule), and ends with a closing brace character.

We just need to define what the parser will interpret as `content`:

rtf/parser.rb

```
rule(:content) {
  (
    unformatted_text |
    control_word     |
    group
  ).repeat
}
```

Content is defined entirely in terms of other rules. We allow it to be any combination of unformatted text, control words, or groups, repeated any number of times (including zero, which will allow for an empty group). We see that we have a circular reference here—the definition of `group` relies on the definition of `content` and vice versa—but that's absolutely fine.

We now have everything we need to parse the document part of an RTF file. All that remains is to parse the header, including in this case the color table and the overall structure of the file:

rtf/parser.rb

```
rule(:header) {
  ( slash >> str("rtf") >> integer.maybe.as(:version) ).as(:rtf) >>
  ( slash >> letter_sequence.as(:charset) ) >>
  ( slash >> str("deff") >> integer.maybe).maybe.as(:deff) >>
  color_table.maybe.as(:color_table) >>
  newline.maybe
}

rule(:color_table) {
  newline.maybe >>
  str("{") >>
  (slash >> str("colortbl;")) >>
```

```
  color_definition.repeat(1).as(:colors) >>
  str("}") >>
  newline.maybe
}
rule(:color_definition) {
  slash >> str("red")   >> (integer.as(:int)).as(:red)   >>
  slash >> str("green") >> (integer.as(:int)).as(:green) >>
  slash >> str("blue")  >> (integer.as(:int)).as(:blue)  >>
  str(";")
}

rule(:file) {
  str("{") >>
  header.as(:header) >>
  content.as(:document) >>
  str("}") >>
  newline.maybe
}

root :file
```

These rules use concepts we've seen before as we gradually progress upward through the document tree. The final rule defines the overall file, which we then tell Parslet to use as the root of its parse tree.

That's it! There are more rules here than there were in our previous example, but the concepts are the same. We started from the leaves of the tree and progressed toward the root, creating rules that defined each element of the text that we're parsing. By composing these manageable chunks together, we slowly but surely built up a grammar for RTF files.

Here's the tree that our parser produces when run over the RTF file with colors in it:

rtf/colors.rtf.tree

```
{
  :header => {
    :rtf => {:version => "1"@5},
    :charset => "ansi"@7,
    :deff => "\\deff0"@11,
    :color_table => {
      :colors => [
        {
          :red => {:int => "0"@33},
          :green => {:int => "0"@40},
          :blue => {:int => "0"@46}
        },
        {
          :red => {:int => "255"@52},
          :green => {:int => "0"@61},
```

```
          :blue => {:int => "0"@67}
        }
      ]
    }
  },
  :document => [
    {:text => "This is some normal text, formatted in black."@71},
    {:control_word => {:word => "line"@117, :delimiter => nil}},
    {:text => "\n"@121},
    {:control_word => {:word => "cf"@123, :delimiter => "2"@125}},
    {:text => "\nThis is some more text, but this time it's colored red."@126},
    {:control_word => {:word => "line"@184, :delimiter => nil}},
    {:text => "\n"@188},
    {:control_word => {:word => "cf"@190, :delimiter => "1"@192}},
    {:text => "\nFinally, this text is back to the normal color, but is "@193},
    {:control_word => {:word => "b"@251, :delimiter => " "@252}},
    {:text => "bold"@253},
    {:control_word => {:word => "b"@258, :delimiter => "0"@259}},
    {:text => ".\n"@260}
  ]
}
```

Just like when parsing the config file, we've taken some raw text and successfully parsed it, transforming it into a structure with the meaning of the text described explicitly. The next step is to write a transformation. There are countless things we might want to do with the parsed RTF text. We could write code to output it to a terminal, including whatever formatting the terminal supported. We could write a transformation that translated it into something a printer understood, so that the document could be printed out. Let's take a look at one particular transformation that might be useful: converting the document to HTML.

Applying a Transformation

Once we've developed a parser for RTF files, we can create transformations for them. These transformations don't then have to reimplement the logic of parsing; they can simply take the parsed tree of the file and transform it into some other form. Let's take a look at a transformation that takes our parsed RTF file and converts it to an HTML representation.

Just like with the config file, we need to create a new class for our transformation:

rtf/transformation.rb

```
require "./parser"

class RtfToHtml < Parslet::Transform
```

We then begin implementing rules, starting from the leaves and working toward the base of the tree. Two rules are simple: converting strings of numbers—such as those in the color values—to actual integers, and converting unformatted text to simple strings:

rtf/transformation.rb
```
rule(int: simple(:n)) { Integer(n) }

rule(text: simple(:t)) { String(t) }
```

The other obvious leaves of our tree are the color values in the header, composed of red, green, and blue values. We can match those and convert them to a string that can later be used in CSS:

rtf/transformation.rb
```
rule(red: simple(:r), green: simple(:g), blue: simple(:b)) {
  "rgb(#{r}, #{g}, #{b})"
```

Next, let's deal with control words. In the sample file that we're parsing, there are four we need to deal with: line breaks, color changes, the start of bold text, and the end of bold text.

rtf/transformation.rb
```
rule(control_word: { word: simple(:_), delimiter: simple(:_) }) {
  ""
}

rule(control_word: { word: "line", delimiter: simple(:x) }) {
  "<br>"
}

rule(control_word: { word: "b", delimiter: simple(:_) }) {
  "<strong>"
}

rule(control_word: { word: "b", delimiter: "0" }) {
  "</strong>"
}

rule(control_word: { word: "cf", delimiter: simple(:n) }) {
  "<span class=\"cf-#{n}\">"
}
```

First, we create a general rule that will match any control word, and we have it return an empty string. This means that any control words that we don't explicitly match will be silently discarded, which is what we want in this case.

Then we define rules for the control words that we want to handle in specific ways. This illustrates the ability of rules in Parslet transformations to match hard-coded values as well as variable ones, and also illustrates that rules defined later take precedence over ones defined sooner.

In this case, the RTF control words map fairly neatly to HTML concepts. The only one that doesn't is the `cf` control word, which controls the foreground color of text. In this case, we output a span with a class attribute.

To generate CSS with these same classes, and therefore actually specify the colors, we'll need to transform the color table block in the header:

rtf/transformation.rb

```
rule(colors: subtree(:c)) {
  html = "<style>\n"

  c.each_with_index do |c, n|
    html << ".cf-#{n + 1} { color: #{c} }\n"
    html << ".cb-#{n + 1} { background-color: #{c} }\n"
  end

  html << "</style>"

  html
}
```

Finally, we need to match the root of the tree, the element that contains the `:header` and the `:document`:

rtf/transformation.rb

```
  rule(header: subtree(:h), document: subtree(:d)) {
    html = <<-HTML
<!DOCTYPE html>
<html>
<head>
  #{h[:color_table]}
</head>
<body>
  #{d.join("\n")}
</body>
</html>
    HTML
  }
```

We transform this element into an HTML document. We include the style tags that replaced the color table in the header. For the body, we simply concatenate the elements of the document, since by this point they've all been replaced with simple elements, so the document is now an array of strings.

Since this final rule returns a string, we've completed the transformation. No trace of the tree remains; it has been fully transformed. If we run the parsing and transforming steps together, we can see that the HTML document is generated for us:

rtf/transformation.rb

```
rtf = Rtf.new
parsed = rtf.parse(File.read("colors.rtf"))
html = RtfToHtml.new.apply(parsed)

puts html
# >> <!DOCTYPE html>
# >> <html>
# >> <head>
# >>   <style>
# >> .cf-1 { color: rgb(0, 0, 0) }
# >> .cb-1 { background-color: rgb(0, 0, 0) }
# >> .cf-2 { color: rgb(255, 0, 0) }
# >> .cb-2 { background-color: rgb(255, 0, 0) }
# >> </style>
# >> </head>
# >> <body>
# >>   This is some normal text, formatted in black.
# >> <br>
# >>
# >>
# >> <span class="cf-2">
# >>
# >> This is some more text, but this time it's colored red.
# >> <br>
# >>
# >>
# >> <span class="cf-1">
# >>
# >> Finally, this text is back to the normal color, but is
# >> <strong>
# >> bold
# >> </strong>
# >> .
# >>
# >> </body>
# >> </html>
```

It's easy to imagine other transforms, things that take the parsed RTF structure and output something totally different. Thanks to Parslet's separation of the parsing logic from the transformation, the amount of repetition between these different transformations will be minimal.

Wrapping Up

We covered an awful lot in this chapter, and it's worth digesting. We first looked at StringScanner, which gave us a way to step through a string while keeping track of our position. This allowed us to implement relatively simple parsers that were an improvement on large and complex regular expressions.

Then we tried out writing more formal grammars, describing the rules of languages and having a library—in this case, Parslet—generate the parsing code for us. We looked first at a simple example, parsing a config file, before moving onto something much more complex—parsing RTF files. We looked at how to write transformations that took the tree generated by a parser and transformed it into a different format.

Next, we'll look at an even larger and meatier subject: natural language processing. Rather than parsing structured text, as we've seen in this chapter, we'll attempt to parse freeform human language and derive meaning from it.

CHAPTER 11

Natural Language Processing

Natural language processing is an enormously broad subject, but in essence it covers any task in which we attempt to use a computer to understand human language. That might mean using a program to extract meaning from text written by a human—to translate it, to determine its subject, or to parse its grammar. Or it might mean using a computer to actually write text for humans to read—think of a computer working as a journalist, writing summaries of sports games, financial events, and so on.

What Is Natural Language Processing?

As a field, natural language processing (or *NLP*) features many of the hardest problems that exist in computer science. A problem like machine translation, for example, involves almost every aspect of artificial intelligence: not just understanding the language syntactically, but also discerning the sentiment behind it, knowing of and deciding between the multiple and contradictory meanings that words and phrases might have, understanding all of the objects and people and places that might be referred to, and using the context of surrounding words to make judgments about potential ambiguities. These are not, for now at least, areas in which computers' greatest strengths lie.

For this reason, many solutions to problems in this area are more about distinguishing between shades of gray than they are about giving clear, black-and-white answers. But if we can get a computer to produce an answer that's good enough for our purposes, then we can exploit the things that computers *are* naturally good at—mainly that they can process text in far greater quantities and at far greater speeds than even an army of people ever could.

NLP, then, is generally a quest toward this *good enough*, which naturally varies from project to project. We're not going to venture very far into this incredibly deep subject in just one chapter; we'll just dip our toes into the water. Even the simpler tasks we can perform with NLP are useful and worth explorating, and its complexity shouldn't dissuade you at all. After all, the thing that makes language processing so useful is that every one of us consumes—and these days creates—vast quantities of natural language text every day. It's easy to think of potential uses for natural language processing.

In our exploration of NLP, we'll look first at *text extraction* and its related problem of *term extraction*. This will allow us to extract the text of an article from its surroundings and then form an understanding about what the article's subject might be by extracting keywords from it.

Then we'll explore *fuzzy matching*. This will allow us to search through text and look not just for exact matches of a search string, as we have done previously, but matches that are slightly different—accounting not just for typing errors in the search term and the source text, but also matching variations of the same word.

In each of these examples, we'll be taking a practical look at when a technique might be useful and what ready-made libraries and tools exist to perform that technique. This isn't about implementing algorithms or exploring theory; it's about solving problems as you would in the real world—and also giving you a taste of what can be done with NLP. Let's get started.

Example: Extracting Keywords from Articles

Let's imagine that we have a list of many hundreds of articles, spread across many different web pages. We'd like to analyze the content of these articles and create a searchable database of them for ourselves. We'd like to store the content of the articles—but not any extraneous text from the web page, such as header text or sidebar content. We'd also like to make an attempt to store some keywords, so that we can search against them and not have to search the whole body of the text. When we're finished, we'll be able to list all the terms mentioned in an article, and by extension we'll be able to list all the articles that match a particular term.

This problem neatly covers two areas of language processing. The first is *text extraction*: how we identify, given a mishmash of HTML, what the primary text on a web page is—the content of the article. The second is *term extraction*: given that text, how we extract just the key ideas and concepts that the article is about, leaving behind the useless *the*s and *he*s and other things that would fail to distinguish between this and any other article.

These two tasks are actually fairly distinct, so let's dive in and explore them both.

Extracting Only the Article Text

Our first step in solving this problem is to download the web pages and, for each of them, extract only the text of the article. We're not interested in anything that might also be on the web page—headers, footers, and so on—but instead want only the text of the article.

As you might expect, this is largely a solved problem. There are several Ruby libraries that perform such extraction. One such library is ruby-readability,[1] a port of a tried and true library that forms the basis of the website readability.com.

Readability's algorithm, like many that tackle language processing problems, is a fuzzy one. It knows several characteristics that generally point to a particular section of a web page being the article's content: the length of the text within an element, whether there is continuous text next to the current element, the density of links within the text (to rule out things like lists of navigation), even things like the names of classes and IDs on the HTML elements themselves. Searching through the document, it assigns a score to each element based on these criteria and then extracts the best-looking matches.

While the algorithm isn't perfect, it's surprisingly capable and will definitely work for our purposes. Let's see how we can use it.

Our first step is to fetch the HTML of the web page, just as it was when we we looked at scraping content. Then we need to pass that HTML to Readability:

nlp/readability.rb
```
require "open-uri"
require "readability"

html = open("http://en.wikipedia.org/wiki/History_of_Luxembourg").read
document = Readability::Document.new(html)
```

That's actually all there is to it. We can now use the `content` method of the document object to access the HTML of the element that the Readability algorithm thinks represents the article text.

nlp/readability.rb
```
article = Nokogiri::HTML(document.content)
article.css("p").first.text
 # => "The history of Luxembourg refers to the history of the country of
 # Luxembourg and its geographical area."
```

1. https://github.com/cantino/ruby-readability

Since the returned article text is HTML, we can use Nokogiri to process it further. This example uses Nokogiri to extract only the first paragraph of the article, but it would be straightforward to return all the text (without HTML tags) or to search for text within the article that matches particular criteria.

Expanding this specific script to cope with multiple articles, by assembling an array of objects containing the article text, should be quite straightforward:

nlp/extracting-text.rb

```
require "open-uri"
require "readability"

urls = File.readlines("urls.txt").map(&:chomp)

Article = Struct.new(:title, :text, :terms)

articles = urls.map do |url|
  $stderr.puts "Processing #{url}..."

  html = open(url).read
  document = Readability::Document.new(html)

  title = document.title.sub(" - Wikipedia, the free encyclopedia", "")
  text = Nokogiri::HTML(document.content).text.strip

  Article.new(title, text)
end
```

First, we extract a list of URLs from a file. We assume that the text file contains one URL per line, and so the only processing we need to do is to strip the final newline from each of the lines. In the sample file, I'm using a list of Wikipedia articles. There's forty of them, arranged like so (here's the first six):

nlp/urls.txt

```
http://en.wikipedia.org/wiki/The_Colour_of_Magic
http://en.wikipedia.org/wiki/The_Light_Fantastic
http://en.wikipedia.org/wiki/Equal_Rites
http://en.wikipedia.org/wiki/Mort
http://en.wikipedia.org/wiki/Sourcery
http://en.wikipedia.org/wiki/Wyrd_Sisters
```

Then we define a Struct called Article for our articles, for convenience. It stores the title of the article and its text. We then loop over the URLs and generate for each of them one of these Article objects. (Since our articles are all from Wikipedia, we also strip out the generic title text that's common to them all.) At the end of the script, we're left with an array of articles that we might then store somewhere on disk or process further; in this case, we're going to be processing them further.

We've solved the first half of our problem: we've searched through our list of URLs and extracted the text of each one of them. The second half of the problem is to parse all of this text and try to figure out what the content is about.

Extracting Terms

Now that we've been able to extract the text of the articles that we're interested in, we need to extract keywords from them to create our index. This task is called *term extraction.*

To do that, we need to know just what we mean by *keyword.* There are infinitely many definitions, naturally, but a common approach is to look at nouns that occur above a certain frequency in the text. That frequency might be in terms of the length of text—nouns that individually make up 1 percent of the words in the text, for example. Or it might be in simple and absolute terms, such as taking the nouns that occur three or more times.

Performing this task, then, involves tagging all of the *parts of speech* in the text and then removing everything that isn't a noun. Typically, a normalization step is performed, often to convert the plural form of nouns to the singular (so that *shoe* and *shoes* are regarded as the same word, for example). The number of times each noun occurs can then be counted, and finally all those nouns that don't meet the given threshold can be removed. The end result is a list of all of the nouns and proper nouns in the text, sorted by frequency, with the *strongest* keywords first.

Again, this is largely a solved problem. There are many Ruby libraries, which implement many different algorithms. One such library is Phrasie.[2]

Phrasie implements exactly this algorithm for term extraction: it pulls all of the nouns out of the text, counts them, and then omits any that occur fewer than three times (though this threshold can be adjusted).

The result is a list of nouns that appear frequently within the text. For most articles, that's a good way to judge the content and a good thing to create an index from.

Let's extend our code to also extract terms for the article text that we've fetched:

nlp/extracting-terms.rb

```
require "open-uri"
require "readability"
```

2. https://github.com/ashleyw/phrasie/

```
require "phrasie"
require "json"
require "json/add/core"

urls = File.readlines("urls.txt").map(&:chomp)

Article = Struct.new(:title, :text, :terms)

ignored_terms = ["^", "pp", "citation", "ISBN", "Retrieved", "[edit"]

articles = urls.map do |url|
  $stderr.puts "Processing #{url}..."

  html = open(url).read
  document = Readability::Document.new(html)

  title = document.title.sub(" - Wikipedia, the free encyclopedia", "")
  text = Nokogiri::HTML(document.content).text.strip

  terms = Phrasie::Extractor.new.phrases(text)
  terms = terms.reject { |term| ignored_terms.include?(term.first) }

  Article.new(title, text, terms)
end

articles.each do |article|
  puts article.title
  puts "Keywords: #{article.terms.take(5).map(&:first).join(", ")}\n\n"
end

File.open("articles.json", "w") do |json|
  json.write(JSON.generate(articles))
end
```

First, we define a list of ignored keywords. There's always going to be something that the term extractor mistakenly thinks is a noun and extracts, or that is a noun but that you don't want to include because it's common to all articles or otherwise irrelevant. In this case, the Wikipedia articles contain several citation- and footnote-related characters that we don't want to include, so we ignore them.

Then it's simply a case of passing the article text into Phrasie's extractor. It returns for us an array of arrays. Each element of the array contains the term, the number of times it occurred in the text, and the term's *strength*. The strength of a term is simply the number of words within it. Terms with multiple words are included even if they don't meet the normal threshold of occurrences, since they're considered to be stronger.

Finally, we store the results in a JSON file so that we can use this index later without having to rerun this script. We might store this information in a database or not at all; it depends on the application.

If we run this script, we'll see Phrasie's guesses for the best five keywords in each article (again, I've shown just the first six here for reasons of space):

nlp/extracting-terms.txt

```
The Colour of Magic
Keywords: Twoflower, Rincewind, novel, book, Magic

The Light Fantastic
Keywords: Rincewind, Twoflower, Discworld, novel, star

Equal Rites
Keywords: Esk, Simon, staff, Discworld, wizard

Mort
Keywords: Mort, Death, novel, princess, Discworld

Sourcery
Keywords: wizard, Rincewind, Coin, Ipslore, Discworld

Wyrd Sisters
Keywords: witch, king, Tomjon, Granny, King
```

Not perfect, sure, but hopefully still impressive: the simple algorithm has yielded genuinely useful keywords for all of the articles here, and there's nothing that's wrong outright. We should hopefully feel confident about building an index based on these criteria.

We've now successfully extracted the core text from a web page, ignoring all of the irrelevant content alongside it. We've then processed that text to extract the most important keywords from it, in effect building an index of the article that we could then search—saving us from having to search the full text of the article.

Next, let's look at how we can actually perform this search, and ways that we can use more language processing techniques to improve the flexibility and accuracy of that search.

Example: Fuzzy Searching

At this point, we've extracted article text from web pages and then created keyword indexes of those articles based on the nouns that occurred most frequently within them.

Now let's explore how we could search our new database for articles that match a given query. More usefully, you'll learn how you can perform a *fuzzy search*—a search that matches not just the exact query you give it, but also things that are similar to it.

Our first step is to write a simple and exact search. Then we can look at how to improve both the storage of the index and the querying process to broaden the text that is matched by it.

A Simple Search

The simplest search we could write would be to, given a search term, list all the articles that have that search term among their keywords. Although it's simple, such a search would actually be quite useful, and given that we only have to search the pre-extracted terms, which are only a fraction of the length of the original articles, it should be relatively efficient, too.

nlp/simple-search.rb

```
require "json"
require "json/add/core"

Article = Struct.new(:title, :text, :terms)
articles = JSON.parse(File.read("articles.json"), create_additions: true)

query = ARGV[0]

articles =
  articles.select { |article| article.terms.assoc(query) }

if matches.length > 0
  matches.each { |article| puts article.title }
else
  puts "No matches"
end
```

We require the necessary libraries, then re-create our Article struct and unserialize the article data from the JSON file it's stored in. We now have an array of Articles, the same data that we created in our extraction script.

Next is the actual searching logic. We take the first argument passed on the command line and use it as our search query, selecting all of the articles where one or more terms matches exactly the query passed on the command line. Since an article's terms are an array of arrays, with each entry containing not just the term itself but also information about the frequency of the term, we can use Array's assoc method for this. Given a value, it returns the first element of an array of arrays for which the first element is equal to the value we pass to it. For each article that matches, we simply output its title.

This logic works perfectly fine. We can run the script as follows and see matching articles:

```
$ ruby simple-search.rb Rincewind
The Colour of Magic
The Light Fantastic
Sourcery
Eric (novel)
Interesting Times
The Last Continent
The Last Hero

$ ruby simple-search.rb 'Granny Weatherwax'
Equal Rites
Wyrd Sisters
Witches Abroad
Carpe Jugulum
A Hat Full of Sky
Wintersmith
```

But the search that we've created is somewhat inflexible. Our first search, for Rincewind, worked fine because the character's name is capitalized and so was our search query. But a search for rincewind produces no results at all:

```
$ ruby simple-search.rb rincewind
```

This is clearly an issue, but we can do two things to solve it. The first is to normalize our index to ignore elements that we don't want to consider in our queries (such as case); this can be done in advance. The second is to be more flexible in what we match. Instead of allowing only for an identical match, we can allow for a *fuzzy* one.

Normalizing the Index

If we want our search queries to ignore some element of the text we're searching—its case, for example—then a simple solution is to account for that in the index. If we want to ignore case, then we make all of the terms lowercase. If we want to ignore accents, then we either strip them out or convert them to some normalized form (converting é to e, for example). Provided we then make the same normalization to our search queries, we'll achieve the desired effect.

In this case, it makes sense to ignore case. It's how a user would expect a search to behave, and it's a straightforward change to make. While we're at it, we'll also ignore dashes, so that Ankh-Morpork will be returned if the user searches for Ankh Morpork.

Let's adapt our term extraction script to store both the original version of the term and a normalized version. Although this increases the size of our index, in this case we're not dealing with tens of thousands of articles, so the trade-off is worth it. First, we can write a method that, given a string, will return the normalized form of that string. To start with, let's just ignore case:

nlp/extracting-normalized-terms.rb

```
def normalize_term(term)
  term.downcase.gsub("-", " ")
end
```

Then we need to make sure that we're storing this normalized version of each term at the point we store the article. Let's modify that portion of the script:

nlp/extracting-normalized-terms.rb

```
terms = Phrasie::Extractor.new.phrases(text)
terms = terms.reject { |term| ignored_terms.include?(term.first) }
terms.each do |term|
  term.unshift normalize_term(term.first)
end
```

Just after extracting the terms, we loop over them and prepend a normalized form of the term onto the array. Since this becomes the first element in the array, it becomes the element checked by `assoc`, so our search script can continue to work in the same way.

Finally, we need to make sure that we're applying the same normalization to our search query:

```
query = normalize(ARGV[0])
```

After making these changes, a search for `rincewind` bears the results our users might have expected:

```
$ ruby simple-search.rb rincewind
The Colour of Magic
The Light Fantastic
Sourcery
Eric (novel)
Interesting Times
The Last Continent
The Last Hero
```

We could adapt our normalization method to do many other things: stripping accents, removing punctuation other than dashes, converting non-ASCII characters to their closest ASCII equivalents (`é` to `e`, for example). There are even normalizations in the realms of language processing that we could perform: reducing every keyword to its stem, for example—so `rowing` would become `row`. This would mean that a search for one of `row` or `rowing` would match *both* the original keywords row and rowing. The sort of normalization we perform will depend on the domain in which we're working.

Fuzzy Matchers

We've developed our search to the point that it's a bit more helpful to users, not forcing them to match the case of the original term in their query. But it still requires them to be pretty exact, particularly when it comes to spelling. Google has spoiled us in this regard: we want to be able to search for, say, rinsewind and have the search know that we really meant rincewind.

There are a variety of techniques within this area, but we're going to focus on two. The first is the concept of *edit distance*, which will catch typos and simple spelling mistakes. For instance, if the user types teh king as a query, this will enable us to match (the probably intended) the king.

The second is the use of *phonetic algorithms*, which will allow the user to search for something they have almost no idea how to spell by searching for terms that sound, when pronounced, like the query. This will allow the user to type reylwey stayshun, for example, and have the term railway station match.

Edit Distance

If we repeatedly add, remove, or modify a single character of a given string of text, it's possible to transform it into any other string, no matter how different in length or in content the two strings might seem. To illustrate this, let's take the string boat. We can transform it into bob by performing the following changes:

```
boat
boa
bob
```

We removed the t, to get boa; that's one transformation. Then we changed the a to a b to get bob; that's a second transformation. Because it required two single-character transformations to get from our first string to our second, we say that these two strings have an *edit distance* of 2.

To transform starring to cart, we perform the following changes:

```
starring
starrin
starri
starr
tarr
tart
cart
```

This time, six transformations are necessary—the two strings have an edit distance of 6. This method of calculating edit distance, by considering the adding, removing, and modifying of characters, is knowing as the *Levenshtein distance.*

By using a Levenshtein distance algorithm in Ruby, we can look for terms that are within a certain edit distance of the query and that are therefore a good—but not necessarily exact—match. A Ruby implementation of this algorithm can be found in Paul Battley's excellent text gem.

Using this library, we can extend our script to look for terms within an edit distance of two from our query:

nlp/levenshtein-search.rb

```
query = normalize_term(ARGV[0])

matches =
  articles
    .select { |article|
      article.terms.find { |term, _|
        Text::Levenshtein.distance(term, query) <= 2
      }
    }

if matches.length > 0
  matches.each { |article| puts article.title }
else
  puts "No matches"
end
```

Previously, we were checking whether the query matched a term exactly. Now we check whether the Levenshtein distance between the query and the term is less than or equal to two. This will cover the previous exact-matching functionality too, since two identical strings will have a Levenshtein distance of zero. But it will also cover cases where the query differs by one or two transformations, allowing for typos and misspellings—in this case the misspelling of the term rincewind:

```
$ ruby levenshtein-search.rb rinsewind
The Colour of Magic
The Light Fantastic
Sourcery
Eric (novel)
Interesting Times
The Last Continent
The Last Hero
```

```
$ ruby levenshtein-search.rb rinsewint
The Colour of Magic
The Light Fantastic
Sourcery
Eric (novel)
Interesting Times
The Last Continent
The Last Hero

$ ruby levenshtein-search.rb rensewint
No matches
```

By altering one or two characters from the actual term, we see that matches are returned. But when we alter a third character, we stray too far from reality, and our criteria are no longer satisfied; we therefore see no results listed.

Searching for terms within a certain level of fuzziness is an improvement, but we're not yet at the slightly magic-feeling Google level, in which we can allow people to search for terms that they've heard of but have no idea how to spell. For that, we'll need another algorithm.

Phonetic Algorithms

English orthography is a strange beast. Many words' pronunciations have little or no resemblance to the way they're spelled. Think of *though*, *through*, *thought*, and *cough*; think of *laugh*, *graph*, and *staff*. Similar spellings don't mean similar sounds, and similar sounds aren't necessarily spelled in similar ways. If English is your second language, you've likely grappled with these bizarre and confusing aspects of its spelling system.

It might seem that translating an English word into its pronounced form would be impossible, but that's actually not the case. While English spelling rules are undoubtedly a hodgepodge, they aren't random. There are rules behind them—rules that are learned to varying degrees by speakers of English —and where there are rules, we can create algorithms.

One such algorithm is called Metaphone.[3] Created by the software engineer Lawrence Philips in 1990, Metaphone is a form of phonetic fingerprinting. If we feed it a string representing an English word or phrase, it will return a representation of that word's approximate pronunciation, allowing for regional differences in accent and pronunciation. This means that the Metaphone values for two words that are pronounced in similar ways will be identical, regardless of how the words are spelled.

3. http://aspell.net/metaphone/

For example, the Metaphone for baron is BRN. The Metaphone for barren, which is pronounced in the same way, is *also* BRN. These values are of course based on the approximate pronunciations of the words. For example, the Metaphone values for pudding and putting, which are pronounced the same in some American accents but not in British English, are the same. But this fuzziness is likely to benefit us in the case of searching, so it's actually desirable—it wouldn't be good if our fuzziness worked only with certain accents.

The text gem, which we used for its Levenshtein distance algorithm, provides us with a implementation of Metaphone in Ruby. For any string, we can obtain its Metaphone representation by using the Text::Metaphone.metaphone method:

```
Text::Metaphone.metaphone("tooth")
=> "T0"
Text::Metaphone.metaphone("tewth")
=> "T0"
Text::Metaphone.metaphone("tuth")
=> "T0"
```

We can introduce Metaphone into our search process in much the same way as we did with edit distance; it just becomes another thing to check against potential terms:

nlp/metaphone-search.rb

```
query = normalize_term(ARGV[0])

metaphone_query = Text::Metaphone.metaphone(query)

matches =
  articles
    .select { |article|
      article.terms.find { |term, _|
        Text::Levenshtein.distance(term, query) <= 2 ||
          Text::Metaphone.metaphone(term) == metaphone_query
      }
    }

if matches.length > 0
  matches.each { |article| puts article.title }
else
  puts "No matches"
end
```

First, we calculate the Metaphone value for the query passed on the command line and store it for later. Then, when looking at each term, we compare the Metaphone value for that term to that of the query. If they're the same—which means that the term sounds like the query—then we consider the term to be a match.

We can now match things that sound similar to valid terms. So, acceptable substitutes for rincewind and vetinari are:

```
$ ruby metaphone-search.rb rensewint
The Colour of Magic
The Light Fantastic
Sourcery
Eric (novel)
Interesting Times
The Last Continent
The Last Hero

$ ruby metaphone-search.rb vetunahree
Men at Arms
Feet of Clay (novel)
Jingo (novel)
The Truth (novel)
The Last Hero
Going Postal
Thud!
Raising Steam
```

That's it; we've now created a fuzzy searcher for our index of articles. It allows users to search using queries that exactly match terms, as you might expect, but also ones that are close misspellings or merely sound like genuine terms. Equally, it allows us to match terms that are misspelled in the original articles—a fairly likely occurrence.

If you wanted to extend this further, you could implement some kind of weighting of the results returned by the search routing (so that "better" matches were listed first), perhaps based on keyword density across the entire database of articles. You could pull out snippets from the article to show the terms in context, helping the user to determine whether the match is a good one. By layering language processing techniques, as we've already seen, we can create powerful tools. It's a subject worthy of exploration.

Wrapping Up

We've now used language processing techniques for several practical tasks. We've fetched web pages and extracted the body text from them. We've used term extraction to pull keywords from within the text, summarizing its contents.

We created a simple search for this index of keywords, then extended it in two ways to make it easier to use and more forgiving: first by using edit distance to allow for typos and misspellings, and then by matching terms that *sounded like* the user's query—allowing them to search for things that they couldn't even spell.

We've barely scratched the surface of language processing, but hopefully you've seen what you can achieve by combining tried and true algorithms and using well-established primitives to perform language processing work. It's not necessary to have a degree in computational linguistics to do some really useful language processing.

That draws to a close the second section of the book. We've now looked at how to read text into our programs and how to perform various types of processing on that text once we have it. The final step in our journey is to explore *writing* text into various formats and to various locations.

Part III

Load: Writing Text

We've looked at how to read text into our programs and at how to manipulate that text once we've read it. The final logical step that we can expect to need to take is to write our processed text somewhere.

This might seem a simple subject, but there's much to get our teeth into. First, we'll look at writing to standard output and to files. Then we'll explore writing to other processes, something that will allow us to exploit the power of text processing pipelines from within our programs. After looking at how to write to structured formats such as JSON, XML, and CSV, we'll finish up by using ERB to create flexibly templated output.

CHAPTER 12

Standard Output and Standard Error

We've completed two pieces of our puzzle: acquiring text and processing it. The final part of a text processing job is usually to output the text somewhere—the "load" part of the "extract, transform, load" process.

There's a bewildering array of places we might want to write our text to and formats in which we might want to write it: to the screen or to files; in JSON or as a CSV; as simple output or using complex, interpreted templates.

The place of first resort, though—for the simplest scripts and at the earliest point of even complex applications—is to write to *standard output*. We investigated its sibling, *standard input*, in Chapter 2, *Processing Standard Input*, on page 19, where we used it to read text both from the user's keyboard and from other processes. Standard output complements standard input well, as you might expect. Let's take a look at what it can do.

Simple Output

At its most basic, standard output is familiar to anyone who's written a Ruby script before. The simplest *hello world* script outputs its message to standard output, and when run from the command line we see that message printed to our screens.

Just like standard input, standard output has two references in Ruby: its constant, `STDOUT`, and the global variable `$stdout`. Just like with standard input, you should prefer the latter since it respects reassignment.

If you want to output to standard output, it's generally not necessary to state this explicitly. The two most used methods for outputting text in Ruby, `print` and `puts`, both operate on `$stdout` implicitly, so while we *could* call:

```
$stdout.puts "Hello, world!"
```

it's not necessary, and seeing such things in the wild is uncommon. It's universal to see the following instead:

```
puts "Hello, world!"
```

But standard output isn't your only option when it comes to writing output. Each Ruby program actually has two output streams, and while the default is standard output, we can and should use the other when appropriate. It's called *standard error*.

Writing to Standard Error

Each process in the world of Unix has two output streams, not just one. The first is standard output. The second is called standard error, and it is used—as you might have guessed—for error output.

Even if you weren't aware of it, you'll definitely have seen it in Ruby; it's where, among other things, exceptions are printed. So the following script:

fail.rb
```
puts "Hello on standard output!"
fail "Error on standard error!"
```

produces the following output on both standard output and standard error:

```
$ ruby fail.rb
Hello on standard output!
fail.rb:2:in `<main>': Error on standard error! (RuntimeError)
```

By default, your shell will display both standard output and standard error in the same way, outputting them to the screen. But they're different streams and can be manipulated separately. For example, let's hide standard error entirely:

```
$ ruby fail.rb 2>/dev/null
Hello on standard output!
```

You might have seen > in your shell before, to redirect standard output to a file. We can do the same with standard error—it's stream two, where standard output is stream one, so we redirect it with 2>. Here, we redirect it to /dev/null, which means to discard it entirely.

Of course, we don't just get output on standard error when we cause an exception. We can write to it ourselves, too, and it's good practice to write error messages there for precisely the aforementioned reason: so that users can handle them separately from the "legitimate" output of your program.

In the same way that we can write to standard output with $stdout.puts, we can write to standard error with $stderr.puts:

```
puts "Non-error on standard output!"
$stderr.puts "Error on standard error!"
```

Of course, there's nothing to say that you have to use standard error only for error messages. If you're expecting your standard output stream to be redirected somewhere else, for example, you can use standard error to output something to the screen despite this redirection and without affecting whatever it is that you're writing to standard output.

This is useful in a long-running filter script that processes a large amount of input or that takes a long time to process. With scripts like this, it's nice to inform the user that progress is being made, and standard error allows you to do that without affecting the script's primary output.

For example, the following script takes URLs as input, fetches them, and then outputs the size of the page that it found at that URL:

stdout/url-sizes.rb

```
require "open-uri"

urls = ARGF.readlines.map(&:chomp)
total_urls = urls.length

urls.each_with_index do |url, n|
  html = open(url).read
  puts "#{html.bytesize} bytes (#{url})"
end
```

If we run the script as follows, its output will be sorted in descending order—showing us the URL of the largest page first:

```
$ printf "http://en.wikipedia.org\nhttp://bbc.co.uk/" \
    | ruby url-sizes.rb | sort -rn
  102434 bytes (http://bbc.co.uk/)
  67953 bytes (http://en.wikipedia.org)
```

However, until we see the final output, we have no idea what's going on—whether the program has hung up or it's actually processing the URLs. We can't output progress messages to standard output, since they'll get mixed up with our actual output. But we can output them to standard error instead:

stdout/url-sizes-progress.rb

```
require "open-uri"

urls = ARGF.readlines.map(&:chomp)
total_urls = urls.length
```

```
urls.each_with_index do |url, n|
  $stderr.print "\rFetching url #{n + 1} of #{total_urls}...   "
  html = open(url).read
  puts "#{html.bytesize} bytes (#{url})"
end

$stderr.print "\r"
```

A couple of things are going on here. First, we're outputting the progress message to standard output. But we're also outputting a carriage return (\r) as the first character of the message and not outputting a newline at the end of it. That means that each progress message will overwrite the previous one, since we'll be continually writing over the same line, and the screen doesn't fill up with progress messages. Once the script finishes, it actually has the same output as the original version:

```
$ printf "http://en.wikipedia.org\nhttp://bbc.co.uk/" \
    | ruby url-sizes-progress.rb | sort -rn
  102434 bytes (http://bbc.co.uk/)
  67953 bytes (http://en.wikipedia.org)
```

This is a nice touch. We see the progress when it's valuable—during the script's execution—but it doesn't hang around after the point that it stops being useful. This idea of using standard error as a second stream for out-of-band communication is a useful one. If you'd like even fancier output, there are various Ruby gems for providing the appearance of animated progress bars. They typically use this same trick under the hood, and can generally be told to output to standard error if you choose.

print vs. puts

Those new to Ruby sometimes wonder about the difference between print and puts. In essence, print is for outputting records on a single line, and puts is for outputting whole records.

This might sound like a cryptic explanation, but it actually makes sense when you get down to the detail. Both methods take multiple arguments. After each argument, print will output $,, or the "output field separator." After the final argument, it will output $\, or the "output record separator."

puts does much the same, except that rather than respecting the global definitions of the output field separator and the output record separator, it always uses a newline for both. So, if you wanted to, you could make print behave like puts by redefining those values yourself. Here's an IRB session that demonstrates:

```
> print "hello", "world"
helloworld
> puts "hello", "world"
hello
world
> $, = "\n"
> $\ = "\n"
> print "hello", "world"
hello
world
```

In practical terms, then, without doing any kind of configuration: puts outputs a newline between each argument and a final newline at the end, while print outputs nothing at all between its arguments and nothing at the end, since both $, and $\ default to nil.

The practical use for this is generally that print can be used to gradually build up a line over multiple calls. For example:

```
print "Your choice is "
if choice == :vanilla
  print "plain old vanilla"
else
  print "something more exciting"
end
puts ". Thanks!"
```

Here we save the puts for the final call. This ensures that the text we previously passed to print appears on a single line and that we output a newline only when we're ready to at the end.

An idiosyncrasy of puts is that the newline is actually printed in a separate operation. Ordinarily, this isn't a problem. But if you're running multiple processes within your script, for example, you might see strange output in which some lines are squashed together and others have too much space after them. This is caused by puts and its separate call to output the newline. There's a race condition possible here, where two simultaneous calls to puts will have their output interleaved. This script illustrates the issue:

stdout/fork-puts.rb

```
5.times do
  fork do
    sleep 0.5
    puts "I'm in a new process!"
  end
end

Process.waitall
```

This script's behavior is unpredictable. Sometimes it might look fine. Other times it might produce output that looks like this:

```
I'm in a new process!I'm in a new process!I'm in a new process!


I'm in a new process!I'm in a new process!
```

The fix is surprisingly simple:

stdout/fork-puts2.rb

```ruby
5.times do
  fork do
    sleep 0.5
    puts "I'm in a new process!\n"
  end
end

Process.waitall
```

All we need to do is to include a trailing newline as part of the string we pass to puts. Internally, Ruby checks whether the string passed to it ends in a new line, and outputs one itself only if that's not the case. This means that we print to the screen only once per call to puts, and the race condition goes away.

Formatting Output with printf

Until now we've been outputting simple strings in a simple way. But if our output is destined to be read by a human being, we're going to need something a bit better.

Very often, when doing data analysis and reporting, the data we're producing isn't for our own benefit. It's destined for the marketing department, for sales, for executives—most of whom would run a mile rather than view output on the command line.

But outputting to the screen is such a cheap thing to do, in terms of development time, that it's often the medium of first resort. Debugging information, programs that are used by developers, and many other applications will need to output to the terminal. Learning to make that output readable is a useful first step—and it's often the only step necessary, especially when the output can easily be copied into a document or email.

An excellent tool for formatting simple output is printf. Inherited from the C programming language, printf allows us to go a step further than a simple print or puts call by allowing us to control in fine detail the formatting of the outputted values. Let's take a look.

Basic Usage

Instead of accepting arguments and outputting them directly and in the order they were specified, as print and puts do, printf takes a *format string*, which states precisely how things should be outputted.

In their simplest forms, these format strings specify the type of data we're outputting. For example, to output a string and an integer:

```
printf "%s %i", "the value is", 2.2678
```

The first argument to printf is our format string, which tells Ruby to format the first value as a string (%s) and the second as an integer (%i), separated by a space. These % values are called *format placeholders*, and they're ultimately replaced by the values we pass them.

If we run this script, we'll see the following output:

```
the value is 2
```

printf converted the floating-point number 2.2678 into an integer for us. If we'd wanted to round it just to a certain number of decimal places, rather than truncating it entirely, we could tell printf to do that, too:

```
printf "%.2f", 2.2678
# >> 2.27
```

In this format string, we specify a precision of two decimal places (.2) and that we'd like the passed value to be treated as a floating-point number (f).

With printf, we determine how the value will be presented only at the point that we output it; we don't actually modify the value in any way. That's usually a good thing. We might want to present the same value in different ways in different places, and that might become impossible if the formatting we're doing is destructive (truncating a string, for example, or rounding a number to a certain number of decimal places).

Used in this basic way, printf doesn't offer many compelling advantages compared to plain old print. Let's dig a little deeper and discover some of its more complex capabilities.

Aligning Values

Probably the most common requirement in making command-line output look a little less ugly is alignment. Generally, that means making sure that columns of output line up with one another, to make scanning through them easy.

Let's imagine we have the following hash, representing the inventory of a hardware store. We'd like to output it to users so they can see a summary of what's in stock:

```
inventory = { "Nuts" => 124, "Bolts" => 2891, "Hammers" => 79, "Nails" => 40 }
```

When outputting this data, alignment is the difference between something that looks a mess:

```
Nuts 124
Bolts 2891
Hammers 79
Nails 40
```

and something that looks much neater and is much more readable:

```
Nuts      124
Bolts    2891
Hammers    79
Nails      40
```

It's much easier to read the amounts in the second example than in the first. What we need to do is to pad the length of each value so that they're always the same—adding spaces to the start or end of each process as appropriate. The name of the product needs to be padded to eight characters to comfortably fit our longest value, and the padding should be added on the right to left-align the text. The numbers, on the other hand, need to be right-aligned and padded to four characters.

With printf we specify padding for our values by prefixing our format placeholder with a number:

```
inventory.each do |product, items|
  printf "%8s %4d\n", product, items
end
```

If we run the previous example, we see the following output:

```
    Nuts  124
   Bolts 2891
 Hammers   79
   Nails   40
```

We're closer, but both our values are right-aligned. That's because right alignment is the default. If we want to left-align a value, we use a hyphen before the width—almost as if we're specifying a negative width:

```
inventory.each do |product, items|
  printf "%-8s %4d\n", product, items
end
```

This produces the output we were hoping for:

```
Nuts       124
Bolts     2891
Hammers     79
Nails       40
```

In these examples, we've hard-coded the width as part of the format string, but that's not always ideal. It's sometimes not possible to know the length of the fields in advance. In these cases, we have two options. The first is to truncate the fields, and the second is to dynamically calculate the field widths.

In the first case, we can specify a precision for a string value. Just as specifying a precision will truncate a float to the appropriate number of decimal places, specifying a precision for a string will truncate it to the appropriate length. To set a precision of 5 in our previous example, then:

```
inventory.each do |product, items|
  printf "%-5.5s %4d\n", product, items
end
```

We'd see the first column set to a minimum of five characters and a maximum of five characters:

```
Nuts   124
Bolts 2891
Hamme   79
Nails   40
```

This isn't the most beautiful option, though; we've sacrificed readability for programmer convenience, which is sometimes the best option but not always. For a little more effort, we can dynamically calculate the widths of the fields, which will produce a much nicer output without us having to hard-code fields. Here's how we do that:

stdout/inventory.rb
```
longest = inventory.max_by { |product, items| product.length }
width   = longest.first.length

inventory.each do |product, items|
  printf "%-*s %4d\n", width, product, items
end
```

Before outputting the table, we discover which product name is the longest and store its length. Then, when actually outputting each row, we specify the first column's width as *. This instructs printf to use the next argument as the width. Then we pass in the width that we've precalculated, and the column will fit its longest value.

By setting the widths of fields, we have the ability to output tabular data in a format that's visually pleasing and easier to read, for a minimum amount of additional effort.

printf has all the accumulated complexities and idiosyncrasies that you might expect of something that's been around for so long. But it's a truly useful tool, and it can perform countless tasks easily that, if you tried to replicate them in Ruby, would otherwise require many lines of code. Learning to use it will be helpful and will—like regular expressions—give you a skill that transfers to many other programming languages.

Redirecting Standard Output

Earlier in the chapter, we saw how methods such as print and puts operated implicitly on $stdout. This is an important point—that is, that they operate on the variable $stdout rather than the fixed STDOUT.

This means that if we reassign $stdout to some other value, all calls to these methods—even ones made by libraries and other code that isn't our own—will be passed to whatever we replaced $stdout with. This enables us to neatly, in a single line, redirect all of the output of our program to another place. Let's take a look at two practical uses for this.

Redirecting All Output to a File

The only expectations that Ruby has of $stdout is that it be an IO object. As we saw in *IO: Ruby's Input/Output Class*, on page 12, the IO class is the foundation of all input and output in Ruby, so there are many things that fit the bill.

One of them is the File class, which means that all that's required to redirect standard output to a file is to reassign $stdout to a File object:

stdout-to-file.rb
```
$stdout = File.open("output.txt", "w")
puts "Hello, world"
```

If we run this script, we'd see no output in the terminal; instead, the call to puts wrote to the file that we opened. That's all that we need to do.

This is particularly handy for long-running processes or daemons, where they're not actually attached to a terminal. Replacing $stdout means that none of our libraries or any other code have to care about where their output is actually going, and they can call puts as they please. The script could then be run with standard output pointing to its original location, and the output would be visible for debugging, without having to alter any of the output calls.

Temporarily Redirecting Output

We might not want to redirect all output for the entire script. It's common to just want to capture output for a short period—to execute a method that outputs directly to the screen, but capture the output instead of printing it, for example.

Since $stdout is a variable, we can easily temporarily reassign it and then assign it back to its original value once we're finished. Let's write a general-purpose method that does just that.

The basic outline of our method will be as follows:

```
def capture_output(&block)
  old_stdout = $stdout
  new_stdout = _____

  $stdout = new_stdout
  block.call
  $stdout = old_stdout

  new_stdout
end
```

Here we save the old value of $stdout. We create a new IO object, too. Then we swap out $stdout for our new object, call the block we were passed, and then return $stdout to its original value.

The only issue is what the new value of $stdout should be—that pesky blank space in the code. In the previous example, *Redirecting All Output to a File,* on page 182, we swapped $stdout out for a file. That worked fine, because File behaves like an IO object and fits the same interface. But that's not appropriate here; we just want to capture the output, not write it to a file. What is there that behaves like an IO object but doesn't actually write anything anywhere?

The answer is StringIO. Part of the Ruby standard library, it looks and feels like an IO object—implementing methods like gets, puts, and so on—but reads from and writes to a string in memory, rather than to a file or network socket.

Using it in the previous example, we get something that looks like this:

capture-stdout.rb

```
require "stringio"

def capture_output(&block)
  old_stdout = $stdout
  new_stdout = StringIO.new

  $stdout = new_stdout
```

```
  block.call

  new_stdout.string
ensure
  $stdout = old_stdout
end

output = capture_output do
  puts "Hello, world"
end

puts output.upcase
```

If we run the script, we should see the output HELLO, WORLD. We were able to capture the output of the block and then modify it.

But it's not quite perfect. We've reassigned $stdout, and all the Ruby code that prints something will respect this reassignment. But our program can generate output from things that aren't Ruby at all, and our script will fail to capture those. If we make a system call that produces output, for example:

capture-stdout.rb

```
output = capture_output do
  puts "Hello, world"
  system "echo 'Hello, world'"
end

puts output.upcase
```

we'll see the following output:

```
Hello, world
HELLO, WORLD
```

The output from our system call wasn't captured at all; it was immediately printed out, as it would have been if we hadn't done this at all. To capture it, we'll need to do a more advanced form of redirection.

Advanced Redirection

To more thoroughly capture the output of our program, we'll need to learn a bit about Unix's plumbing: we're going to be creating some pipes. I first learned this specific technique from Avdi Grimm,[1] who in turn credits Ara T. Howard. But at its heart is a technique that asks Unix to do the hard work for us. This sort of code could easily be written in any language that exposes Unix's plumbing to us.

1. Ruby Tapas, episode 29, "Redirecting Output"

Here's the new capture_output method:

redirecting-stdout.rb

```
def capture_output(&block)
  stdout = STDOUT.clone

  read_io, write_io = IO.pipe
  read_io.sync = true

  output = ""
  reader = Thread.new do
    begin
      loop do
        output << read_io.readpartial(1024)
      end
    rescue EOFError
    end
  end

  STDOUT.reopen(write_io)
  block.call
ensure
  STDOUT.reopen(stdout)
  write_io.close
  reader.join

  return output
end
```

Let's step through it bit by bit, since it's a fair bit more complex than our original.

redirecting-stdout.rb

```
stdout = STDOUT.clone
```

First, we clone STDOUT, saving its existing form into a variable. We'll need this in order to restore the original output stream after our method is done.

redirecting-stdout.rb

```
read_io, write_io = IO.pipe
read_io.sync = true
```

Next, we create a pipe. IO's pipe method returns two IO objects for us, each representing one end of a pipeline. (If it helps, you can think of this just like a pipeline in your shell, like the ones we covered in Chapter 2, *Processing Standard Input*, on page 19; it functions in exactly the same way.) The first object reads data from the pipe. The second object writes data to it. We could then use these from different threads, or even different processes, giving us the ability to communicate between concurrent tasks.

By setting the sync flag to true, we tell Ruby that we want data written to this pipe to be passed through instantly; otherwise, Ruby will store it up in a buffer first. (Buffering is often a good idea, since it allows the write end of the pipe to write as quickly as it wants without worrying about how slow the reading end is, but here it's unnecessary.)

redirecting-stdout.rb
```
output = ""
reader = Thread.new do
  begin
    loop do
      output << read_io.readpartial(1024)
    end
  rescue EOFError
  end
end
```

Here, we do just that: create a new thread. Its responsibility will be to wait for input to be received by monitoring the read end of the pipeline. Until it receives some, it will sit patiently waiting. It'll also wait for more after it receives its first input, and it will stop only once it receives an "End of File" notice—that's what the rescue EOFError does.

redirecting-stdout.rb
```
STDOUT.reopen(write_io)
block.call
```

Now that we've got our pipeline and have spawned a thread to monitor the read end of it, we need to hook up the write end to standard output somehow, so that when text is written there it actually gets sent down our pipeline to be captured.

For that we use the reopen method, available on all IO streams. This allows us to replace the source of the stream with an entirely new IO object—in this case, the write end of our pipe.

After reopening STDOUT, we execute our block. Any output written to standard output within the block will, since we reopened STDOUT, be sent down our pipe and be captured by our thread.

redirecting-stdout.rb
```
ensure
  STDOUT.reopen(stdout)
  write_io.close
  reader.join

  return output
end
```

At this point, our block has finished executing; everything that we wanted to capture has now been output. First, we restore STDOUT to the IO object that it originally pointed to. Next we close the write end of the pipe; this is what sends the "End of File" signal to our thread, shutting it down. Then we use join to wait for the thread to finish—since it might currently be writing to our output variable—and then finally we return the output that we've captured.

Although this might seem like a complex technique, we've created a really robust output capturing method. It captures output written to $stdout, output written to STDOUT, and output from subprocesses. It's something we could use time and time again, and it's worth the upfront increase in complexity.

Wrapping Up

We've covered quite a lot in this chapter. We started with a *hello world* script, the simplest possible use of standard output. Then we looked at standard error, the other output stream, and how we could use it to distinguish between and treat separately two different sorts of output from the same program.

We learned the difference between print and puts, and then looked at a more advanced form of them both: printf, with its flexible and powerful format strings that can be used to format values, convert values from one type to another, and help us generate readable tabular data by aligning our columns for us.

Finally, we explored redirecting standard output from within our script, so that we could use ordinary output methods to write to a different location—including the ability to capture output our script wrote, even down to the level of capturing system commands' output.

Our next subject is closely related to standard output. We're going to look at how we can write to the standard input streams of other processes, forming pipeline chains within our programs, and also how to write to the filesystem.

CHAPTER 13

Writing to Other Processes and to Files

We've looked at writing to standard output, a useful technique that allows our programs' output to either be read by people or be redirected into another process as part of a pipeline chain. Sometimes, though, we don't want to leave the choice of redirecting output up to the user of our program; we want to write directly to a file or to another process ourselves.

This might be so that we can persist our output between invocations of our program, storing up more data over time, in which case it would be useful to be able to write data to a file. Or it might be to harness the power of other programs, so that we can avoid reimplementing logic ourselves. We could achieve this by constructing our own pipeline chains within our program, sending input in one and capturing the transformed output.

Let's take a look at this latter case first. It's a natural extension of writing to standard output but will give us great power and flexibility.

Writing to Other Processes

In Chapter 3, *Shell One-Liners*, on page 29, we looked at how powerful chaining processes together in pipelines could be. The chapter culminated in our mixing Ruby with other Unix commands to process text in an ad hoc fashion, with multiple processes linked together in a *pipeline chain*. Each took some text as input and then passed it along, in some transformed form, as output to the next process.

Here, for example, we use Ruby to extract only those rows of a file that we're interested in, and then use sort, uniq, and head to further process those lines:

```
$ cat error_log \
  | ruby -ne '$_ =~ /^\[.+\] \[error\] (.*)$/ and puts $1' \
  | sort | uniq -c | sort -rn | head -n 10
```

By using a pipeline chain like this, we speed up our development by having to solve only the novel parts of the problem. We're not forced to reimplement solutions to long-solved problems such as sorting, counting unique lines, and so on.

But in this case, the decision to use those further commands, to perform this extra logic, was taken by the user. Ruby had no knowledge of them. It just wrote its text to standard output, and that was that.

There's a certain usefulness and generality to that approach, but it doesn't always fit. Sometimes we know in advance that we want to harness the power of other processes and that we don't want to have to reinvent the wheel. In these cases, we'll need to be able to use these external utilities from within our scripts, not just on the command line.

Simple Writing

To write to another process, we need to do two things. First, we have to spawn the process that we want to communicate with. Second, we need to hook its standard input stream up to something in our script, which we can then write to, so that our data will be passed into the script in the same way as it would be on the command line.

Ruby offers us a short and simple way to do both of those things, and it's with our trusty friend open. (We've previously used open to read from files, in Chapter 1, *Reading from Files*, on page 3, and to fetch URLs, in Chapter 6, *Scraping HTML*, on page 63.)

As well as allowing us to read from files and URLs, open has a third function: it can read to and write from other processes. We achieve this by passing open a pipe symbol followed by a command name:

open-pipe.rb
```
open("| sort | uniq -c | sort -rn | head -n 10", "w") do |sort|
  open("data/error_log") do |log|
    log.each_line do |line|
      if line =~ /^\[.+\] \[error\] (.*)$/
        sort.puts $1
      end
    end
  end
end
```

Here we open the same pipeline chain as we saw earlier on the command line. By passing w as the second argument to open, we tell Ruby that we want to write to the process. Then we open up the log file—the step that was performed by cat in our manual pipeline chain—and loop over the lines within it. If a line matches our conditions, we write the error message to the pipeline chain, causing it to be passed to the standard input stream of the first process.

When we execute this script, Ruby will dutifully start all of the processes we requested, hooking each one's standard output stream to the standard input stream of the next. It then creates a pipe, the output end of which is attached to the first process in the chain and the input end of which is passed to our block.

This works in exactly the same way as the command-line version did and produces the same output. Just like in the command-line version, we haven't had to reimplement any logic that isn't part of our core problem.

This technique is even more useful when used to perform tasks that would be impossible—or at least difficult—to perform in Ruby alone, but for which there exists ready-made command-line utilities. Let's imagine that we wanted to compress some text generated by our script and write that compressed data to a file.

There's a command called gzip that will do this for us. Like other filter commands, it takes standard input, compresses it, and outputs that compressed data to standard output. That means we can use it exactly like we did our previous pipeline, writing data to gzip's standard input stream and getting compressed data back into our program from gzip's standard output stream.

Unlike our first example, though, we don't want to have the output from the final process printed to our screen. We want to write it to a file. open has us covered here, too:

open-gzip.rb

```
open("|gzip", "r+") do |gzip|
  gzip.puts "foo"

  gzip.close_write

  File.open("foo.gz", "w") do |file|
    file.write gzip.read
  end
end
```

In this case, we specify a mode of r+ to the pipe, to specify read and write mode. We then write to the pipe as we did in the first example, and then close it for writing. This sends the "End of File" notice to the gzip command, signaling that the input is complete. We then use read to read gzip's entire output, and we write that to a new file.

By doing this, we've been able to harness the power of an existing command-line tool, rather than needing to either implement gzip encoding ourselves (which would be infeasible) or use a Ruby library that does it for us (which might be impractical or undesirable).

A Practical Example: Paging Output

If you've ever used the version-control software Git, you might have noticed a particular behavior it has. If you use, for example, the git log command in a project with a lot of history, Git won't dump thousands of lines on your screen in one go, swamping you and making it difficult to see what was at the top of the output. Instead, it uses less to allow you to scroll through the output—a nice touch that makes using Git much easier.

If we're writing a script that outputs a large amount of text, we can achieve this same effect to make things easier for the people running it. By combining what we learned about redirecting standard output in the previous chapter with our newfound ability to write to other processes, we should be able to do just that.

Here's the code:

paging-output.rb
```
def page_output
  stdout = STDOUT.clone

  less = open("|less", "w")
  STDOUT.reopen(less)

  at_exit do
    STDOUT.reopen(stdout)
    less.close
  end
end
```

Just like in the previous chapter, we first clone STDOUT so that we can restore it later. Next we use open to spawn the less process for us. This, as we saw earlier in the chapter, will give us an IO object that will allow us to write to the less process's standard input stream. Then we use reopen to point the standard output stream of our own process to the standard input stream of less, ensuring that everything we write from this point on will be paged correctly—even output from subshells.

The final part of the method uses an exit handler to tell Ruby that once our script finishes, we should restore the original standard output stream and, critically, close the IO object that we have pointing to less. This allows less to function properly, since it allows it to know how many lines it's been given.

Everything output after we call the page_output method will be passed into less. Here's an example that checks for the presence of a terminal and, if it finds one, chooses to page the output. It then outputs a thousand lines of text:

paging-output.rb

```
page_output if STDOUT.tty?

500.times do |n|
  puts "#{n + 1}: Hello from Ruby"
  system "echo '#{n + 1}: Hello from a sub-shell'"
end
```

If we run this example, we should see the top of the output first—however many lines will fit in our terminal. We can then use the arrow keys to scroll up and down the text (and horizontally, if the lines were very long or if our terminal was very narrow). Compared to the experience of dumping a thousand lines of text into the terminal normally, this is a huge improvement.

There's an added bonus, though. Because we're checking for the presence of a terminal before redirecting our output to less, we've not broken the usual Unix model, so we can still use our script in a pipeline. For example, we could count the number of lines being output:

```
$ ruby paging-output.rb | wc -l
1000
```

This is the same behavior as Git, incidentally. It will page output when a terminal is present but do nothing when one isn't.

If we think about it, the implementation cost of all this is basically nothing. We don't have to reimplement paging ourselves; we just need to point a single stream to a different place. Our users also get the same behavior that they're familiar with from elsewhere. They don't get some poorly implemented subset of less; we give them the real deal. This is a great thing. Thanks to fundamental design decisions made decades ago, the hard work is done for us.

Writing to Files

Compared to writing to other processes, writing to files is a relative breeze—there's only a limited number of ways to do it. This isn't really surprising, I suppose, but what's interesting is typically the content—what's actually being written—rather than the mechanism of writing.

In Chapter 1, *Reading from Files*, on page 3, we looked at how we could use open to obtain a File object that enabled us to read from a file. It looked like this:

```
File.open("file.txt") do |file|
  contents = file.read
end
```

What if, rather than using read to read from the file, we tried to use write or puts to write to it—something like this?

```
File.open("file.txt") do |file|
  file.puts "Hello, world"
end
```

If we ran this code, we'd get the following exception:

```
IOError: not opened for writing
```

That's because the default behavior of File.open is to open the file in read-only mode. Attempts to write the file, as we've just seen, are met with resistance.

We can control this behavior through the second argument to File.open or open. It tells Ruby the mode to use when opening our file. Its possible values are:

r
: Read-only mode. We can read from the file freely, but we can't write to it. This is the default mode, which is why we saw our error when trying to use the File object to write to the file.

  If the file doesn't exist, we'll quite reasonably get an error telling us so, since it doesn't make sense to read from a file that doesn't exist.

r+
: Read-write mode. This allows us to both read from and write to the file. If the file doesn't exist, we'll get an error just like we would when opening the file in read-only mode.

  This mode is useful when you care about the current contents of the file but will be overwriting them. You can read the file and then when you're done, use puts or write to write the new content—allowing you, for example, to do some sort of substitution of the contents or to insert new content into the start or middle of the file.

w
: Write-only mode. If the file doesn't exist, it will be created. If it does exist, opening it in this mode will cause it to be truncated (that is, it will cause all of its content to be deleted).

  This mode is useful when you're writing the entire content of the file, and you don't care if the file exists or has any current contents. This is perhaps the most common mode to use when writing files.

`w+` Read-write mode. This allows us the same flexibility as opening the file in `r+` mode but will create the file for us if it doesn't exist (and if it does, it will truncate the file). Rarely seen in the wild, it's occasionally useful.

`a` Append mode. Like `w` mode, the file will be created if it doesn't exist. If the file does exist, though, content will be written to the end of the file, hence the name.

Perhaps the most common use of append mode is to write to a log file. In such a file, we want the content to be ordered chronologically, so that the oldest lines are first and the newest lines are last. Using append mode will do this for us.

For example, if our log file currently contains:

```
21:00 Did a thing
```

then the following code:

```
File.open("log.txt", "a") do |log|
log.puts "21:01 Did another thing"
end
```

will result in `log.txt` having the following content:

```
21:00 Did a thing
21:01 Did another thing
```

No other mode will preserve the contents of the file when writing to it in this way. It's not possible, then, to prepend a line to a file. If you want to keep the existing contents and merely add to them, you're limited to append mode.

`a+` Read-write append mode. If the file exists, it will open it for both reading and writing, and content will be written to the end of the file. If the file doesn't exist, it will be created.

In our previous example, this would enable us to both read the current contents of the log and write new log entries with the same `File` object.

Temporary Files

Sometimes, when writing to a file, we don't care about the data sticking around. We just want it to be there for the duration of our script's execution, after which it can safely be discarded.

The reasons for doing this are many. We might be using a library that needs to read from a file, but have data in memory. In this case, we can write the data to a temporary file and then pass that file into our library's code. We might be dealing with data that's too big to fit in memory but that won't ultimately be written to the filesystem—buffering an upload before passing it to another service, for example.

On the face of it, the problem seems like a very simple one, and it's tempting to create our own solution for it. All we need to do is to create a new file with a unique name, store it somewhere on the filesystem, and then remove it once our script exits.

As in many similar cases, though, there's already a solution in the Ruby standard library: a class called Tempfile. It behaves very similarly to a normal File object, and indeed delegates almost all of its methods to a File object that it keeps track of internally. A Tempfile can be used, then, in any place that's expecting a File. However, it has two special features that set it apart.

The first is that it will deal with the problem of coming up with a unique name for us, so that our temporary file is guaranteed to be new and we won't get a clash. Unlike a normal file, where the path that we pass to open is used as the identifier for the file we want, with Tempfile we have no idea in advance what the name of the file will be, and one is generated for us.

We can see this from the following simple example. We pass a basename argument to create, which forms part of the final filename, but the rest is unique and generated:

tempfile-create.rb

```
require "tempfile"

Tempfile.create("test") do |file|
  puts file.path
end
```

On my machine, this produces the following filename:

```
test20140917-10996-17txawv
```

We see that the filename begins with "test," the value of the basename argument that we passed to create. Then we have some generated data. The first portion is the current date, the next is the ID of the current process, and the final portion is a random number between 0 and 4,294,967,296 (2^{32}), expressed in base 36. The chances of a collision here—that is, of a filename being generated twice, and so a clash with an existing file occurring—are absolutely minuscule, but nevertheless Tempfile will check for this and regenerate the filename if it detects a clash.

The second feature of Tempfile is that it will automatically clean up the file for us when we're done. In the case of our earlier example, in which we pass a block to Tempfile.create, the file will automatically be deleted for us when the block exits. We can see this behavior in the following example:

tempfile-cleanup-block.rb

```
require "tempfile"

path = nil

Tempfile.create("test") do |file|
  path = file.path
  puts File.exist? path
end

puts File.exist? path
```

Running it, we get the output:

```
true
false
```

That is, the temporary file exists within the block, and we can reference it, write to it, and use it like any other file. Once the block has finished executing, however, the file is automatically cleaned up for us, and it no longer exists on the filesystem.

If we'd like to keep a reference to the file around for longer—if our use of the file can't fit easily into a single block—then we can do so. However, the automatic cleanup isn't as simple in this case: the file will be deleted when the script exits. For web apps this might be far into the future.

For that reason, it's advisable to close and unlink the file when you're finished with it. For example:

tempfile-cleanup-new.rb

```
require "tempfile"

file = Tempfile.new("test")
path = file.path

begin
  puts File.exist? path
ensure
  file.close
  file.unlink
end

puts File.exist? path
```

Again we see our expected output, the same as with the block example:

```
true
false
```

Using Tempfile in this way is marginally more complex than passing a block, but is still significantly easier and more robust than rolling your own solution.

Wrapping Up

We've looked at two different techniques in this chapter, one used more frequently than the other, but both useful in their way. First, we explored how to write to other processes, allowing us to leverage the power of existing utilities within our scripts. We then looked at how we could use this in combination with redirecting our own standard output stream, in this case to page the output from our script.

Then we looked at writing to files, which, while straightforward, is the single most common task we face when wanting to write data somewhere. We also looked at the Ruby standard library's capacity to create temporary files that are cleaned up after our script finishes its execution.

Now that we've looked at the mechanisms of writing, it's time to explore the format of what we actually write. Our next chapter will explore the subject of serialization, allowing us to convert our Ruby data structures to structured formats like JSON and XML.

CHAPTER 14

Serialization and Structure: JSON, XML, CSV

In looking at writing data in various ways, all we've dealt with has been the writing of unstructured text. We haven't thought much about the form that the text takes, only the mechanism of how and where to write it. But in reality, we typically want our text to have some sort of structure, and it's especially common for that structure to be something that a computer can read—in other words, we want the ability to write the data our program creates to a particular location, and then in the future read that data back into the program.

This process—of transforming a data structure into a format that can be written somewhere, typically to disk or over the network—is called *serialization*. There's generally a reverse process, *unserialization*, that takes this data and transforms it back into the original data structure again.

Sometimes, this unserialization is a process of perfect fidelity and requires no configuration or further processing. The data is, as soon as it's unserialized, in its final state. This is usually true only of serialization formats that work with a single language, though. There are simply too many differences between languages—different data types, different ways of representing different values—to make a universal serialization format that can be serialized to and unserialized from with no loss of data in between.

So we generally work with serialization formats that give up some fidelity in exchange for universality. They might require a bit more effort to reconstruct the original data in some cases, but they have the enormous benefit of being interchangeable between any programming language, operating system, or physical hardware architecture.

In this chapter, we'll look at three common serialization formats, each with its advantages and disadvantages and all commonly found in the real world: JSON, XML, and CSV.

JSON

Once upon a time, all was XML. Java dominated the world, and for better or for worse the result was that XML dominated both as an interchange format and as a serialization format. It was the format of choice when you needed to pass data from one platform, process, or computer to another. It was the format of choice to store objects and data that programs later reconstructed into in-memory objects. It was everywhere.

In recent years, though, the move away from XML has been swift. Thanks to the predominance of JavaScript and the explosion in the world of web development, you're now more likely to encounter JSON in the real world than you are XML.

In fact, it's everywhere. Query any API over the web, and JSON is likely to be the default format—or even the only one. Download a complex dataset from a purveyor of statistics, and there's a strong chance it'll be stored in JSON.

JSON stands for *JavaScript Object Notation*, and as its name suggests, it has its origins in JavaScript. Its syntax is actually a subset of JavaScript's, which means that you could evaluate a JSON file as JavaScript without issue. This made it incredibly useful in the world of web development, since neither specific libraries nor browser support were necessary to parse it: you could simply evaluate it.

If we want to make the data that we're processing available to others, either dynamically through an API or as static files, then JSON is an excellent choice. It allows us to store complex data, including large hierarchies of nested objects, in a format that's not only supported by every mainstream programming language, but is also relatively straightforward for humans to read and edit.

Like most languages, Ruby offers JSON support in its standard library. All we need to do to use it is to `require "json"`.

JSON allows us to store six data types, each of which maps fairly neatly to a type, or types, in Ruby:

- Numbers, like `42`, `26.76`, or `4.13e15`. Although these have only one representation in JSON, in Ruby they'd be an `Integer`, `Float`, and `Float` again.

- Strings, like "hello, world". Straightforwardly, these are equivalent to the String class in Ruby.
- Booleans—true or false. These are equivalent to Ruby's own true and false.
- Arrays of multiple values, like [1, 1, 2, 3, 5]. Again, these map simply to Ruby's Array class.
- Objects, a set of key-value pairs. For example, { "name": "Alice", "age": 38 }. In Ruby's terms, JSON objects are closest to a Hash. More accurately, they offer a subset of Hash's functionality, since keys can only be strings, whereas hashes in Ruby can use arbitrary values as keys. In practice, though, this is rarely an issue.
- Simplest of all, null, used to indicate the absence of a particular value. This maps neatly to Ruby's nil and has the same behavior.

After require-ing the JSON library, all we need to do to convert data in Ruby to its JSON representation is to call the to_json method, available on all Ruby's built-in types. For example:

to-json.rb
```
require "json"

"hello, world".to_json
# => "\"hello, world\""
42.to_json
# => "42"
[1, 1, 2, 3, 5].to_json
# => "[1,1,2,3,5]"
{ "name" => "Alice", "age" => 32 }.to_json
# => "{\"name\":\"Alice\",\"age\":32}"
```

That's it! to_json works recursively, so even the most complex nested hash with as much data as you can imagine will work perfectly with a single call.

Converting Custom Classes to Primitives

What doesn't work out of the box is the serialization of custom classes, with custom attributes and custom methods. This isn't surprising. The JSON library can't know how to translate these into JSON—which attributes to include and which to ignore, for example, or how to descend into a nested structure, or how to convert something that can't be obviously represented using one of the JSON data types.

But we can define our own to_json method for a class, which sets out how to translate objects of this type into JSON. By implementing this interface, we also get the benefit of supporting deeply nested structures, since the JSON library will recursively call to_json on each nested element we return.

To make this more concrete, let's imagine we have a Person class for representing people. It has two attributes, name and age:

person-to-json.rb
```
class Person
  attr :name, :age

  def initialize(name, age)
    @name = name
    @age  = age
  end
```

If we do nothing else to this class, when we call to_json on an instance of Person, we'll unhelpfully get the result of calling person.to_s.to_json—in other words, an ugly and useless identifier, something like this:

```
"\"#<Person:0x007f8073d07118>\""
```

Clearly, this isn't how we want our data to be stored in JSON. We've lost the name and age of the person, for a start. There's no getting around it: we need to define our own to_json method.

Doing so is straightforward, though. We just need to reduce our object to the primitive types that JSON does know about. In this case, our person has a name and an age, and we can express these as a string and an integer, respectively. To group both of these values together, we can just use a hash. This will let us communicate which value is which.

Putting it together, our to_json method will look something like this:

person-to-json.rb
```
def to_json(*)
  { "name" => name, "age" => age }.to_json
end
```

Now let's see what happens when we call to_json on our object:

person-to-json.rb
```
person = Person.new("Alice", 32)
person.to_json
# => "{\"name\":\"Alice\",\"age\":32}"
```

That's more like it! Although we have lost some information—that this was once an instance of a class called Person—we've maintained the critical information that our class is storing. For someone consuming this data, who probably doesn't care what the name of our class was, this is perfect. And, because to_json is called recursively, things just work even if we have a Person object within a hash or an array:

person-to-json.rb
```
person = Person.new("Alice", 32)
[ 14, 42, person ].to_json
# => "[14,42,{\"name\":\"Alice\",\"age\":32}]"
```

Here we can see that our Person object is correctly represented as a hash within the array. In other words, we've expressed the data in our Person object in terms of JSON primitives.

Serialization of Objects

Defining a to_json allows us to outline how an object should be expressed in terms of JSON primitives. This is the approach that we'd take if we wanted to create JSON for consumption external to our program—if we were outputting JSON for an API, for example, or for a human to read.

But another form of serialization involves data that we know will be consumed primarily or exclusively by our own program. In these cases, we don't want to convert objects entirely into JSON primitives, because doing so involves losing some information about their original form.

In the previous example, we converted a Person object to a hash, with each element of the hash representing an instance variable of the object. But nowhere did we record in the JSON that this was ever a Person object; the final JSON makes no distinction between this Person and a simple hash containing the same data.

If we adapt our to_json method, though, we can retain this information in a way that will tell the JSON library to automatically create an object of the correct class when we later load the JSON. The new method looks like this:

person-serialize-json.rb
```
def to_json(*)
  {
    "json_class" => self.class.name,
    "data" => { "name" => name, "age" => age }
  }.to_json
end
```

Instead of returning a simple hash of the attributes, we return a hash that contains some metadata. We tell JSON what class to create the object as, and then pass the attributes along in the data section.

We need to do one more thing: the reverse part of the process, the bit that tells the JSON library how to construct our object when it comes to unserialize it. That means defining a class method on Person called json_create:

person-serialize-json.rb
```
def self.json_create(object)
  data = object["data"]
  new(data["name"], data["age"])
end
```

When some JSON that has a json_class of Person is unserialized, this method will be called, with the hash of data passed into it. All that it needs to do then is extract the name and age values from the data element of the hash and pass them to new to create a new Person object.

We can test this behavior:

person-serialize-json.rb
```
person = Person.new("Alice", 32)

json = person.to_json
# => "{\"json_class\":\"Person\",\"data\":{\"name\":\"Alice\",\"age\":32}}"

person = JSON.load(json)
person.class
# => Person
person.name
# => "Alice"
person.age
# => 32
```

When we call to_json on our object, we see the extra metadata as we expect. When we call JSON.load and pass in that JSON, we can see that the JSON library dutifully creates an object of class Person for us, rather than just a simple hash.

The choice between whether to create JSON that's "pure" or JSON that contains Ruby-specific information depends on your use case. If the JSON we're creating will be consumed by programs written in different languages or for different platforms, or is intended to be primarily edited or written by people, it doesn't make sense to include that extra information. You're just creating more work for those other consumers of the information. But if you're using it primarily to serialize data to and from Ruby programs, the extra convenience is almost certainly worth the Ruby-specific detail; you won't have to write custom logic to convert the JSON into your Ruby objects at the point that you deserialize it.

XML

Although JSON has become perhaps the most common serialization format—in certain circles, anyway—that's not been wholly at the expense of XML. Many APIs still return it and expect it as input; many applications use it for configuration and storage. At some point, you will definitely need to write XML.

XML as a Tree

XML is fundamentally a representation of a tree. There is a root node, which has children, which may also have children, and so on down a hierarchy of arbitrary depth.

If we represented information about a car, for example, we might end up with XML that looks like this:

```
<car>
  <make>Ford</make>
  <model>Model T</model>
  <engine>
    <size>2.9 L</size>
    <power>20 hp</power>
  </engine>
</car>
```

Our root node is car, representing a car. A car node has three children, each representing a different attribute of the car: its make, its model, and its engine. Within the engine element we have further children, representing the properties the engine has—in this case, its size and power.

Building a Tree

Building such a nested tree in Ruby is straightforward, especially if you utilize the late Jim Weirich's wonderful library Builder.[1]

Builder is a *domain-specific language* (DSL) for building XML. Thanks to Ruby's flexible syntax and to Jim Weirich's enormous creativity, it allows you to write code like this:

builder-example.rb

```
require "builder"

builder = Builder::XmlMarkup.new(:indent => 2)

xml = builder.car do |car|
  car.make "Ford"
```

1. https://github.com/jimweirich/builder

```
  car.model "Model T"
  car.engine do |engine|
    engine.size "2.9 L"
    engine.power "20 hp"
  end
end
```

When we output xml, implicitly converting it to a string, we see that all of the XML has been generated for us:

builder-example.rb
```
puts xml
# >> <car>
# >>   <make>Ford</make>
# >>   <model>Model T</model>
# >>   <engine>
# >>     <size>2.9 L</size>
# >>     <power>20 hp</power>
# >>   </engine>
# >> </car>
```

Thanks to the indent option that we passed when setting up the builder object, it's even generated "pretty" output for us, indented correctly according to the nesting of the document.

It looks a lot like magic, but it's not. The object returned from Builder::XmlMarkup.new, that we assigned to builder, is a special one. It has no methods of its own, but instead responds to any message passed to it (in this case, things like car, make, model, and so on). When these methods are called, a new element is introduced into the document. If a block has been passed to the method, the block is executed with the builder passed as an argument, so that the block can add elements below the current one.

This simple concept underpins the entirety of Builder and is what makes it feel so natural. Read through the code, and it feels like we've described, in plain English, the attributes of the car. It doesn't feel like we're constructing XML at all.

So far we've just looked at creating new elements. But a key part of XML is *attributes*—modifiers on elements, such as:

```
<painting name="Anna and the Blind Tobit" artist="Rembrandt" year="1630"/>
```

Let's imagine we wanted a whole gallery of such paintings, each with those particular attributes. Let's see if we can do this while maintaining the readability of the first example:

builder-attributes.rb

```
require "builder"

builder = Builder::XmlMarkup.new(:indent => 2)

xml = builder.gallery do |gallery|
  gallery.name "The National Gallery"
  gallery.location "London, UK"

  gallery.collection do |collection|
    collection.painting(
      name: "Anna and the Blind Tobit",
      artist: "Rembrandt",
      year: 1630
    )

    collection.painting(
      name: "The Stonemason's Yard",
      artist: "Canaletto",
      year: 1725
    )
  end
end

puts xml
# >> <gallery>
# >>   <name>The National Gallery</name>
# >>   <location>London, UK</location>
# >>   <collection>
# >>     <painting name="Anna and the Blind Tobit" artist="Rembrandt" year="1630"/>
# >>     <painting name="The Stonemason's Yard" artist="Canaletto" year="1725"/>
# >>   </collection>
# >> </gallery>
```

This maintains all the readability of the first example. It flows naturally, and the difference between attributes and new elements is tangible without one being more clumsy than the other.

That's about all there is to the core of Builder's functionality, and yet with it we can construct even the most complex of documents. Whatever your thoughts on XML, generating it in Ruby should never be painful and can even be fun.

CSV

In Chapter 5, *Delimited Data*, on page 51, we looked at reading from CSV files, a common need when it comes to acquiring text for your program. But it's often necessary to write CSV files, too.

We can do this using the same CSV library that we used to read the files. It has a capable interface for generating CSV data, writing directly to files, and modifying existing CSVs.

There are generally two reasons we'd want to write a CSV file. The first is when we want to take a data structure from our Ruby code and write it out to a CSV. The second is when we want to take an existing CSV file and modify it. These two different tasks have two different approaches. Let's take a look at them in turn.

Serializing Existing Data

If we're generating the data that we want to write to a CSV ourselves, or if we're importing it from a different source, then we need to create a CSV file from scratch.

When we looked at writing to files generally, in Chapter 13, *Writing to Other Processes and to Files*, on page 189, we saw how we could pass different *modes* to `File.open` in order to write, rather than read, a file. Well, `CSV` is no different. Just like `File`, it has an `open` method, and just like `File` that method takes a `mode` argument:

```
CSV.open("path/to/file.csv", "w") do |csv|
  # do something with csv
end
```

Where we depart from ordinary files is within the block. With a plain text file, we use methods such as `puts` and `write` to write content to the file. With a CSV, we use the *shovel operator* (<<) to append rows to the file:

csv-writing.rb
```
require "csv"

CSV.open("data/writing.csv", "w") do |csv|
  csv << ["field one", "field two", "field three"]
  csv << ["another field one", "another field two", "field three, again"]
end

puts File.read("data/writing.csv")
# >> field one,field two,field three
# >> another field one,another field two,"field three, again"
```

The CSV library will take care of quoting fields for us as necessary; we can see in the second row that the third field, which contains a comma, has been quoted as a result.

Modifying Existing CSVs

Sometimes, the data that we want to write to a CSV also comes from a CSV in the first place. In this case, our task is more like modifying the original CSV than it is serializing a new data structure to CSV format, so it would make more sense if we could do this as a single step rather than separate parsing and regenerating steps. The CSV library provides us with a shortcut interface for doing just that.

In Chapter 5, *Delimited Data*, on page 51, we used the example of a shopping list:

data/shopping-with-header.csv

```
"Item","Price","Shop"
"White Bread","£1.20","Baker"
"Whole Milk","£0.80","Corner Shop"
"Gorgonzola","£10.20","Cheese Shop"
"Mature Cheddar","£5.20","Cheese Shop"
"Limburger","£6.35","Cheese Shop"
"Newspaper","£1.20","Corner Shop"
"Ilchester","£3.99","Cheese Shop"
```

Let's imagine that we want to update our shopping list to convert the prices from British pounds, as they are at the moment, to US dollars. We then want to output the modified CSV content so that it can be written to another file.

We could use foreach to loop over the records in the CSV, modify the resulting array, convert that array to CSV form, and then output the resulting CSV row. That feels like a lot of boilerplate, though, and what about the step where we convert the row to a CSV string—do we have to do that ourselves?

The answer is, as ever, no. CSV provides a filter method for just this sort of task. Here's how we'd use it to implement the previous example:

csv-filter.rb

```
require "csv"

File.open("data/shopping-with-header.csv") do |input_file|
  File.open("data/shopping-dollars.csv", "w") do |output_file|
    CSV.filter(input_file, output_file, headers: true) do |record|
      dollars = record["Price"].sub(/^£/, "").to_f * 1.58
      record["Price"] = "$%.2f" % dollars
    end
  end
end

puts File.read("data/shopping-dollars.csv")
# >> White Bread,$1.90,Baker
# >> Whole Milk,$1.26,Corner Shop
```

```
# >> Gorgonzola,$16.12,Cheese Shop
# >> Mature Cheddar,$8.22,Cheese Shop
# >> Limburger,$10.03,Cheese Shop
# >> Newspaper,$1.90,Corner Shop
# >> Ilchester,$6.30,Cheese Shop
```

For our input object, we pass a File object pointing to our CSV file. For each of the records in the file, we then convert the item's price to dollars, modifying the "Price" element of the row directly. CSV then outputs the modified CSV content to standard output for us.

We can also see that this example neatly combines the three steps that we've talked about throughout the book. We first extract the information we need by parsing the CSV, we then transform it by performing the currency conversion, and finally we load it by outputting the modified CSV.

Filtering CSVs from the Command Line

The filter method of the CSV class allows us to easily take a CSV as input and then output that same CSV in a modified form from within a script. But we can also easily use it from the command line, in the sort of one-line scripts we saw in Chapter 3, *Shell One-Liners*, on page 29.

That's because the method has two helpful defaults. The first is that, if we don't specify an input file to read from, filter will use ARGF. The second is that filter writes to standard output unless we tell it otherwise. Taking input from ARGF and writing to standard output is exactly the behavior of a typical filter program, so this behavior allows us to easily write such programs that work on CSVs.

But it also makes it easy to process CSV files from the command line in the form of one-liners. Let's revisit our shopping list example. Imagine we wanted to output only the first two fields. This simple task isn't worth writing a full script for, but we also should avoid the naive solution—simply splitting the string on all commas—because that's error-prone.

With the filter, though, the task becomes straightforward in a one-liner:

```
$ ruby -r csv -e 'CSV.filter(headers: true) { |row| row.delete "Shop" }' \
    data/shopping-with-header.csv
```

We invoke Ruby with two options. The first, -r csv, tells it to require the CSV library. The second is the -e flag that allows us to pass code as a string.

In the code, we call the CSV.filter method without passing an input source or output destination explicitly, causing it to default to ARGF and $stdout. In the block, executed for each row, we delete the Shop field, leaving the others intact.

Finally, we pass the filename of the CSV that we want to process. This will then be read by `ARGF` as the source of the CSV data.

The result of running this one-liner is that we see the CSV's contents, minus the final column, output to the terminal. We could then redirect them to a file or pipe them into another process—or just inspect them by eye. The process of using `CSV.filter` in this way is quick and concise, and it allows the easy exploration and transformation of data that's locked away in CSV files.

Wrapping Up

The world of serialization is dominated by three main formats, each with their strengths and weaknesses, and we've looked at all three of them here. The first was JSON, which is common on the web and will allow us to communicate with many different APIs—as well as being the easiest of the formats to edit by hand.

Then we looked at XML, which is still found in many places despite perhaps declining from its mid-2000s heyday. We used the DSL specified by the Builder library to build up our XML element by element in a readable way.

Finally, we looked at the CSV file. CSVs are common in data that's destined for databases, spreadsheets, and the import routines of many online services, so being able to write data into this format will allow us to write files that can be consumed by these services.

Sometimes, though, we need to write data into much more complex or ad hoc formats. In these cases we can define templates that specify exactly how our output will be structured. The next chapter explores how we can do this in Ruby.

CHAPTER 15

Templating Output with ERB

We've looked at writing data either in an unformatted way or into standard formats like XML, JSON, and CSV. Sometimes, though, we need to conform to more complex or more unusual formats, ones that don't have ready-made libraries but that are nevertheless still text formats.

For example, imagine that we want to generate a financial report for a bar, outlining the purchases made by the bar in the past month. We want the final output to look something like this:

```
                                         The Bistro Illegal
                                               Sector RT 74
                                                Lazgar Beta

Purchase ledger, October 2014

Generated: 4 October 2014, 12:49pm

Product                                Units          Price

Ol' Janx Spirit                          282     $27,918.00
Eau de Santraginus V                     300        $600.00
Arcturan Mega-Gin                        150      $7,500.00
Fallian Marsh Gas                      1,000      $2,000.00
Qalactin Hypermint Extract                25        $500.00
Algolian Suntiger, teeth of              300     $30,000.00
Zamphuor                                   3        $120.00
Olives                                   200         $24.00

Total                                            $68,662.00
```

This isn't too complex. It's something that we could achieve with some standard puts and printf statements, as we did in Chapter 12, *Standard Output and Standard Error*, on page 173. But this leaves us in a state where we're combining the formatting of our output with the logic of how the data is being generated.

We're combining business logic with presentation logic, which will make things harder to maintain in the long run. If you've done any web development, especially in an MVC framework such as Rails, this principle is likely to be familiar to you: there, we keep our *model* logic separate from our *view* logic.

When things get to this point, we can help ourselves out by using a *templating system* to split out the presentation side of things. This will allow us to calculate the values in one place, and in another define the formatting of our final output. Changing one of these things won't require us to change the other, and when trying to make such a change we won't have to wade through irrelevant information to get to the parts we want to modify.

Using a templating system will allow us to create significantly more complex output than we would otherwise be able to. Looping over collections, using branching to alter our output based on particular conditions—we have all the power of a programming language from within our templates.

Ruby comes with a powerful templating system included in its standard library. It's called ERB—short for *Embedded Ruby*—and it allows us to embed Ruby code inside of other text. That text might be HTML if our output is for the web. It might be an email. Or it could just be a plain-text document intended for a person to read. The beauty of ERB is that we can use it to generate any sort of text output. Let's take a look at how to use it.

Writing Templates

To use ERB, we need to learn two things. First, we need to learn how to write the content of our ERB templates and how to use flow control, conditionals, and other Ruby constructs within them. And second, we need to learn how to actually execute these templates from within our Ruby code, including how to pass data into them.

ERB files are, in essence, plain text files. You don't need to use any special invocations or formatting; any plain text file is, by definition, a valid ERB file. If we had a file containing the following text:

```
Hello, world
```

it would, when compiled as ERB, produce the output `Hello, world`. This is the key advantage of using a templating language like ERB: boilerplate content—such as the address in our purchase ledger example or the headings of the table—requires no special treatment and can be output directly. This is especially advantageous if we're generating HTML output, where there's typically more static, presentational content than there is dynamic.

But we do need *some* dynamic content, or else we wouldn't be using a templating system at all. For this, ERB gives us some special tags that we can use, the contents of which will alter the behavior of our template. These give us the ability to do three things: output Ruby expressions, execute Ruby code without outputting it, and write comments that won't be included in our final output. Let's take a look at each of these tags and how they differ.

Outputting Ruby Expressions

Perhaps the most common task we'll need to perform within a template is to output the result of a Ruby expression. Typically, that means outputting the contents of a variable or the return value of a method call, but it could be any Ruby expression at all.

We can do this in Ruby by using the <%= %> tags. The content of the tag will be evaluated as Ruby code, and the result will be placed into the template. In essence, the tag itself is replaced with whatever the expression returns.

If we wanted to include the current date and time in our template, then, we could do so:

```
This template was generated at <%= Time.now %>
```

If we compiled and ran this ERB template, we'd see output similar to the following:

```
This template was generated at 2015-06-06 15:44:27 +0100
```

In this case, the expression is a method call, but it could just as easily be a variable passed into the template. We'll discuss variable bindings and passing data into templates later in the chapter, when we look at how to actually render ERB templates.

Flow Control

Outputting dynamic content is one element of a templating language. But we also need to be able to control flow, to be able to change output based on a particular condition, for example, or to loop over a collection and do something with each of its members.

For this, ERB offers the <% %> tags—note the lack of an =. Ruby code inside these tags won't be outputted. The expression will be discarded, but it will still be executed. So we can do things like `if`/`else` conditions:

erb/if.erb
```
<% if @price == 0 %>
  Free
<% else %>
  $<%= @price %>
<% end %>
```

We can also iterate over members of a collection, just as we would in normal Ruby:

erb/each.erb
```
<% @products.each do |product| %>
  Price: $<%= product.price %>
<% end %>
```

In fact, we can execute any Ruby code we like within these tags, even code that has side effects. But we should exercise caution not to introduce too much logic into our templates; regularly using <% %> blocks for anything beyond looping and conditionals is generally frowned upon.

Comments

Sometimes, despite our best efforts, templates can become complex—or at least unintuitive. In these cases, it can be helpful to document them for the benefit of others. ERB allows you to write comments, which won't appear in the final output of the template, by using the <%# %> tags:

erb/comment.erb
```
<%# This won't appear in the final output %>
<%= "This will" %>
```

In practice, it's unusual to write too many comments in ERB templates, but like anything else they have their place.

The key takeaway here is that, inside ERB's special tags, it's just plain old Ruby. Anything you can do in a Ruby script you can do in ERB, and outside ERB's special tags, you're free to do as you please without worrying about accidentally doing something that has a special meaning within Ruby and causing a problem.

This clear separation of template logic from other content gives us an enormous amount of flexibility. We can use ERB to generate HTML, XML, JSON, or any other text format you can imagine. ERB doesn't know or care what's going on outside its special tags, so we can put anything we like outside them.

Example: Generating a Purchase Ledger

At the start of the chapter, we saw an example of something that we might write a template for: a purchase ledger for a fictional bar:

```
                                                   The Bistro Illegal
                                                         Sector RT 74
                                                          Lazgar Beta

Purchase ledger, October 2014

Generated: 4 October 2014, 12:49pm

Product                                    Units            Price

Ol' Janx Spirit                              282       $27,918.00
Eau de Santraginus V                         300          $600.00
Arcturan Mega-Gin                            150        $7,500.00
Fallian Marsh Gas                          1,000        $2,000.00
Qalactin Hypermint Extract                    25          $500.00
Algolian Suntiger, teeth of                  300       $30,000.00
Zamphuor                                       3          $120.00
Olives                                       200           $24.00

Total                                                  $68,662.00
```

Let's write an example ERB template for this type of file. We won't worry about where the data is coming from just yet; we'll write our idealized template and then investigate how to pass data into it afterward.

First, let's deal with the header. We have some static content—the address of the bar—followed by two dates, which should be dynamic:

erb/purchase-ledger.erb

```
                                                   The Bistro Illegal
                                                         Sector RT 74
                                                          Lazgar Beta

Purchase ledger, <%= Time.now.strftime("%B %Y") %>

Generated: <%= Time.now.strftime("%-d %B %Y, %l:%M%P") %>
```

Just as we saw earlier, we dynamically output the date, using the strftime method to format it differently in the two places that we use it.

Next, we generate the line items within the purchase ledger. Let's assume that we've been passed these in a variable called @line_items:

erb/purchase-ledger.erb
```
Product                                          Units          Price

<% @line_items.each do |item| %>
<%= "%-40s%5d%15.2f\n" % [item.name, item.units, item.price / 100] %>
<% end %>
```

Hopefully the only somewhat cryptic part here is the format string, which aligns the values so that the output resembles a table. (We looked at these formatting strings in *Formatting Output with printf*, on page 178, if you need a refresher.) Here we specify a left-aligned, 40-character string for the product name; followed by a right-aligned, 5-character integer for the quantity; and then finally a right-aligned, 15-character floating-point number rounded to two decimal places for our price. (We're dividing by 100 here because we're assuming prices will be passed in as cents, rather than dollars.) This will ensure that, unless our values overspill these generous allocations, everything will line up nicely in the final report.

Finally, we output the total value of all the items. In keeping with the theme of separating business logic from presentation logic, we'll assume that this is being calculated elsewhere and passed in as another variable, this time called @total:

erb/purchase-ledger.erb
```
<%= "Total%55.2f" % @total / 100 %>
```

Hopefully this example illustrates not only the power of ERB, but also its simplicity. We haven't had to learn new syntax for a new language: the logic we've written is Ruby, the same as we'd write in an ordinary Ruby script. We use each to loop over the items in the @line_items collection. We access properties on the line item to output information about it.

The key advantage, though, is that we've successfully separated our presentation logic from our business logic. If we suddenly needed to generate this same report in HTML format, to publish on the web, we could do so easily: it would just mean creating a new template, without touching the logic at all.

Evaluating Templates

We've looked at ERB from the perspective of writing templates. Once we've created a template, though, we need to know how to evaluate it and capture its output, and how to pass data into it.

Let's first take a look at how we can load a simple template and get its output.

Simple Templates

Since ERB is part of Ruby's standard library, it's just a require away; we don't need to install a third-party gem. Once we've required it, we use it by creating an ERB object for each of our templates, passing in the template content. We then execute the template and capture the resulting string. For example:

erb/simple-template.rb
```
require "erb"

template = "The time is <%= Time.now.strftime('%T') %>"

renderer = ERB.new(template)
puts renderer.result
```

We define a variable, template, which contains a string of ERB. Then we create a new ERB object, passing in our template. Finally, we call result, which returns the template output as a string. It's only at this point that our template is actually executed—not before. This might not seem important and isn't necessarily important now, but it will be once we start passing variables into our templates. We can demonstrate that the template isn't actually executed until we call result by putting an artificial delay into our code:

erb/render-time.rb
```
require "erb"

puts "The time is #{Time.now.strftime('%T')}"
template = "The time is <%= Time.now.strftime('%T') %>"

renderer = ERB.new(template)

sleep 2

puts renderer.result
```

Running this example, you should see output similar to the following:

```
The time is 15:02:16
The time is 15:02:18
```

Even though the template is defined at the same point that we output the time directly with puts, it isn't actually executed until we call result. Since that's after our sleep-induced delay, we see two different times displayed in our output.

By default, templates are evaluated as though they were at the top level of our Ruby script. That means they can access variables that are also in that scope. For example:

erb/top-level-variables.rb
```
require "erb"

time = Time.now.strftime("%T")
template = "The time now is <%= time %>"

renderer = ERB.new(template)
puts renderer.result
```

Trying to access variables not within that scope will produce an error:

erb/local-variables.rb
```
require "erb"

def display_time
  time = Time.now.strftime("%T")
  template = "The time now is <%= time %>"

  renderer = ERB.new(template)
  puts renderer.result
end

display_time
# ~> (erb):1:in `<main>': undefined local variable or method `time'
#         for main:Object (NameError)
# ~>    from .../ruby-2.2.2/lib/ruby/2.2.0/erb.rb:863:in `eval'
# ~>    from .../ruby-2.2.2/lib/ruby/2.2.0/erb.rb:863:in `result'
# ~>    from -:8:in `display_time'
# ~>    from -:11:in `<main>'
```

Later in this chapter, we'll look at how to avoid this issue and gain access to variables in scopes other than the global one.

Loading Templates from Files

In reality, we're unlikely to define templates in this way. It would be unwieldy and wouldn't help us separate our presentation logic from our business logic. We're more likely to have our templates reside in dedicated template files instead.

ERB doesn't read from files itself, but it's trivial to do so ourselves. To adapt the simple template example from earlier:

erb/template-file.rb
```
require "erb"

template = File.read("simple-template.erb")

renderer = ERB.new(template)
puts renderer.result
```

In this case we're still passing a string to ERB; we're just fetching that string from a file. This means we can store the template anywhere we like—a database, for example—and ERB will happily render it for us.

Trim Modes

By default, ERB will preserve and output all of the newlines in a file—even when a line contains only Ruby tags. For template formats where whitespace isn't significant, such as HTML, that's typically not an issue. In other cases, though, it can be problematic.

We can control Ruby's behavior in this regard by altering its *trim mode.* It's the third argument to `ERB.new`, and there are four behaviors we can choose:

`%` Allows lines beginning with % to be parsed as Ruby, making the following two examples equivalent:

```
<% if @price == 0 %>
  Free
<% end %>

% if @price == 0
 Free
% end
```

<> Suppresses newlines after lines that start with <% and end with %>. This generally means that newlines are suppressed after lines that contain only Ruby code.

> Suppresses newlines after lines that end with %>. This behaves like <>, but will also suppress newlines after <%= %> blocks.

\- Suppresses newlines after lines that end in -%>. This allows you to control, per line, whether a newline will be output:

```
<%= "We'll get a newline after this line" %>
<%= "...but not this one." -%>
```

We can specify which of these behaviors we want by passing a string as the third argument of `ERB.new`. For example, to allow the -%> behavior:

```
renderer = ERB.new(template, nil, "-")
puts renderer.result
```

Passing Data to Templates

We've skirted around one of the more complex areas of ERB: how to access variables from within our templates. We've seen that, by default, our templates are evaluated as though they were top-level Ruby code, allowing them access to variables in that scope. But in practice, that's unworkable. We don't want to create variables in the top-level scope if we can help it.

We need to be able to control the scope that our templates are evaluated in. We do this by passing a *binding* to ERB when our template is compiled. This binding holds information about the variables currently in scope. (These bindings aren't a feature of ERB; they're a concept within Ruby itself.)

It's much easier to illustrate this with an example. So, let's take our purchase ledger example again and start to build up the data that we'll actually need.

In the template, we're referencing the variables @line_items and @total. First, we need to populate these instance variables, which means creating a class that will render our template; then, we'll look at how we can execute our template in the context of that object.

First, though, let's create a class to represent a line item in our ledger. In this case, we need only some simple properties, so we'll use a Struct:

```
LineItem = Struct.new(:name, :units, :unit_price) do
  def price
    units * unit_price
  end
end
```

Each line item has a name, a quantity, and the unit price of an individual item. We then define a method, price, that calculates the total price of this line item by multiplying the quantity by the price of an individual item.

Next, we'll create the overall class for our purchase ledger. It needs to generate a list of line items and calculate the total, and have a method for generating the report that we're looking for. Let's take a look:

erb/purchase-ledger.rb

```
class PurchaseLedger
  def initialize
    @line_items = [
      LineItem.new("Ol' Janx Spirit",              282,   9900),
      LineItem.new("Eau de Santraginus V",         300,   200),
      LineItem.new("Arcturan Mega-Gin",            150,   5000),
      LineItem.new("Fallian Marsh Gas",            1_000, 200),
      LineItem.new("Qalactin Hypermint Extract",   25,    2000),
      LineItem.new("Algolian Suntiger, teeth of",  300,   10000),
      LineItem.new("Zamphuor",                     3,     4000),
      LineItem.new("Olives",                       200,   12),
    ]
    @total = @line_items.reduce(0) { |t, i| t + i.price }
  end
```

```
  def report
    template = File.read("purchase-ledger.erb")
    renderer = ERB.new(template, nil, ">")
➤   renderer.result(binding)
  end
end
```

(In reality, of course, our data would likely come from a database, or from a CSV that we've parsed, or from some other source; for now, though, we're making them up and simply storing them statically.)

The key line is marked with an arrow; it might slip your notice unless you're looking for it. Rather than calling result without any arguments, as we have been doing up until now, we pass it an argument: binding. This isn't a local variable; we're calling the binding method on Kernel. This method returns a Binding object that has attached to it all of the variables that are available at the point that we call it. In practice, this means that our template can access instance variables and methods on the current instance of PurchaseLedger—which means it can access the @line_items and @total variables it requires.

To use our new code, we create a new PurchaseLedger and run the report:

erb/purchase-ledger.rb

```
ledger = PurchaseLedger.new
puts ledger.report
```

The output looks similar to example we saw at the start of this chapter:

```
                                       The Bistro Illegal
                                             Sector RT 74
                                               Lazgar Beta

Purchase ledger, October 2014

Generated: 4 October 2014,  7:21pm

Product                              Units          Price

Ol' Janx Spirit                        282       27918.00
Eau de Santraginus V                   300         600.00
Arcturan Mega-Gin                      150        7500.00
Fallian Marsh Gas                     1000        2000.00
Qalactin Hypermint Extract              25         500.00
Algolian Suntiger, teeth of            300       30000.00
Zamphuor                                 3         120.00
Olives                                 200          24.00

Total                                            68662.00
```

It's almost there, but it's missing some niceties that the first example had. There are no thousands separators in the numbers, for example, or currency symbols on the prices. While we can do this logic in the template, that doesn't feel right. We'd be violating the business-logic/presentation-logic divide again, but in the other direction by putting business logic in our templates.

Controlling Presentation with Decorators

It's common to need to alter an object in some way purely for presentation. In the previous example, we saw two such cases. In the first, we wanted to output numbers with thousands separators, and in the second we wanted to prefix prices with the correct currency symbol.

In essence, we want to create some methods to help with the formatting and display of our data. The only question is where to put them. We could create them as top-level methods, but just like creating top-level variables, this doesn't feel right. We could *monkey patch* the built-in Ruby classes in question—in this case, Numeric—to add helper methods like with_commas or with_currency_prefix, but this will pollute all numbers and might well lead to conflicts with other code.

A popular approach that avoids the ugliness of global methods, the dangers of monkey patching, and the unpleasantness of performing such logic in the templates themselves is the *decorator pattern*.

The principle of a decorator is that we create a class that wraps an existing one and either adds some extra functionality or modifies the existing functionality in some way, while still preserving all of the other original functionality. In this case, we need to be able to comma-separate numbers; for currency, we need to round to two decimal places and then add the $ symbol—as well as performing the same comma separation.

This implies two decorators: let's call them Number and Dollars. The first needs to decorate the existing Numeric object with a method called with_commas, which will return a string representation of the number with commas added as thousands separators.

The dollars decorator needs to wrap a number representing a quantity of cents. It then needs to convert this to dollars and round to two decimal places. It then needs to override the to_s method to return the number prefixed with "$".

In both cases, we want the classes to behave otherwise exactly like the classes they're wrapping, so we'll use Ruby's SimpleDelegator to delegate all methods to the wrapped objects. This will pass through any methods that don't exist to whatever object we pass into the initialize method—which in this case is the object we're wrapping.

Here's what the final decorators look like:

erb/purchase-ledger-decorators.rb

```
class Number < SimpleDelegator
  def initialize(number)
    @number = number
    super
  end

  def with_commas
    @number.to_s.reverse.gsub(/(\d{3})(?=\d)/, '\\1,').reverse
  end
end

class Dollars < SimpleDelegator
  def initialize(cents)
    @cents = cents
    super
  end

  def to_s
    "$" + Number.new("%.2f" % (@cents / 100)).with_commas
  end
end
```

We can then use these decorators in our view:

erb/purchase-ledger-decorators.erb

```
<% @line_items.each do |item| %>
<%=
  "%-40s%5s%15s\n" % [
    item.name,
    Number.new(item.units).with_commas,
    Currency.new(item.price)
  ]
%>
<% end %>
```

We've converted our quantities to Numbers and our prices and totals to Currency objects. By doing so, we gain the extra functionality those decorators give us, and we don't have to be at all aware of the implementation of this functionality in our view. This includes things like the conversion from cents (hundredths of a dollar) to whole dollars, which shouldn't be the responsibility of the template at all (and yet was in our previous example).

Wrapping Up

In this chapter, you learned how to use templates to generate truly flexible output. In doing so, we separated our presentation logic from our business logic, just as we might when writing a web application.

We looked at the more advanced options we can pass through to ERB to alter its behavior, and how we can use variable bindings to pass data into our templates.

With this, we've reached the end of our exploration of text processing. We learned how to acquire text from any source, a host of techniques for processing that text once we've gotten it into our Ruby programs, and finally where we can write that transformed text once we're finished.

With the techniques in this book, you should have built up a formidable data-wrangling arsenal and be capable of tackling the vast majority of text processing problems you're likely to encounter. I hope you've found the book interesting and useful!

Part IV

Appendices

APPENDIX 1

A Shell Primer

It's common, even among programmers with some significant experience, to have used the command line only in the most basic way: to type commands one at a time and observe their output. But the Unix shell is a powerful programming environment in its own right.

In case you're not familiar with using the shell in this way, here is a basic primer. The examples in it will work whether you use bash or zsh, the two most common shells, and the principles hold for any Unix shell—so if your computer is running Linux, BSD, or Mac OS X, all of the examples will work without any additional effort from you. Windows users who install Cygwin[1] can use all of this functionality, too.

Running Commands

Every shell has a *prompt* at which you can type commands. Often the prompt character is `$` for a normal user and `#` for an administrator, but it's also common to see `%`, `>`, and virtually any other character.

Prompts also commonly include information about the environment: what directory you're in, the name of the user your session is running under, or even things like the status of version control repositories or the battery status of your laptop.

When you open a new terminal window, you should see your prompt. It's likely to look something like this:

```
user@computer:~ $
```

A cursor should be flashing just after the dollar sign, inviting you to type. If you type a single command and hit the Enter key, the shell will run that

1. https://www.cygwin.com/

command for you and display its output on the screen. Try ls for a start, to list the contents of the current directory:

```
user@computer:~ $ ls
Documents Pictures        Movies
```

Virtually all commands accept *options* (also known as *flags* or *switches*) that alter their behavior in different ways, and *arguments*, which generally specify actions to take or the target the tool should work on. We type these after the command, each one separated by a space. ls, for example, accepts many different *options* that change its behavior, and then zero or more *arguments* that specify what files or directories to list. For example:

```
user@computer:~ $ ls -l Pictures
-rw-r--r--    1 rob  staff     75130  2 May  2015 ollie.jpg
-rw-r--r--    1 rob  staff      6688  7 May  2015 hendrix.jpg
```

Here we specify one option, -l, which tells ls to list files in long format (showing things like the permissions, owner, and size of the files), and then specify one argument, Pictures, which tells ls to list the contents of that particular directory.

That's all there is to it. You can get quite far using the shell in this way. The capabilities of the commands that come with your operating system are pretty vast. But you're using only a tiny fraction of the shell's power.

Controlling Output

If you just type single commands and do nothing else with them, you'll see the output printed to your screen. The shell also lets you send this output elsewhere, though, using two important techniques: first by *stream redirection* and second by creating *pipelines*.

Stream Redirection

We can redirect streams using > and >> after the command whose output we want to redirect. The first will write the output to a file, clearing the file's contents if it exists. The second will also write to a file, but will append to the existing content if the file already exists.

To revisit the ls example:

```
user@computer:~ $ ls -l Pictures > files.txt

user@computer:~ $ cat files.txt
-rw-r--r--    1 rob  staff     75130  2 May  2015 ollie.jpg
-rw-r--r--    1 rob  staff      6688  7 May  2015 hendrix.jpg
```

This time, we see no output from ls. When we output the contents of files.txt, we see that it contains the output instead. Appending is similar:

```
user@computer:~ $ ls -l Documents >> files.txt

user@computer:~ $ cat files.txt
-rw-r--r--   1 rob  staff     75130  2 May  2015 ollie.jpg
-rw-r--r--   1 rob  staff      6688  7 May  2015 hendrix.jpg
-rw-r--r--   1 rob  staff     12481  7 June 2015 birthday-list.doc
```

By using >> rather than >, we see that the original contents of files.txt are preserved and that we've added a third line rather than replacing what was there before.

If we want to redirect a process's standard error stream, rather than standard output, we can use 2>:

```
user@computer:~ $ ls non-existent-file
ls: non-existent-file: No such file or directory

user@computer:~ $ ls non-existent-file 2>/dev/null
```

This example illustrates two concepts. First, we redirect standard error by using 2>. Second, we redirect to a device rather than file—in this case /dev/null, which will discard the input, in effect hiding it. We can see that the error message from the first example, which was printed on standard output, is hidden in the second.

Pipelines

Pipelines are similar to redirection, except that instead of redirecting output to a file we redirect it to the input of another process. We explore these pipelines in much more detail in Chapter 2, *Processing Standard Input*, on page 19, but they're created by simply separating each command, and therefore each stage of the *pipeline chain*, with the pipe symbol (|):

```
user@computer:~ $ ls -l Pictures | grep hendrix
-rw-r--r--   1 rob  staff      6688  7 May  2015 hendrix.jpg
```

Here we list the files in the Pictures directory and then use grep to output only those lines the contain the word hendrix.

Pipelines can be of arbitrary length. It's not uncommon to see five or ten commands strung together in this way, each performing its own distinct step of a larger process.

If you want to pipe the contents of a file, you have two options. The first is to use cat. The second is to have the shell pass the file as input, something we can achieve with >:

```
user@computer:~ $ cat Documents/birthday-list.txt | grep Ruby
Text Processing with Ruby by Rob Miller

user@computer:~ $ grep Ruby < Documents/birthday-list.txt
Text Processing with Ruby by Rob Miller
```

(In this case neither is strictly necessary, as grep accepts a filename, but it illustrates the point.) Some purists will bristle at the first example, considering the use of cat to be unnecessary, but others prefer it for maintaining the left-to-right reading of the pipeline chain.

Exit Statuses and Flow Control

In programming languages, functions and methods generally *return* a value. Unix processes are the same. At the point that they exit, they set an *exit status* that tells you something useful about what happened when the process ran.

This exit status is always a number between 0 and 255. Convention dictates that 0 indicates success and that anything greater than 0 indicates some sort of failure. Individual programs are allowed to use whichever non-zero codes they like for whichever purpose, though it's common to find programs that simply set a status of 0 for success and 1 for all failure states.

After running a command, we can check the value of the exit status that it set by inspecting the $? variable:

```
user@computer:~ $ ls -l Pictures | grep hendrix
-rw-r--r--   1 rob  staff     6688  7 May  2015 hendrix.jpg

user@computer:~ $ echo $?
0

user@computer:~ $ ls -l Pictures | grep slartibartfast

user@computer:~ $ echo $?
1
```

Here the exit status is 0 when grep successfully found a match and 1 when it didn't. We could then act on this knowledge, perhaps taking a different course of action depending on whether it matched.

We can do this flow control easily by using *short-circuiting Booleans*. For example:

```
user@computer:~ $ ls -l Pictures | grep -q hendrix && echo "found"
found

user@computer:~ $ ls -l Pictures | grep -q slartibartfast || echo "not found"
not found
```

Here we use && to run a command only if grep finds a match, and || to run a command only if it doesn't. (By passing the -q, or *quiet*, option to grep, we tell it to hide its normal output, so we see only the output from our echo command.)

These basics will allow us to progress from using our shell as a place to enter commands to using our shell as a programming environment and will give us enough knowledge to understand all of the various ways that the shell is used in this book.

APPENDIX 2

Useful Shell Commands

Although this is first and foremost a book about text processing *with Ruby*, it's also about an approach to text processing that fits in with existing tools. If you're not particularly experienced with the Unix command line and the utilities it offers, this list might help you find the right tool for the job.

There are only 16 commands here, but together they form a considerable arsenal and—along with Ruby—will provide you with the tools you need for virtually all text processing tasks.

These commands are all part of GNU's coreutils project and are invariably packaged with Linux distributions. Mac OS X ships with virtually all of them, and those that it doesn't can be installed using Homebrew:[1]

```
$ brew install coreutils
```

Windows users should install Cygwin[2] to get them.

The rest of the chapter gives a summary of each of these 16 commands.

1. http://brew.sh/
2. https://www.cygwin.com/

cat Outputs the content of the filenames passed to it. Its name comes from the word *concatenate*, since it concatenates the files one after another. If no files are given, it outputs standard input.

```
$ cat foo.txt
foo
$ cat bar.txt
bar
$ cat foo.txt bar.txt
foo
bar
```

tac Exactly like cat, but outputs the lines of the files in reverse—that is, starting from the last line of the first file and working backward, then the last line of the second, and so on.

```
$ cat foo.txt
foo
bar
$ tac foo.txt
bar
foo
$ cat baz.txt
baz
$ tac foo.txt baz.txt
bar
foo
baz
```

shuf Randomizes the order of lines in standard input or in the specified file. If the -n option is specified, will output at most that many lines; otherwise, all of the lines in the input will be shuffled.

Display five random dictionary words:

```
$ shuf -n 5 /usr/share/dict/words
gasification
merrymake
thingum
chiliastic
zygose
```

head	Outputs the first *n* lines of a file, where *n* is by default 10 but can be altered by passing a number to head.
	
	Output the first ten lines of foo.txt:
	
	`$ head foo.txt`
	
	Output the first two lines of foo.txt:
	
	`$ head -2 foo.txt`
	
	Output the first five lines of foo.txt:
	
	`$ head -5 foo.txt`

tail	Similar to head, but with the last *n* lines rather than the first.
	
	Output the last ten lines of foo.txt:
	
	`$ tail foo.txt`
	
	Output the last two lines of foo.txt:
	
	`$ tail -2 foo.txt`
	
	Output the last five lines of foo.txt:
	
	`$ tail -5 foo.txt`

split	Takes a file and splits it into new files every *n* lines, where *n* is by default 1,000.
	
	Split a file every 1,000 lines:
	
	`$ split big.txt`
	
	Split a file every 500 lines:
	
	`$ split big.txt -l 500`
	
	Split a file every 100 bytes:
	
	`$ split big.txt -b 100`

grep Outputs only those lines that match a given pattern. Accepts regular expressions, allowing complex patterns to be matched, and supports recursing through the filesystem itself—allowing you to search across whole directories of files.

Show lines in standard input that match a given pattern:

```
$ echo "foo\nbar" | grep foo
foo
```

Show lines that don't match a given pattern:

```
$ echo "foo\nbar" | grep -v foo
bar
```

Match against a regular expression:

```
$ echo "foo\nbar" | grep '^f'
foo
```

Case-insensitive matching:

```
$ echo "foo\nbar" | grep -i FOO
foo
```

Search through all files in the current directory and below:

```
$ grep -r foo .
./foo.txt: foo
./bar.txt: foo
```

cut Splits lines into fields, allowing you to process delimited data and only output particular columns. cut splits on tab by default but can be configured to separate fields by any character using the -d option.

Split fields on the space character and output the fourth field:

```
$ date
Tue 30 Jun 2015 11:37:52 BST

$ date | cut -d ' ' -f 4
2015
```

Output multiple fields, illustrating both ranges and comma-separated lists of fields:

```
$ date | cut -d ' ' -f 1-3,5
Tue 30 Jun 11:37:52
```

tr Performs a substitution on the input, allowing you to replace certain characters with others. tr is flexible about how characters are specified, allowing you to define ranges and use character classes.

Convert uppercase input to lowercase:

```
$ echo 'HELLO WORLD' | tr A-Z a-z
```

The same, but accounting for non-ASCII characters:

```
$ echo 'HËLLØ WÔRLD' | \
  tr '[:upper:]' '[:lower:]'
hëllø wôrld
```

Delete numbers from the input:

```
$ echo 'HELLO 123 WORLD' | tr -d 0-9
HELLO  WORLD
```

Delete anything that isn't a letter from the input (the -c stands for *complement*):

```
$ echo 'HELLO %^!@$()' | tr -cd a-zA-Z
HELLO
```

Compress multiple-space characters into one:

```
$ echo 'Hello    world' | tr -s ' '
Hello world
```

wc Counts the number of characters (with the -c option), words (with the -w option), or lines (with the -l option) in a given file or in standard input. If no options are specified, will output all three metrics.

Show statistics for a file. The first column shows lines, the second words, and the third characters:

```
$ wc foo.txt
     103     392    3944 foo.txt
```

Display the number of lines in a file:

```
$ wc -l foo.txt
103
```

Display the number of characters in standard input:

```
$ echo "Hello world" | wc -c
12
```

sort Sorts input or the content of files. Takes options to treat sort data as numeric, to sort insensitively to case, and to ignore leading whitespace, among other things.

Sort a file alphabetically:

```
$ cat foo.txt
foo
bar

$ sort foo.txt
bar
foo
```

Sort input numerically:

```
$ echo "12\n111\n1" | sort
1
111
12

$ echo "12\n111\n1" | sort -n
1
12
111
```

Sort input in reverse order:

```
$ echo "ant\nmole\nzebra" | sort -r
zebra
mole
ant
```

column Converts data into columnar format. Very useful for performing alignment that would otherwise take painstaking manual adjustment.

Display a delimited file as an aligned table, with a header row:

```
$ cat people.txt
Samantha 57 Pianist
Alice 31 Biochemist
Terence 90 Retired
Alex 20 Student

$ ( echo "NAME AGE JOB"; cat people.txt ) | column -t
NAME        AGE  JOB
Samantha    57   Pianist
Alice       31   Biochemist
Terence     90   Retired
Alex        20   Student
```

uniq Outputs its input, but for all consecutively identical lines, outputs those lines only once. So if a line containing foo was followed by three identical lines all containing foo, these four lines would be compressed to one in uniq's output.

Compress consecutively identical lines:

```
$ cat foo.txt
foo
foo
bar
foo

$ uniq foo.txt
foo
bar
foo
```

Display only lines that are unique across the whole file, by using sort to ensure identical lines always appear together:

```
$ sort foo.txt | uniq
bar
foo
```

Display lines that are unique across the whole file, along with a count of how many times those lines occurred:

```
$ sort foo.txt | uniq -c
 1 bar
 3 foo
```

paste Nothing to do with the clipboard—as its name might suggest to modern ears, at least. paste joins together two files so that line one from file two is placed on the same line as line one from file one, joined by a tab. This effectively creates tabular data.

Join two files horizontally:

```
$ cat first-names
Avdi
Katrina
David

$ cat last-names
Grimm
Owen
Brady

$ paste first-names last-names
Avdi    Grimm
Katrina Owen
David   Brady
```

Join two files vertically:

```
$ paste -s first-names last-names
Avdi    Katrina David
Grimm   Owen    Brady
```

Separate fields with spaces, rather than tabs:

```
$ paste -d' ' first-names last-names
Avdi Grimm
Katrina Owen
David Brady
```

join Joins two files together. Unlike paste, which does this based on the position of the lines in each file, join functions much more like a join in a relational database: it looks for fields with the same values and joins based on that equality.

Join two files based on the equality of values in the first column:

```
$ cat users
bob@example.com         Bob     Smith
alice@example.com       Alice   Jones

$ cat orders
bob@example.com         Chips   $1.95
alice@example.com       Beer    $3.50

$ join users orders
bob@example.com Bob Smith Chips $1.95
alice@example.com Alice Jones Beer $3.50
```

Output only certain fields:

```
$ join -o 1.2,2.2 users orders
Bob Chips
Alice Beer
```

comm Given two sorted files, displays the lines that occur only in file one, the lines that occur only in file two, and the lines that occur in both. Can be configured to show any number of these columns. (For example, just the lines that are in both or just the lines that are unique to one or more files, but not the lines that are in both, etc.)

Display lines that occur only in file one, that occur only in file two, and that occur in both:

```
$ cat 1.txt
bar
foo

$ cat 2.txt
bar
baz

$ comm 1.txt 2.txt
                bar
        baz
foo
```

Display only the lines that are in both files:

```
$ comm -1 -2 1.txt 2.txt
                bar
```

Display only the lines that occur only in file one:

```
$ comm -2 -3 1.txt 2.txt
foo
```

By composing together these various commands in different ways, you'll be able to perform many text processing tasks without having to reach for anything else. When you find them limiting, you can reach for Ruby to fill in the gaps.

Index

SYMBOLS

" (quotes)
- CSV data, 59
- escaping, 59
- fields, 208
- parsers, 138

"" (double quotes), 59

character, regular expressions, 113

shell prompt, 229

#! shebang, 22

$ (dollar sign)
- anchor, 107
- shell prompt, 229

$& global match variable, 118

$' global match variable, 119

$+ global match variable, 118

$, output field separator, 176

$/ variable, 53

$; field separator, 57

$= attribute selector, 70

$? variable, exit status, 232

$[1-9] global match variables, 118

$\ output record separator, 176

$` global match variable, 119

$~ global match variable, 117, 125

$_ variable, 31, 34

% ERB trim mode, 221

% format placeholders, 179–180

&& and flow control, 233

() (parentheses)
- arbitrary text, 131
- capture groups, 108

* (asterisk)
- alignment with printf, 181
- regular expressions, 106
- wildcards, 104

+ quantifier, regular expressions, 106, 120

, (comma)
- separating CSS selectors, 71
- with_commas, 224–225

- ERB trim mode, 221

. character
- class shortcut, 71
- regular expressions, 110

/ (forward slash), regular expressions, 109

// literal, 109

<% %> tags, 215

<%# %> tags, 216

<%=%> tags, 215

<< (shovel operator), appending rows, 208

<> ERB trim mode, 221

= sign, attribute selectors, 70

=~ operator, 115, 117

> operator
- child selectors, 68
- ERB trim mode, 221
- piping with, 232
- redirecting streams, 230

>> operator
- joining atoms, 137
- redirecting streams, 230

? quantifier, regular expressions, 106

@ prefix, attribute selectors, 69

[] (square brackets), HTML attribute selectors, 69

[] (subscript operator)
- accessing fields, 62
- attr shortcut, 74

\ (backslash)
- capture groups, 124
- control words, 144
- escaping, 145
- escaping line breaks, 33
- escaping quotes, 59

^ (carat)
- anchors, 107, 120
- negative character classes, 106

_ (unused value), 56

{} (braces), regular expressions, 107

| (pipe symbol)
- about, 231
- alternation, 146
- CSS selectors, 71
- writing to other processes, 190

|| and flow control, 233

||= conditional assignment operator, 36

~=, HTML attribute selectors, 70

A

a (append mode), 195

\A anchor, 107

-a flag, 57–58
a+ (read-write append mode), 195
absent?, 146
accents, ignoring, 163
aligning
  aligning values, 179–182
  in ERB templates, 218
  HTML scraping, 87
alternation, 108, 146
anchors, regular expressions, 107, 120
ANSI, RTF documents, 143
Apache
  parsing log with shell one-liner, 37–39
  processing log file line-by-line, 5–10
append mode, 195, 230
appending
  append mode when writing to files, 195, 230
  ARGV, 48
  command shell one-liner, 35–39
  rows to CSV files, 208
apply, 142
ARGF, 41–49, 210
arguments
  ARGV and, 47
  shell commands, 230
ARGV, 47–49
arrays
  converting to hashes, 142
  JSON data type, 201
articles, fuzzy search, 161–169
as, tagging in Parslet, 138
ASCII
  converting to UTF-8, 94–99
  history, 90
  Ruby support, 93–95
  in UTF-8, 92
assignment operator, 137
assoc, 162, 164
asterisk
  alignment with printf, 181
  regular expressions, 106
  wildcards, 104
atoms, 137
attr, 74
attributes
  reading HTML, 74
  selectors, 69
  XML, 206
autosplitting, 57

B

\b control word, 144, 150
backslash
  capture groups, 124
  control words, 144
  escaping, 145
  escaping line breaks, 33
  escaping quotes, 59
bar examples, 213, 217, 221–224
basename, 196
Battley, Paul, 166
BEGIN blocks, 35
binding, ERB templates, 222–223
Binding object, 223
blocks, replacement, 125
boilerplate
  avoiding lengthy, 29, 31
  ERB, 214
bolding, RTF documents, 144, 150
Booleans
  JSON data type, 201
  short-circuiting, 232
braces, regular expressions, 107
brackets, HTML attribute selectors, 69
browsers, scraping HTML, 78, 82
buffering, standard input and output, 25–27, 186
builder, 206
Builder library, 205–207
business logic, separating from presentation logic, 213, 216, 218
bytes
  invalid byte sequences, 89, 93, 97
  reading fixed-width files, 12–18

C

-c argument, 38
calculations, TSV data, 55
capture groups, 108, 116, 118, 122–125
capture_output, 184–187
carat
  anchors, 107, 120
  negative character classes, 106
carriage return, overwriting when outputting, 176
case
  converting, 20
  normalization, 163
  regular expressions, 105, 109–110
case statements, 141
cat
  about, 41, 236
  memory and, 26
  piping with, 232
\cf control word, 144, 150
character classes, 105
characters
  counting, 12, 239
  encodings, 89–100
  ignoring accents, 163
  matching with regular expressions, 105, 110, 120
  rules for RTF parsing, 145
  streaming files by, 11
Charlock Holmes, 98
check, 130
check_until, 131
cheese shop example, 55–58
children
  child selectors, 67–69, 71–77
  navigating HTML from nodes, 75
  XML, 205
children method, 75
chmod, 23
chomp, 20
cleanup, temporary files, 196
code
  for book, xiii
  executing from command line, 30–34
  prepending and appending, 35–39
code points, UTF-8, 91, 99
collection pipelines, 10, 226, *see also* pipeline chains
color, RTF parsing, 144, 148, 150
\colortbl control word, 144

column, 240
columns, aligning output, 179–182, 240
comm, 244
command shell
  arguments and ARGV, 47
  commands table, 235–244
  delimited data processing, 56–58
  filtering CSVs from, 210
  global match variables, 117–119, 125
  Nokogiri from, 77, 79
  one-liners, 29–40, 56–58, 80, 210
  output from, 174, 178–182, 230–232, 236
  prepending and appending code, 35–39
  primer, 229–233
  redirecting to standard error, 174, 231
  resources, 48
  ruby arguments, 30–35
  standard output with printf, 178–182
commas, *see also* CSV
  separating CSS selectors, 71
  with_commas, 224–225
comments
  ERB templates, 216
  regular expressions, 113
comparison operator, 117
compressing text, 191
concurrency and buffering, 25–27
conditional assignment operator, 36
conditional output, 32–34, 38
conditionals, ERB, 214–215
config file parsing examples, 132–143
constant time, 16
content, 147, 157
context, keyword in, 169
control words, 144, 146, 150
converting
  accents, 163
  arrays to hashes, 142
  ASCII to UTF-8, 94–99
  case, 20
  cents to dollars, 224
  character encodings, 94–99
  currency, 209–211
  custom classes to primitives, 201–203
  floats, 15, 179
  RTF to HTML, 149–152
  spelling, 45
coreutils, 235
count, streaming files, 12
counting
  characters, 12, 239
  lines, 38, 44, 239
  words, 239
country populations example, 119–122
create, temporary files, 196
cryptic globals, *see* pipeline chains
CSS
  converting RTF to HTML, 150
  selectors, 65–72, 74
css method, 66
CSV
  creating file, 208
  modifying existing files, 209–211
  parsing, 51, 58–62
  serialization, 207–211
currency
  converter example, 209–211
  converting cents, 224
  decorator, 224–225
custom classes, converting to primitives, 201–203
cut
  about, 238
  delimiting with, 34
  using flags instead, 58
Cygwin, xiii, 229, 235

D

\d, regular expressions, 106
daemons, redirecting output to a file, 182
dashes, ignoring, 163
data types, JSON, 200
decorators, ERB templates, 224–225
delays, 219
delegating, 224
deleting
  elements with ARGV, 47
  temporary files, 196
delimited data, 51–62
  CSV, 51, 58–62, 207–211
  cut, 238
  TSV, 51–58
descendant selectors, 68, 73
detect_encoding, 99
detect_encoding!, 99
directories, scripts, 23
discography example, 123–125
@doc variable, 80
:document, 138, 151
Document Object Model (DOM), 63
dollar
  converting cents, 224
  decorator, 224–225
dollar sign
  anchor, 107
  shell prompt, 229
domain-specific languages, 205
dot character
  class shortcut, 71
  regular expressions, 110
double quotes, 59

E

-e flag, 30, 37–39, 57–58, 80, 210
each, 8, 10
each_char, 11
each_line
  ARGF, 42
  processing standard input, 23
  splitting files into records, 52
  streaming files, 7
edit distance, 165–167
elements
  ARGV and, 47–49
  exploring pages, 77–80, 82
  selectors, 65–72, 77, 79, 82–83
  types, 66
  web inspectors, 79
  working with, 72–77
Embedded Ruby, *see* ERB
encode method, 94

encodings, 18, 89–100
END blocks, 35–36
End of File, 186, 191
ENOENT error, 42
Enumerable
  calculations, 55
  league table example, 85
  streaming files, 8–11
  uses, 56
Enumerator, streaming files, 11
env, 23
eos?, 133
equality operator, 115
ERB, templating with, 213–226
errors, *see also* standard error
  ENOENT, 42
  invalid byte sequences, 89, 93, 97
  parsing Apache error log with shell one-liner, 37–39
  raising parsing, 133
escaping
  backslashes, 145
  line breaks, 33
  quotes, 59
evaluating ERB templates, 218–221
exit status, 232
extended regular expressions, 113
external encodings, 95
external_encoding method, 96
extract, transform, and load process, overview, xi, *see also* extracting; loading; transforming
extracting
  ARGF, 41–49
  command shell one-liners, 29–40
  delimited data, 51–62
  encodings, 89–100
  error messages from Apache log, 38
  in extract, transform, and load process, xi
  fixed-width files, 12–18
  HTML, 63–88
  line-by-line, 5–10, 31–34
  reading from files, 3–18
  standard input, 19–27
  streaming files, 7–12, 42–45
  term extraction, 156, 159–161
  text extraction, 156–161
  URL example, 22–25
  whole file at once, 4

F

-F option, 57
FasterCSV, 59
fields
  aligning output, 179–182
  header rows, 61
  output field separator, 176
  quoting, 59, 208
  separator option, 57
  splitting records into, 54, 56–57
File class
  opening File object, 3
  reading from, 4, 14–18
  redirecting output, 182
file method, 44
filename method, 44
files
  appending, 48, 195, 208, 230
  compressed, 191
  delimited data, 51–62
  encodings, 93
  filtering with ARGF, 41–49
  loading templates from, 220
  opening, 3, 208
  read-write modes, 4, 191, 194–195
  reading fixed-width, 12–18
  reading from, 3–18, 51–62
  reading line-by-line, 5–10
  reading whole, 4
  redirecting standard output, 182
  splitting, 52, 237
  streaming, 7–12, 42–45, 60
  writing temporary, 195–198
  writing to, 191, 193–198, 230
filter, 209–211
filtering
  with $_ variable, 32–34, 38
  ARGF, 41–49
  in-place mode, 45
  modifying CSV files, 209–211
financial report example, 213
find, 26
fixed-width files, reading, 12–18
flags, shell commands, 230
flexibility
  scraping HTML, 78
  scripts, 20
floats
  converting temperatures to, 15
  converting to integers, 179
flow control
  command shell, 232
  ERB, 214–215
fonts, RTF documents, 143
football league table example, 80–88
force_encoding, 94, 99
foreach, 8, 60
foreground, RTF documents, 144
format placeholders, 179–180
format strings, 179, 218
formatting
  ERB templates, 218
  RTF documents, 144
  standard output with printf, 178–182
forward slash, regular expressions, 109
fuzzy searching, 156, 161–169

G

gets, 20, 31
Git, 192
global match variables, regular expressions, 117–119, 125
global substitute, *see* sub
GNU, 235
grep
  about, 21, 238
  flow control, 233
  pipeline chain example, 231
Grey II, James Edward, 59
Grimm, Avdi, 184

group_by, 9
grouping, regular expressions, 108, 116
groups, RTF documents, 144, 146
gsub
  $_ variable, 32, 35
  replacing text, 122–125
gsub!, 35, 123
gzip, 191

H

hashes, converting from arrays, 142
head, 39, 237
header rows
  CSV files, 61
  scraping HTML, 77
headers
  ERB templates, 217
  RTF parsing, 143, 147, 151
Hello World examples
  ERB, 214
  redirecting output, 184
  RTF parsing, 143–152
  simple output, 173, 176
Howard, Ara T., 184
HTML
  converting RTF to, 149–152
  exploring pages, 77–80, 82
  extracting keywords, 156–161
  league table example, 80–88
  navigating from nodes, 74–77
  scraping, 63–88
  searching document, 64–72

I

-i (in-place) flag, 45
i option, regular expressions, 109–110
iconv library, 93
ICU library, 98
IDs, selectors, 71, 77, 82
ignoring
  ARGV, 47
  case, 163
  dashes, 163
  keywords, 160
in-place mode, 45
indentation, serialization, 206
index, normalizing, 159, 163–165
initialize, 133
input, external encodings, 95, *see also* standard input
input record separator, 53–54, 57
inspection tools, 79
intermediate tree, Parslet, 136, 140–143, 150–152
International Components for Unicode (ICU) library, 98
interpolation, regular expressions, 109, 111–113
invalid byte sequences, 89, 93, 97
IO
  about, 12
  redirecting output, 182, 185
ISO-8859 encodings
  converting to UTF-8, 95
  history, 91

J

JavaScript Object Notation, *see* JSON
join, 187, 243
joining, atoms, 137
JSON
  data types, 200
  reading whole files, 5
  serialization, 200–204
  term extraction, 161–162

K

\k option, regular expressions, 124
keywords
  in context, 169
  defining, 159
  extracting, 156–161
  reducing to stem, 164

L

-l flag, 230
language
  domain-specific, 205
  natural language processing, 155–170
languages, *see* encodings
league table example, 80–88
less, 192
Levenshtein distance, 166
lexing, 127
libraries, requiring, 59
line breaks
  escaping, 33
  in RTF documents, 145, 150
\line control word, 145, 150
line-by-line processing, 5–10, 31–34
lineno, ARGF, 44
lines
  anchors for regular expressions, 107, 120
  counting, 38, 44, 239
  input record separator, 53
  line breaks in RTF documents, 145, 150
  multiline regular expressions, 110
  printing with -p flag, 32, 34
  processing line-by-line, 5–10, 31–34
  sorting, 38
listing options, 230
loading
  data into ERB templates, 221–224
  in extract, transform, and load process, xi
  serialization, 199–211
  templates from files, 220
  templating with ERB, 213–226
  writing to other files, 193–198
  writing to other processes, 189–193
  writing to standard error, 174–176, 231
  writing to standard output, 173–187
log file examples
  parsing with shell one-liner, 37–39
  processing line-by-line, 5–10
log files, append mode, 195
long format option, 230
lookaheads, 121, 131, 134, 146

lowercase
  converting, 20
  regular expressions, 105, 110
ls options, 230

M

m option, regular expressions, 110
magic comments, 93, 96
Main, 48
map, 9, 56
map!, 10
Marino, Brian, 98
match
  Parslet, 137
  regular expressions, 116
MatchData objects, 116–117
matching, *see* parsing; regular expressions; searching
maybe, 137, 146
memory
  CSV files, 60
  extracting standard input, 23
  processing line-by-line, 6
  streaming files, 7
Metaphone, 167
Microsoft Windows, Cygwin for Unix, xiii, 229, 235
model logic, separating from view logic, 213, 216, 218
modes, reading and writing, 194–195, 208
modifiers, regular expressions, 110–114
modifying
  CSV files, 209–211
  files with ARGF, 45–47
multi-byte encoding, 18, 91, 226, *see also* UTF-8
multiline mode, regular expressions, 110
multilingualization, *see* encodings

N

-n flag, 31–34, 37–39, 57–58
\n variable, 53
name, HTML elements, 74
names
  capture groups, 124
  files, 44, 196
  reading elements', 74
  temporary files, 196
  values, 56
National Oceanic and Atmospheric Administration example, 13–18
natural language processing, 155–170
  fuzzy searching, 161–169
  text extraction, 156–161
navigating, HTML documents, 74–77
negative forms, regular expressions, 106
negative lookaheads, 146
nesting
  descendant selectors, 68
  parsers and, 127–128
newlines
  ERB templates, 221
  escaping line breaks, 33
  output separators, 176–177
  reading fixed-width files, 15
  regular expressions, 111
  removing from standard input, 20
  trailing, 178
next_sibling, 76
NOAA temperature data example, 13–18
nodes
  navigating HTML documents, 74–77
  searching HTML documents, 66–72
  working with HTML elements, 72–77
NodeSet
  navigating HTML documents, 74–77
  searching HTML documents, 66–72
  working with HTML elements, 72–77
Nokogiri, 63–88
  about, 64
  command-line, 77, 79
  exploring pages, 77–80, 82
  extracting text from HTML, 158
  league table example, 80–88
  navigating from nodes, 74–77
  searching document, 64–72
  working with elements, 72–77
normalization, 159, 163–165
nouns, extracting terms, 159
null, JSON data type, 201
numbers
  converting floats, 15, 179
  decorators, 224–225
  JSON data type, 200
  regular expressions, 105–106
Numeric class decorators, 224–225

O

o option, regular expressions, 111–113
objects
  JSON data type, 201
  serialization, 203
one-liners, *see also* pipeline chains
  command shell, 29–40, 80
  delimited data processing, 56–58
  filtering CSVs, 210
  Nokogiri, 80
open
  files, 3, 208
  global method, 4
  HTML, 85
  uses, 4
  writing to other processes and files, 190–193
open-uri library, 64
OptionParser library, 48
options, shell commands, 230
order of rules, 150
orthography, *see* spelling
output, *see also* standard output
  command shell basics, 230–232, 236
  conditional, 32–34, 38
  external encodings, 95
  field separators, 176
  paging, 192
  Ruby expressions in ERB templates, 215
overwriting, progress messages, 176

P

-p flag, 32, 34, 37–39

padding, aligning values, 180

paging output, 192

paintings example of XML serialization, 206

parent method, 75

parentheses
- arbitrary text, 131
- capture groups, 108

parents
- child selectors, 67–69, 71–77
- navigating HTML from nodes, 75

parse method, 85

parse_file, 133

parse_item, 133

parsers, *see also* Nokogiri
- creating in Parslet, 137–140, 145–149
- JSON, 5
- rule-based parsers, 135–152
- StringScanner, 128–135
- writing parsers, 127–153

parsing, *see also* extracting; reading
- defined, 127
- delimited data, 51–62
- HTML, 63–88
- natural language processing, 155–170
- RTF example, 143–152

parsing expression grammars (PEG), 135, 226, *see also* Parslet

parsing generators, 136, 226, *see also* Parslet

Parslet, 136–152
- about, 136
- creating parser, 137–140, 145–149
- RTF example, 143–152
- transformations, 136, 140–143, 149–152

passwd file example, 58

paste, 242

patterns, decorators, 224–225, *see also* regular expressions

PEGs (parsing expression grammar), 135

percent literal, 109

performance
- filtering and conditional output, 34
- interpolation, 112–113
- seeking through files, 16

Person class example of JSON conversion, 202–203

Philips, Lawrence, 167

phone number example, 108

phonetic algorithms, 165, 167–169

phonetic fingerprinting, 167

Phrasie, 159

pipe method, 185

pipe symbol
- about, 231
- alternation, 146
- CSS selectors, 71
- writing to other processes, 190

pipeline chains
- ARGF, 43
- collection pipelines, 10
- command shell one-liners, 29–40, 58
- concurrency and buffering, 25–27
- defined, 20
- delimited data processing, 56–58
- filtering CSVs from, 210
- flexibility, 20
- Nokogiri, 80
- output basics, 230–231
- redirecting standard output, 184–187
- standard input, 19–20, 23
- standard output, 20
- writing to other processes, 189–193

pos method, 129

positive lookaheads, 122, 134

postcodes example, 114

precision, specifying, 181

prepending
- ARGV, 48
- command shell one-liner, 35–39

presentation logic, separating from business logic, 213, 216, 218

previous_sibling, 76

primer, shell, 229–233

primitives, converting custom classes to, 201–203

print
- vs. puts, 176–178
- standard output, 173

printf, 87, 178–182

printing
- aligning text, 87
- formatted, 178–182
- lines with -p flag, 32, 34
- print vs. puts, 176–178
- simple standard output, 173

processes, writing to, 189–193

processing, *see* extracting

progress bars, 176

progress messages, writing to standard error, 175

prompt, shell, 229

pronunciation, *see* phonetic algorithms

purchase ledger examples, 217, 221–224

push, 49

puts
- vs. prints, 176–178
- standard error, 175
- standard output, 173

Q

-q flag, 233

quantifiers, regular expressions, 106, 120

query methods, StringScanner, 129

question mark, regular expressions, 106

quotes
- CSV data, 59
- escaping, 59
- fields, 208
- parsers, 138

R

\r, outputting carriage return, 176

r (read-only mode), 194

-r flag, 210

%r literal, 109

r+ (read-write mode), 191, 194

race condition, puts, 177

random access, read, 15–17

ranges, regular expressions, 105
read
  compressed text, 191
  CSV files, 60
  fixed number of bytes, 14–18
  random record access, 15–17
  whole files, 4
read-only mode, 4, 194
read-write append mode, 195
read-write mode, 191, 194–195
readability, regular expressions, 113
Readability library, 157
readability.com, 157
reading
  ARGF, 41–49
  delimited data, 51–62
  encodings, 89–100
  from files, 3–18, 42–45, 51–62
  fixed-width files, 12–18
  HTML, 63–88
  line-by-line, 5–10
  standard input, 19–27
  streaming files, 7–12, 42–45
  whole file at once, 4
readlines, 6
read–evaluate–print loop (REPL), 79
records
  output record separator, 176
  splitting files into, 52
  splitting into fields, 54, 56–57
  streaming by, 60
recursion, parsers and, 127–128
redirecting
  to standard error, 174–176, 231
  standard output, 20, 182–187, 192, 231
  streams, 230
reduce, 56
regex, *see* regular expressions
Regexp class, 109–114
regular expressions
  $_ variable, 31–32, 34
  anchors, 107, 120
  basics, 103–114
  capture groups, 108, 116, 122–125
  character matching, 105, 110, 120
  defined, 104
  escaping backslashes, 145
  extracting with, 115–122
  global match variables, 117–119, 125
  grep, 238
  HTML parsing, 63
  limits of, 127
  lookaheads, 121, 131, 134, 146
  matching strings, 115–119
  matching without capturing, 122
  parsing Apache error log, 38
  pattern modifiers, 110–114
  quantifiers, 106, 120
  replacement blocks, 125
  in Ruby, 108–114
  syntax, 104–108
  transforming text, 122–126
  URL extraction example, 24
reopen, 186, 192
REPL (read–evaluate–print loop), 79
replacement blocks, 125
replacement character, UTF-8, 97
replacing
  -n and -p switches, 32
  regular expressions transformations, 122–126
  tr command, 239
require, 59, 210
rescue EOFError, 186
resources
  for book, xiv
  command-line applications, 48
  source code, xiii
result, 219, 223
Rich Text Format, *see* RTF parsing example
-rn argument, 39
robustness and scraping HTML, 78, 82
root, 138
rounding, 179, 224
rows
  aligning output, 179–182
  appending, 208
  CSV files, 61
  scraping HTML, 85
RTF parsing example, 143–152
Ruby
  regular expressions, 108–114
  versions and code samples, xiii
  versions and encodings support, 92–98
ruby command, arguments, 30–35
ruby-readability, 157
rule, 141
rule-based parsers, 135–152
rules, order of, 150

S

\s, regular expressions, 106
scan
  extraction with regular expressions, 121
  URL extraction, 24
  writing parser with StringScanner, 129, 134
scan pointer, 128
scan_until, 131, 134
scanning
  regular expressions, 121
  StringScanner, 129–135
  URL extraction, 24
scope, variables and ERB templates, 219, 221–224
scraping HTML, 63–88
  exploring pages, 77–80, 82
  league table example, 80–88
  searching document, 64–72
  working with elements, 72–77
screen scraping, *see* scraping HTML
scripts, *see also* pipeline chains
  flexibility, 20

prepending and appending code, 35–39
shebang, 22
storing, 23
scrub, 97
searching
buffering and concurrency, 26
fuzzy, 156, 161–169
HTML scraping, 64–72
-n and -p switches, 32
simple, 162
security and anchors, 107
seek, 16–18
select, 56
selectors
from command-line, 79
HTML elements, 65–72, 77, 82–83
separators
fields, 57, 176
input record separator, 53–54, 57
serialization, 199–211
CSV, 207–211
JSON, 200–204
objects, 203
XML, 205–207
shebang, 22
shell, *see* command shell
shopping list examples
CSV, 59–62, 209–211
TSV, 52–58
short-circuiting Booleans, 232
shovel operator, appending rows, 208
shuf, 236
siblings, HTML nodes, 75
simple value, 142
SimpleDelegator, 224
size, file, 44
skip
ARGF, 44
StringScanner, 130, 134
skip_until, 131
skipping
parsers, 130–131, 134
reading files, 16, 44
sleep, 219
Slice objects, 141
sort
about, 21, 240
error log example, 38
spaces, splitting files into records, 54
spawning, writing to other processes, 190
specificity and scraping HTML, 77, 84
spelling
ARGF example, 45
edit distance, 165–167
fuzzy search, 156, 161–169
phonetic algorithms, 165, 167–169
regular expressions, 106
split
about, 237
records into fields, 54, 57
streaming files, 9
splitting
from command line, 57
files, 52, 237
lines, 9, 238
records into fields, 54, 56–57
spreadsheet examples
CSV, 59–62
TSV, 52–58
square brackets, HTML attribute selectors, 69
standard error, writing to, 174–176, 231
standard input
ARGF, 41–49
concurrency and buffering, 25–27
hooking to other processes, 190
reading from, 19–27
standard output
concurrency and buffering, 25–27
filter, 210
formatting with printf, 178–182
pipeline chains, 20
print vs. puts, 176–178
redirecting, 20, 182–187, 192, 231
simple output, 173–178
writing to, 173–187
$stderr, writing to, 174–176, 231
$stdin, processing standard input, 20–27
$stdout
filter, 210
redirecting output, 182–187, 192
simple output, 173–178
STDOUT constant, 173, 185–187
storing scripts, 23
str, 137
streaming
ARGF, 42–45
concurrency and buffering, 25–27
files, 7–12, 42–45, 60
line-by-line, 7–10, 31–34
record-by-record, 60
redirecting, 230
standard input, 22–25
strength, keywords, 159–160
String class, detecting encodings, 98
StringIO, redirecting standard output, 183
strings, *see also* parsers; parsing
edit distance, 165
encodings, 94
escaping backslashes, 145
force encoding, 94
format, 179
global match variables, 118–119
HTML attribute selectors, 70
JSON data type, 201
multi-byte encodings, 92
reading files into, 4
regular expressions, 115–119, 122–126
truncating, 181
writing parser with StringScanner, 128–135
StringScanner, 128–135
strip, 15
stripping
invalid byte sequences, 97
whitespace, 15
Struct, text extraction, 158
structure and serialization, *see* serialization
sub, 32, 122
sub!, 123
subscript operator
accessing fields, 62
attr shortcut, 74

substitutions
- -n and -p switches, 32
- regular expressions, 111–113
- replacing text, 122–125
- tr command, 239

subtree, 142

switches, shell commands, 230

sync
- redirecting standard output, 186
- streaming, 26

syntax
- errors when parsing, 133
- regular expressions, 104–108
- tree when parsing, 127

SyntaxError class, 133

T

tabs, *see* TSV

tac, 236

tail, 237

temperature data example, 13–18

Tempfile class, 196–198

templating with ERB, 213–226

term extraction, 156, 159–161

Terry Pratchett example, 158–169

test scores example, 33

text extraction, 156–161, 226, *see also* extracting

text gem, 166, 168

text method, 72

text processing pipelines, *see* pipeline chains

text() node, 73

Thor, 48

time, constant, 16

time utility, 112

to-uppercase.rb script, 20

to_f, 15

to_h, 142

to_json, 201–204

tokens, parsing, 127

tr, 239

transformations, Parslet, 136, 140–143, 149–152

transforming
- in extract, transform, and load process, xi
- natural language processing, 155–170
- regular expressions basics, 103–114
- regular expressions extraction, 115–122
- regular expressions transformations, 122–126
- writing parsers, 127–153

tree
- intermediate, 136, 140–143, 150–152
- XML, 205–207

trim modes, 221

truncating
- keywords, 164
- strings, 181

TSV, parsing, 51–58

U

Unicode, *see* encodings; UTF-8

union operator, *see* pipe symbol

uniq, 38, 241

UNIX
- commands table, 235–244
- redirecting standard output, 184–187
- shell primer, 229–233
- Windows, xiii, 229, 235

unless /^#/, 58

unserialization, 199, 204

unshift, 49

uppercase, converting, 20

URLs
- extracting standard input example, 22–25
- extracting text from HTML, 158
- injecting, 85
- pattern matching example, 115–117

UTF-8
- about, 91
- ASCII in, 92
- converting to, 94–99
- Ruby support, 93–98
- stripping invalid byte sequences, 97
- transition to, 89, 92

utilities
- commands table, 235–244
- writing with ARGF, 41–49

V

values
- aligning output, 179–182
- attribute selectors, 70
- format placeholders, 179–180
- naming, 56
- parsers, 134, 138, 141
- regular expressions, 109, 111–113
- simple, 142

variables
- ERB templates, 219, 221–224
- global match, 117–119, 125
- initializing with BEGIN blocks, 36

versions, Ruby
- code samples for book, xiii
- encodings support, 92–98

view logic, separating from model logic, 213, 216, 218

W

\w, regular expressions, 106

w (write-only mode), 194

w option, writing to other processes, 190

w+ (read-write mode), 195

wc (word count), 239

web browsers, scraping HTML, 78, 82

web scraping, *see* scraping HTML

weighting, fuzzy search, 169

Weirich, Jim, 205

whitespace
- ERB templates, 221
- HTML attribute selectors, 70
- parsers, 134, 137–138
- regular expressions, 106, 113
- separating lines on, 9
- splitting records into fields, 54
- stripping, 15

width
- aligning values, 180

- reading fixed-width files, 12–18
- variable width encoding, 91
- zero-width lookaheads, 122, 131

wildcards, 104

with_commas, 224–225

words
- control, 144, 146, 150
- counting, 239
- regular expressions, 106

write-only mode, 194

writing
- CSV, 207–211
- ERB templates, 213–226
- to files, 191, 193–198, 230
- JSON, 200–204
- to other processes, 189–193
- simple, 190
- to standard error, 174–176, 231
- standard output, 173–187
- temporary files, 195–198
- XML, 205–207

X

x option, regular expressions, 113

XML, serialization, 205–207

xpath method, 66

XPath selectors, 65–72, 74

Z

\z anchor, 107

zero-width lookaheads, 122, 131

zipped files, 191

Get Deeper Into Ruby

You've seen the power of Ruby. Now learn to exploit it fully with the definitive Ruby book, and the book that shows you how to make your scripts into powerful command line tools.

Programming Ruby 1.9 & 2.0 (4th edition)

Ruby is the fastest growing and most exciting dynamic language out there. If you need to get working programs delivered fast, you should add Ruby to your toolbox.

This book is the only complete reference for both Ruby 1.9 and Ruby 2.0, the very latest version of Ruby.

Dave Thomas, with Chad Fowler and Andy Hunt
(888 pages) ISBN: 9781937785499. $50
https://pragprog.com/book/ruby4

Build Awesome Command-Line Applications in Ruby 2

Speak directly to your system. With its simple commands, flags, and parameters, a well-formed command-line application is the quickest way to automate a backup, a build, or a deployment and simplify your life. With this book, you'll learn specific ways to write command-line applications that are easy to use, deploy, and maintain, using a set of clear best practices and the Ruby programming language. This book is designed to make *any* programmer or system administrator more productive in their job. This is updated for Ruby 2.

David Copeland
(224 pages) ISBN: 9781937785758. $30
https://pragprog.com/book/dccar2

Long Live the Keyboard!

Use tmux for incredible mouse-free productivity, and learn how to edit like a pro using Vim.

tmux

Your mouse is slowing you down. The time you spend context switching between your editor and your consoles eats away at your productivity. Take control of your environment with tmux, a terminal multiplexer that you can tailor to your workflow. Learn how to customize, script, and leverage tmux's unique abilities and keep your fingers on your keyboard's home row.

Brian P. Hogan
(88 pages) ISBN: 9781934356968. $16.25
https://pragprog.com/book/bhtmux

Practical Vim

Vim is a fast and efficient text editor that will make you a faster and more efficient developer. It's available on almost every OS—if you master the techniques in this book, you'll never need another text editor. In more than 100 Vim tips, you'll quickly learn the editor's core functionality and tackle your trickiest editing and writing tasks.

Drew Neil
(346 pages) ISBN: 9781934356982. $29
https://pragprog.com/book/dnvim

The Pragmatic Bookshelf

The Pragmatic Bookshelf features books written by developers for developers. The titles continue the well-known Pragmatic Programmer style and continue to garner awards and rave reviews. As development gets more and more difficult, the Pragmatic Programmers will be there with more titles and products to help you stay on top of your game.

Visit Us Online

This Book's Home Page
https://pragprog.com/book/rmtpruby
Source code from this book, errata, and other resources. Come give us feedback, too!

Register for Updates
https://pragprog.com/updates
Be notified when updates and new books become available.

Join the Community
https://pragprog.com/community
Read our weblogs, join our online discussions, participate in our mailing list, interact with our wiki, and benefit from the experience of other Pragmatic Programmers.

New and Noteworthy
https://pragprog.com/news
Check out the latest pragmatic developments, new titles and other offerings.

Save on the eBook

Save on the eBook versions of this title. Owning the paper version of this book entitles you to purchase the electronic versions at a terrific discount.

PDFs are great for carrying around on your laptop—they are hyperlinked, have color, and are fully searchable. Most titles are also available for the iPhone and iPod touch, Amazon Kindle, and other popular e-book readers.

Buy now at *https://pragprog.com/coupon*

Contact Us

Online Orders:	*https://pragprog.com/catalog*
Customer Service:	*support@pragprog.com*
International Rights:	*translations@pragprog.com*
Academic Use:	*academic@pragprog.com*
Write for Us:	*http://write-for-us.pragprog.com*
Or Call:	+1 800-699-7764

CPSIA information can be obtained at www.ICGtesting.com
Printed in the USA
BVOW09s1815111115

426713BV00022B/147/P

9 781680 500707